5e

W9-CEM-769

Foundations in Strategic Management

Jeffrey S. Harrison

Robins School of Business
University of Richmond

Caron H. St. John

College of Business and Behavioral Science
Clemson University

SOUTH-WESTERN
CENGAGE Learning

Australia • Brazil • Japan • Korea • Mexico • Singapore • Spain • United Kingdom • United States

SOUTH-WESTERN
CENGAGE Learning

Foundations in Strategic Management, 5e
Jeffrey S. Harrison and Caron H. St. John

Vice President of Editorial, Business:
Jack W. Calhoun

Editor-in-Chief: Melissa Acuña

Senior Acquisitions Editor: Michele Rhoades

Developmental Editor: Ruth Belanger

Marketing Manager/Director:
Nathan Anderson

Marketing Coordinator: Suellen Ruttkay

Content Project Management:
Pre-Press PMG

Media Project Manager: Danny Bolan

Production Technology Analyst:
Starratt Alexander

Senior Manufacturing Buyer: Sandee
Milewski

Production Service: Pre-Press PMG

Copyeditor: Melody Feist

Senior Art Director: Tippy McIntosh

Image Permissions Manager: Deanna
Ettinger

Text Permissions Manager:
Mardell Glinski Schultz

Cover Designer:
Stuart Kunkler, triartis communications

Cover Image: ©Getty Images, Paul Price

For product information and technology assistance, contact us at
Cengage Learning Customer & Sales Support, 1-800-354-9706
For permission to use material from this text or product,
submit all requests online at **www.cengage.com/permissions**
Further permissions questions can be emailed to
permissionrequest@cengage.com

Library of Congress Control Number: 2009930439

ISBN-13: 978-1-4390-8046-7

ISBN-10: 1-4390-8046-1

South-Western Cengage Learning
5191 Natorp Boulevard
Mason, OH 45040
USA

Cengage Learning products are represented in Canada by Nelson Education, Ltd.

For your course and learning solutions, visit **www.cengage.com**

Purchase any of our products at your local college store or at our preferred online store **www.ichapters.com**

Printed in the United States of America
2 3 4 5 6 7 13 12 11 10

Foundations in Strategic Management treats core topics and current issues in the field directly and concisely without compromising learning. With just eight chapters, it flows at a brisk pace. While it is half the size of standard texts, *Foundations* covers all major strategic management topics, including classic and modern theory, draws on the contributions of leading authors in the field, and interlaces all its presentations with current debates, current perspectives, and current examples. *Foundations* gives you strategy at its most essential along with the option to build a course to your own particular specifications: to add your own readings, to run a simulation, to select your own cases, to experiment with exercises—in short, to customize your course to suit your teaching style and goals.

Three theoretical foundations, above all other concerns, influenced the shape of this book:

(1) *The traditional strategic management process model.* This approach is based primarily on applications of industrial organization economics and other classic writings from a wide range of the pioneers in the field.

(2) *The resource-based view (RBV) of strategic management.* The emphasis in RBV is on acquiring and managing resources that help a firm develop sustainable competitive advantage.

(3) *Stakeholder theory.* The stakeholder perspective views the firm at the center of a network of contacts with whom mutually beneficial relationships are formed. Effective management of these relationships, and the stakeholder network itself, can enhance competitive performance. Stakeholder theory is also inherently ethics based, which provides a nice balance for the more economically based theories.

CURRENT TOPICS

Issues of current relevance—including global competitiveness, innovation and entrepreneurship, social networks and strategic alliances, economic cycles, restructuring, corporate governance, business ethics, and social responsibility—are treated with depth and sophistication and incorporate cutting-edge research findings. Combined with traditional discussions of environmental analysis, organizational analysis, strategic thinking, strategic leadership, strategic direction, strategy formulation and strategy implementation, the field's newest trends stay linked to our focus on strategic management—that is, on strategies and strategic decisions that seek to create a future for an organization with long-range, or "strategic," planning as a central concern. Issues associated with the service sector and technology-focused businesses are reflected throughout the text in examples, concepts, assumptions, and inferences.

ACADEMICALLY SOLID, GLOBALLY ENGAGED

Foundations pays particular attention to the fundamentals of strategic management and takes a traditional approach to topical organization. Chapter 1 covers the strategic management process and strategic thinking. Chapter 2 discusses the external environment, including both the broad and the task environments. Chapter 3 treats the internal environment and examines how internal resources are associated with competitive advantage. Chapter 4 covers elements of strategic direction, including missions, visions, and organizational values and purpose. Chapter 5 discusses business-level strategy, including Blue Ocean strategies. Corporate-level strategy is tackled in Chapter 6. Chapter 7 focuses on implementation issues, including creation and integration of functional-level strategies, organizational structure and fostering innovation and entrepreneurship. Chapter 8 treats strategic control and restructuring. The important topic of global strategy is covered in each of the chapters through integration of international concepts and examples.

For Instructors

Instructors of strategic management face significant challenges fitting all the material they may want to cover into a single capstone course. We are mindful of these challenges and believe we have written a text that is uniquely supportive of including a broad range of supplemental materials such as cases, exercises, simulations, and research projects. We also provide standard teaching resources with the text, including an instructor's manual, test bank and presentation slides.

Instructor's Manual with Test Bank. The Instructor's Manual with Test Bank includes lecture outlines and a bank of test questions.

PowerPoint™ Presentation Slides. Over 150 PowerPoint slides are available to supplement course content. To download now, visit *Foundations'* supporting Web site at http://harrison.swcollege.com.

For Students

The decision-making tools you develop during this course are relevant to all levels of an organization and should also help you in your own personal planning. You won't be long on the job before you discover that the techniques of strategic management, such as those required to pull together an industry or organizational analysis, are highly applicable to all types of firms, including small entrepreneurial firms and nonprofits. In addition, the material contained in this book will help you understand, appreciate, and think critically about trends of current and future importance to the business community.

Studying strategic management will help you become better prepared to deal with important issues in our increasingly complex, increasingly global business environment, regardless of your position or of the industry in which you work. We strongly encourage you to apply the concepts of strategic management to your own employment and career planning decisions. Many of our students have told us that their understanding of strategic management impressed recruiters and allowed them to ask perceptive questions during interviews.

ACKNOWLEDGMENTS

In developing this text, we would like to acknowledge the efforts of an outstanding staff at Cengage, as well as the many reviewers, students and colleagues who have contributed so much to enhancing the value of this book. We are also grateful to our families for their continuing support that made this project possible.

To Marie, for unbounded enthusiasm and never-ending support
—Jeff

To my daughters, Ashley and Kimberly
—Caron

Jeffrey S. Harrison is the W. David Robbins Chair of Strategic Management and Director of the Innovation and Entrepreneurship Program at the Robins School of Business, University of Richmond. Prior to his current appointment he served as the Fred G. Peelen Professor of Global Hospitality Strategy at Cornell University. He has served on several review boards, including nine years with the *Academy of Management Journal* and eleven years with the *Academy of Management Executive*. He and R. Edward Freeman guest edited special issues on stakeholder themes at both of these journals. Dr. Harrison's research interests include strategic management and business ethics, with particular expertise in the areas of corporate strategy and stakeholder theory. Much of his work has been published in prestigious academic journals such as *Academy of Management Journal*, *Strategic Management Journal* and *Journal of Business Ethics*. He has authored or coauthored numerous books, including *Strategic Management of Organizations and Stakeholders*, *Managing for Stakeholders: Survival, Reputation and Success*; and *Mergers and Acquisitions: A Guide to Creating Value for Stakeholders*. Dr. Harrison has also provided consulting and executive training services to many companies on a wide range of strategic, entrepreneurial and other business issues. His clients have included Lockheed Martin, Siemens, American Express, Southdown, and Volvo Group North America. He has provided training in Brazil, Argentina, Singapore and across the United States.

Caron St. John is a full professor in the Department of Management and serves as Director of the Arthur M. Spiro Institute for Entrepreneurial Leadership at Clemson University. Dr. St. John has participated in grants receiving over $1.5 million in funding from U.S. SBA, the U.S. Department of Commerce, and the National Science Foundation. She has published over 30 articles in leading scholarly journals including *Academy of Management Review*, *Strategic Management Journal*, *Journal of Operations Management*, *Production and Operations Management*, and *Organizational Research Methods*, as well as two textbooks in strategic management. She teaches undergraduate and graduate courses that address the business, operations, and technology strategies of firms. During her tenure as Director of the Spiro Institute, she has developed several new curriculum initiatives in entrepreneurship, planned and implemented several outreach programs that link graduate business students and experienced business executives with inventors and entrepreneurs for assistance and mentoring, created a competitive research grants program for faculty and graduate students, and raised the profile of entrepreneurship activities on campus. She has also involved the Spiro Institute in several collaborations on campus and in the state that are intended to spur economic development through technology-based entrepreneurial initiatives. She is a founding board member of the Upstate Coalition for Entrepreneurial Development, serves on the Clemson University Research Foundation board, and serves on the advisory boards of various start-up firms and seed capital funds.

Brief Contents

Contents

Foundations in Strategic Management

1

The Strategic Management Process

IBM

IBM provides computer hardware, software and services in more than 170 countries. Several years ago, the company saw fundamental changes coming. Developing economies were growing rapidly, a new computing architecture was providing unprecedented computing power and an ability to transform oceans of data into usable information, and companies were seeking to integrate their advanced information technologies with other business operations to improve efficiency and facilitate innovation and growth.

In response to these trends, IBM made several bold moves. First, the company remixed its businesses to take advantage of the most attractive business segments. The company exited commodity businesses such as PCs and disk drives as well as acquiring over 100 companies in less than ten years, including PricewaterhouseCoopers Consulting. Internally, the company has formed new units in areas such as analytics, which employs four thousand IBM consultants. Now the company's historically large hardware operations provide less than 10 percent of its revenues, with approximately 40 percent each coming from software and services (the rest is from financing operations). Also, about one third of IBM's revenues now come from non-U.S. operations. Growth is especially strong in Brazil, Russia, India and China.

Moving forward, IBM's CEO Samuel J. Palmisano envisions a "smarter planet". He explains:

This isn't a metaphor, and I'm not talking about the Knowledge Economy—or even the fact that hundreds of millions of people from developing nations are gaining the education and skills to enter the global workforce. I mean the infusion of intelligence into the way the world actually works: the systems and processes that enable physical goods to be developed, manufactured, bought and sold; services to be delivered; everything from people and money to oil, water and electrons to move; and billions of people to work and live.

Through pervasive instrumentation and interconnection, almost anything—any person, any object, any process or any service, for any organization, large or small—can become digitally aware, networked and intelligent. This means that industries, infrastructures, processes and

entire societies can be more productive, efficient and responsive. And problems that have heretofore been insoluble can now be tackled.

Palmisano envisions IBM at the center of smarter technologies to help save energy, save time, and increase efficiency and innovation. For instance, a team of 70 IBM scientists and engineers worked for five years to develop what the company calls "stream" computing. The technology allows companies to analyze data as it is received rather than waiting until it is in a database. An early application of the technology at TD Securities allows the company to analyze 5 million pieces of options trading information per second and make automatic trading decisions. According to Riswan Khalfan, chief information officer at TD Securities, "In this business, quicker decisions are better decisions."[1]

The most successful organizations are able to acquire and manage resources and capabilities that provide competitive advantages. Furthermore, they are capable of managing and satisfying a wide range of external constituencies, called stakeholders. CEOs play a pivotal role in this process, as they help their companies interpret trends in the external environment, lead in the development of strategies and oversee their execution. In the IBM example, we see a company that has transformed itself as a result of changes in the external environment. The processes associated with evaluating the competitive situation of a company, acquiring and managing resources, and developing and executing strategies are a part of the field generally referred to as Strategic Management.

WHAT IS STRATEGIC MANAGEMENT?

Strategic management is the process through which organizations analyze and learn from their internal and external environments, establish strategic direction, create strategies that are intended to help achieve established goals, and execute those strategies, all in an effort to satisfy key organizational stakeholders. A simple model of the strategic management process is illustrated in Exhibit 1.1. The model is not rigid, but simply represents a useful sequence in which to frame the central topics of strategic management. For a firm engaged in a formal strategic planning process, the activities will likely occur in the order specified in the model. In other situations, the activities may be carried out in some other order or simultaneously. The dotted arrows in Exhibit 1.1 indicate that organizations often cycle back to earlier activities during the strategic management process.

External and Internal Environmental Analysis

External environmental analysis, discussed in Chapter 2, involves evaluation of the broad and task environments to determine trends, threats, and opportunities and

Exhibit 1.1   The Strategic Management Process

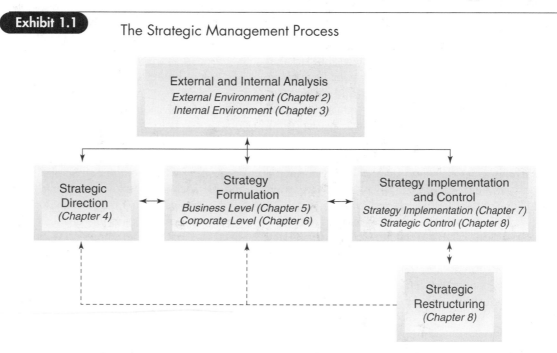

The Organization and Its Environments   **Exhibit 1.2**

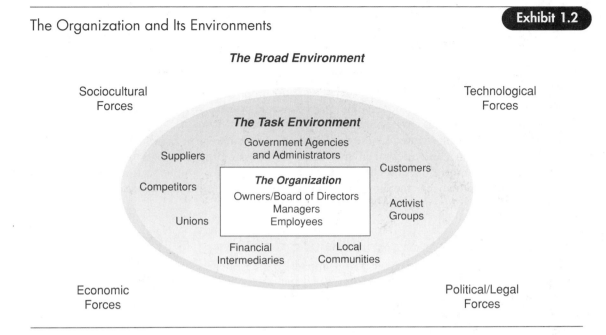

The Broad Environment

Sociocultural
Forces

Technological
Forces

The Task Environment

Suppliers

Government Agencies
and Administrators

Customers

Competitors

The Organization
Owners/Board of Directors
Managers
Employees

Activist
Groups

Unions

Financial
Intermediaries

Local
Communities

Economic
Forces

Political/Legal
Forces

to provide a foundation for strategic direction. The **broad environment** consists of domestic and global environmental forces such as socio cultural, technological, political and economic trends. The broad environment forms the context within which the firm and its task environment exist. The **task environment** consists of external stakeholders. **External stakeholders** are groups or individuals outside the organization that are significantly influenced by or have a major impact on the organization.[2] Examples of external stakeholders include customers, suppliers, competitors, government agencies and administrators, and a variety of other external groups that have a stake in the organization. Many of the stakeholders and forces that have the potential to be most important to organizations are shown in Exhibit 1.2. All of the external stakeholders should be analyzed at both the domestic and international levels. In all of the countries in which a company operates, managers must interact with government agencies, competitors, and activist groups, and manage the organization within the countries' sociocultural, political, economic, and technological context. Thus, Exhibit 1.2 contains both a global and a domestic dimension.

Internal stakeholders, including managers, employees and the owners and their representatives (e.g., board of directors), also have a stake in the outcomes of the organization. A fully developed internal analysis includes a broader evaluation of all of the organization's resources and capabilities to determine strengths, weaknesses, and opportunities for competitive advantage, and to identify organizational vulnerabilities (threats) that should be corrected. Internal analysis is the subject of Chapter 3.

Often the results from external and internal analysis are combined into a SWOT analysis, which stands for strengths, weaknesses, opportunities and threats. **Strengths** are firm resources and capabilities that can lead to a competitive advantage. **Weaknesses** are resources and capabilities that the firm does not possess but that are necessary, resulting in a competitive disadvantage. **Opportunities** are conditions in the broad and task environments that allow a firm to take advantage of organizational strengths, overcome organizational weaknesses and/or neutralize environmental threats. **Threats** are conditions in the broad and task environments that may stand in the way of organizational competitiveness or the achievement of stakeholder satisfaction. An organization's managers then consider this analysis as they identify strategic alternatives and formulate strategies. The general idea is that strategies should be formulated to take advantage of internal strengths and opportunities arising from the external environment, to overcome internal weaknesses, or to neutralize threats found in the external environment.

As illustrated by the downward pointing arrows in Exhibit 1.1, analysis of the external and internal environments provides an organization with a foundation for all of the other tasks of strategic management. For example, strategic direction is an outcome of melding the desires of key organizational stakeholders with environmental realities.

Strategic Leadership and Strategic Direction

Strategic leaders have a large impact on the strategies and performance of the firm.[3] Consider, for example, Jeffrey Katzenberg, CEO of DreamWorks Animation, the company that has produced successful movies such as Shrek. Employees of DreamWorks are not traditional nine-to-five workers. Consequently, Katzenberg sees himself as more of a cheerleader rather than a boss:

Create a haven. Artistic people tend to be more vulnerable. From the outset, our hope and our ambition was that we could create a safe place where any ideas are welcome, and failure is okay. We can only succeed when what we do is original.

Tell people a story about themselves. We're not firemen climbing into burning buildings. We're storytellers who are trying to give people a good laugh.

Celebrate often. When a movie opens, when a DVD comes out, or when awards are won, all of those milestones are celebrated in a big way.

Treating departing employees well. We try to be very generous when someone has an opportunity outside the company, because we usually want them back. It's more important that there be a red carpet for valued people when they leave than when someone joins.[4]

One of the most important responsibilities of a strategic leader is to establish direction. Strategic direction pertains to the enduring goals and objectives of the organization. It encompasses a definition of the businesses in which a firm operates, its vision for the future, and its purpose. As a practical matter, there is no way to discuss purpose without also including a discussion of the ethics of the organization. **Ethics** are the moral standards by which people judge behavior. **Business ethics**, then, pertain to the moral obligations of businesses to individuals, groups (such as stakeholders) and society as a whole. More often than not, an organization's ethics are discussed in terms of its values. Organizational **values** define what matters when making decisions and what is rewarded and reinforced. For instance, organizations may promote values such as honesty, service, hard work, quality, or responsible treatment of stakeholders.

Strategic direction may be contained, in part, in a **mission** statement. Unlike shorter-term goals and strategies, the mission is an enduring part of planning processes within the organization. Some missions are short. For example, "Google's mission is to organize the world's information and make it universally accessible and useful."[5] This mission focuses on defining Google's business. Other mission statements contain more of the elements of strategic direction, such as its values.

Barnes and Noble, a major U.S. bookstore with over 600 locations in 49 states, has a more comprehensive mission statement. It is particularly interesting because, although the statement clearly defines the company as a bookseller, it also leaves the door open for the company to engage in other specialty retail businesses:

> Our mission is to operate the best specialty retail business in America, regardless of the product we sell. Because the product we sell is books, our aspirations must be consistent with the promise and the ideals of the volumes which line our shelves. To say that our mission exists independent of the product we sell is to demean the importance and the distinction of being booksellers. As booksellers we are determined to be the very best in our business, regardless of the size, pedigree or inclinations of our competitors. We will continue to bring our industry nuances of style and approaches to bookselling which are consistent with our evolving aspirations. Above all, we expect to be a credit to the communities we serve, a valuable resource to our customers, and a place where our dedicated booksellers can grow and prosper. Toward this end we will not only listen to our customers and booksellers but embrace the idea that the Company is at their service.[6]

A well-established strategic direction provides guidance to the managers and employees who are largely responsible for carrying it out. It also can provide external stakeholders with a greater understanding of the organization and what it is seeking to accomplish. Since strategic leadership and strategic direction are so important to strategic management, Chapter 4 is devoted to these topics.

Business and Corporate Strategy Formulation

A **strategy** is an organizational plan of action that is intended to move an organization toward the achievement of its shorter-term goals and, ultimately, toward the achievement of its fundamental purposes. Strategy formulation is often divided into three levels—corporate, business, and functional, as shown in Exhibit 1.3.

Business strategy formulation, discussed in Chapter 5, pertains to domain direction and navigation. In other words, it describes how businesses compete in the areas they have selected. Business strategies are also sometimes referred to as competitive strategies. **Corporate strategy formulation**, the subject of Chapter 6, refers primarily to domain definition, or the selection of business areas in which the organization will compete. Although some firms, such as Southwest Airlines, are involved in just one basic business, diversified organizations such as

---

Strategy Formulation in a Multibusiness Organization   **Exhibit 1.3**

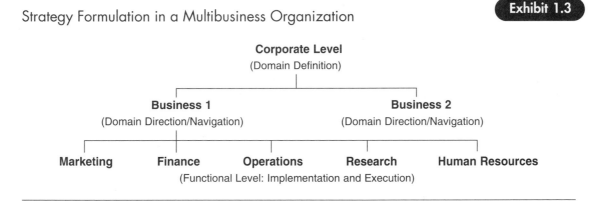

General Electric are involved in several different businesses and serve a variety of customer groups. **Functional strategy formulation** contains the details of how the functional areas such as marketing, operations, finance, and research and development should work together to achieve the business-level strategy. Thus, functional strategy is most closely associated with strategy implementation, found in Chapter 7.

Another way to distinguish among the three strategies is to determine the organizational level at which decisions are made. Corporate strategy decisions typically are made at the highest levels of the organization by the CEO and/or board of directors, although these individuals receive input from other managers. If an organization is only involved in one area of business, then business strategy decisions tend to be made by the same people. In organizations that have diversified into many areas, the different areas may be represented by different operating divisions or lines-of-business. In those situations, business strategy decisions are made by division heads or business unit managers. Functional decisions are made by functional managers, who represent organizational areas such as operations, finance, personnel, accounting, research and development, or information systems.

Strategy Implementation and Control

Strategy formulation results in a plan of action for the organization and its functions, business units, and divisions. On the other hand, strategy implementation represents a pattern of decisions and actions that are intended to carry out the plan. **Strategy implementation** (Chapter 7) involves creating the functional strategies, systems, structures, and processes needed by the organization in achieving strategic ends.

Functional strategies outline the specific actions that each function must undertake to convert business- and corporate-level strategies into actions. Without a translation of all of the plans into specific actions, nothing will change. Organizational systems are developed to train and compensate employees, assist in planning efforts, reinforce organizational values, and gather, analyze and convey information. Organizational structures reflect the way people and work are organized, which includes reporting relationships and formation into work groups, teams and departments. Processes, such as standard operating procedures, are developed to create uniformity across the organization and promote efficiency. Strategy implementation may require changes to any of these factors as the organization pursues new strategies over time.

Good control also is critical to organizational success. **Strategic control**, the topic of Chapter 8, refers to the processes that lead to adjustments in strategic direction, strategies, or the implementation plan when necessary. Managers may collect new information that leads them to reevaluate their assessment of the environment. They may determine that the organizational mission is no longer appropriate or that organizational strategies are not leading to the desired outcomes. On the other hand, the strategic control system may tell managers that the environmental assumptions, mission and strategies are appropriate, but the strategies have not been well executed. In such an instance, adjustments should be made in the implementation process.

As noted earlier, the strategic management process is usually not as sequential or linear as implied by the previous discussion. The activities are usually performed simultaneously, with constant adjustments to assumptions, direction, strategies, and processes as new information is learned and new assessments are made.

Strategic Restructuring

At some point in the life of every organization, growth will slow and some stakeholders will begin to feel dissatisfied. For example, for years American automakers have been having great difficulty competing with foreign automakers. Satisfaction levels of customers, workers and shareholders reached new lows during the economic downturn of 2008 and 2009, which led to substantial restructuring in the industry. Many banks also restructured during this downturn. Regardless of the reason, organizations eventually feel the need to re-evaluate their strategies and the way they are executing them. **Restructuring**, discussed in Chapter 8, typically involves a renewed emphasis on the things an organization does well, combined with a variety of tactics to revitalize the organization and strengthen its competitive position. Popular restructuring tactics include refocusing corporate assets on a more limited set of activities, retrenchment, Chapter XI reorganization, leveraged buyouts and changes to the organizational structure. Chapter 8 also includes a section on dealing with economic cycles.

Now that the strategic management process has been described, we will establish a theoretical foundation upon which the rest of the book will be based. Then we will turn our attention to the trends that are moving organizations quickly into a global playing field.

ALTERNATIVE PERSPECTIVES ON STRATEGY DEVELOPMENT

The field of strategic management blends a wide variety of ideas representing many functional areas of business. This diversity may be one reason that scholars and practitioners have not been able to agree on a standard set of theories (i.e., paradigm) to guide the field. Nevertheless, some ideas are more widely adopted than others. For example, you have already been introduced to a very popular strategy formulation technique called SWOT analysis (strengths, weaknesses, opportunities and threats). The next several sections contain a brief explanation of some of the other major theories and ideas upon which our model of the strategic management process is based. These theories are summarized in Exhibit 1.4. Other important theories are woven into the chapters where they are most applicable.

Determinism versus Enactment

The traditional process for developing strategy consists of analyzing the internal and external environments of the organization to arrive at organizational strengths, weaknesses, opportunities and threats (SWOT). The results from this "**situation analysis**," as this process is sometimes called, are the basis for developing missions, goals and strategies.[7] In general, an organization should select strategies that (1) take advantage of organizational strengths and external opportunities or (2) neutralize or overcome internal weaknesses and external threats.

The traditional approach to strategy development is conceptually related to **environmental determinism**, which suggests that good management is associated with determining which strategy will best fit environmental, technical and human forces at a particular point in time, and then working to carry it out.[8] From this perspective, the most successful organization will be the one that best *adapts* to existing forces. In other words, the environment is the primary determinant of

Exhibit 1.4 — Ideas and Theories Regarding the Strategic Management Model

Situation Analysis	The traditional process for developing strategy, consisting of analyzing the internal and external environments of the organization, to arrive at organizational SWOT. The results form the basis for developing missions, goals, and strategies.
Environmental Determinism	Management's task is to determine which strategy will best fit environmental, technical, and human forces at a particular point in time and then work to carry it out.
Principle of Enactment	Organizations do not have to submit to existing forces in the environment. They can, in part, create their environments through strategic alliances with stakeholders, advertising, political lobbying, and a variety of other activities.
Deliberate Strategy	Managers plan to pursue an intended strategic course. Strategy is deliberate.
Emergent Strategy	Strategy simply emerges from a stream of decisions. Managers learn as they go.
Resource-Based View	An organization is a bundle of resources. The most important management function is to acquire and manage resources in such a way that the organization achieves sustainable competitive advantages leading to superior performance.
Stakeholder Management	The organization is viewed from the perspective of the internal and external constituencies that have a stake in the organization. Stakeholder analysis is used to guide the strategy process. Stakeholder management is central to the development of mutually beneficial relationships and alliances with external stakeholders.

strategy. After a critical review of environmental determinism, a well-known researcher once argued:

> There is a more fundamental conclusion to be drawn from the foregoing analysis: the strategy of a firm cannot be predicted, nor is it predestined; the strategic decisions made by managers cannot be assumed to be the product of deterministic forces in their environments . . . On the contrary, the very nature of the concept of strategy assumes a human agent who is able to take actions that attempt to distinguish one's firm from the competitors.[9]

The principle of **enactment** assumes that organizations do not have to submit to existing forces in the environment—they can, in part, shape their environments through strategic alliances with stakeholders, advertising, political lobbying and a variety of other activities.[10]

It is not necessary to completely reject determinism and the view that organizations should adapt to their environments or the more modern view that organizations can alter their environments through enactment. In reality, the best-run organizations are engaged in both processes simultaneously, influencing those parts of the environment over which the firm can exercise some control and adapting to environmental circumstances that are either uncontrollable or too costly to influence.

Deliberate versus Emergent Strategy Formulation

The traditional school of thought concerning strategy formulation also supports the view that managers respond to the forces discussed thus far by making decisions that are consistent with a preconceived strategy. In other words, strategy is deliberate. **Deliberate strategy** implies that managers *plan* to pursue an *intended* strategic course. On the other hand, in some cases strategy simply emerges from a stream of decisions. Managers learn as they go. An **emergent strategy** is one that was not planned or intended, but involves recognizing an opportunity and reacting quickly. According to this perspective, managers *learn* what will work through a process of trial and error.[11] Supporters of this view argue that organizations that limit themselves to acting on the basis of what is already known or understood will not be sufficiently innovative to create a sustainable competitive advantage.[12]

The story of the small Honda motorcycle offers support for the concept of emergent strategy. When Honda executives decided to market a small motorcycle, they had no idea it would be so successful. In fact, the prevailing wisdom was that small motorcycles would not sell very well. But Honda executives broke the rules and made the decision to market a small motorcycle. As sales expanded, they increased marketing, and ultimately captured two-thirds of the American motorcycle market. In spite of many such examples of successful emergent strategies, it is not a good idea to completely reject deliberate strategy. In other words, firms should engage in both planning and learning. One of the strongest advocates of the emergent strategy perspective once confessed, "we shall get nowhere without emergent learning alongside deliberate planning."[13] Both processes are necessary if an organization is to succeed.

The Resource-Based View of the Firm

Another perspective on strategy development has gained wide acceptance in recent years. It is called the **resource-based view of the firm** and has its roots in the work of the earliest strategic management theorists.[14] According to this view, an organization is a bundle of resources, which fall into the general categories of (1) financial resources, including all of the monetary resources from which a firm can draw; (2) physical resources such as plants, equipment, locations and access to raw materials; (3) human resources, which pertains to the skills, background and training of individuals within the firm; (4) knowledge and learning resources, which help the firm to innovate and remain competitive and (5) general organizational resources, which includes a variety of factors that are peculiar to specific organizations. Examples of general organizational resources include the formal reporting structure, management techniques, internal planning systems, knowledge found in the organization and the systems that help to create it, organizational culture, organizational reputation and relationships within the organization as well as relationships with external stakeholders.[15]

If a resource that a firm possesses has value in allowing a firm to take advantage of opportunities or neutralize threats, if only a small number of firms possess it, if the organization is aware of the value of the resource and is taking advantage of it, and if it is difficult to imitate, either by direct imitation or substitution for another resource, then it may lead to a **sustainable competitive advantage**. A sustainable competitive advantage is an advantage that is difficult to imitate by competitors and thus leads to higher-than-average organizational performance over a long time period.[16] For example, Toyota has been able create and maintain a high-performance knowledge-sharing network with its suppliers and other stakeholders that has led to very high levels of efficiency and innovation.[17] Also, the success of Marriott is largely attributable to advantages created by resources that have been difficult to duplicate by other companies in the hotel industry, such as outstanding financial controls and a very strong reputation. Many strategy scholars believe that effective acquisition and development of organizational resources is the most important reason that some organizations are more successful than others. There is substantial research evidence to support the idea that firms that possess resources that are valuable, rare, have no viable substitutes, and are hard for competitors to imitate have high financial performance.[18]

Stakeholder Analysis and Management

The stakeholder perspective of strategic management considers the organization from the perspective of the internal and external constituencies that have a strong interest in the organization. High priority, or "primary," stakeholders include shareholders, employees, managers, customers, suppliers, communities and a variety of other individuals and groups that vary in their importance depending on the situation of the firm and its industry. For instance, labor unions are a primary stakeholder in unionized industries.

It is helpful to draw a distinction between stakeholder analysis and stakeholder management. **Stakeholder analysis** involves identifying and prioritizing key stakeholders, assessing their needs, collecting ideas from them, and integrating this knowledge into strategic management processes such as the establishment of strategic direction and the formulation and implementation of strategies. Organizations can use the information they collect from stakeholders to develop and modify their strategic direction, strategies and implementation plans. Organizations also can use information from stakeholders to predict stakeholder responses to their own strategic actions.

Stakeholder management, on the other hand, includes communicating, negotiating, contracting, and managing relationships with stakeholders, and motivating them to behave in ways that are beneficial to the organization and its other stakeholders. In reality, the processes associated with stakeholder analysis and management are overlapping. For example, a firm may use a survey both to collect information on customer needs and communicate information about a new service.

Many successful organizations have learned that productive and mutually beneficial relationships with stakeholders can lead to competitive advantages.[19] Some of these advantages, and the value they create, are outlined in Exhibit 1.5. Research evidence supports the view that firms that are vigilant in serving the needs

---

Exhibit 1.5   Managing for Stakeholders and Value Creation

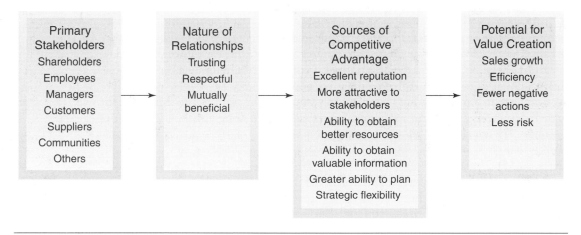

Primary Stakeholders	Nature of Relationships	Sources of Competitive Advantage	Potential for Value Creation
Shareholders	Trusting	Excellent reputation	Sales growth
Employees	Respectful	More attractive to stakeholders	Efficiency
Managers	Mutually beneficial	Ability to obtain better resources	Fewer negative actions
Customers		Ability to obtain valuable information	Less risk
Suppliers		Greater ability to plan	
Communities		Strategic flexibility	
Others			

of a broad group of stakeholders have higher financial performance and may have lower risk in terms of variability of returns.[20] This sort of management is sometimes called "**managing for stakeholders.**" According to Jeffrey Harrison, Douglas Bosse and Robert Phillips, "A firm that manages for stakeholders allocates more resources to satisfying the needs and demands of its legitimate stakeholders than what is necessary to simply retain their willful participation in the productive activities of the firm. Firms that exhibit this sort of behavior develop trusting relationships with stakeholders based on principles of distributional, procedural and interactional justice."[21]

Distributional justice means that firms give more value back to the stakeholders that helped to create it than what they really need to provide simply to retain their involvement in transactions with the firm.[22] For instance, Starbucks, a stakeholder-oriented company, gives medical benefits to its part-time employees.[23] This practice is unusual in its industry, but Starbucks feels strongly that its employees deserve to be treated well because they are on the front lines creating value for the company. Firms that practice distributional justice also tend to provide exceptional products at prices that are below what their competitors might charge for a comparable product. Honda and Toyota are examples. These sorts of firms also allocate more value back to other stakeholders, such as suppliers, shareholders and the communities in which they operate.

Distributional justice leads to relationships with stakeholders that are mutually beneficial. Mutual benefit motivates stakeholders to do business with the firm and may also motivate them to reveal valuable information that the firm can use to create even more value. For instance, a supplier may be willing to provide information about a new technology to a firm if it believes that it will share in some way in the value that is created from the technology. Such information can spur innovation and help a firm to plan better for the future. Strategic flexibility is increased as the firm is presented with a larger number of better business opportunities from which to select.[24] In addition, highly skilled potential employees are likely to be attracted to the best employers.[25] Stakeholder cooperation and innovation can also enhance the efficiency of a firm's operations. Finally, costs associated with creating and enforcing contracts are minimized because there is a higher level of confidence that the parties will actually follow through on agreements.[26]

Trust is essential to unlocking these benefits. Although distributional justice is important, procedural and interactional justice also help a firm build trusting relationships. **Procedural justice** refers to a stakeholder's perception of how fair a decision-making process is and **interactional justice** pertains to fairness in the way that stakeholders are treated in transactions with the firm.[27] According to Harrison, Bosse and Phillips, "Together, procedural and interactional justice compensate for the fact that a genuinely fair distribution of tangible value among stakeholders is elusive. In other words, although a stakeholder may not believe that their portion of the value distributed to them is precisely fair, they may still believe that processes are fair and that they have been treated with respect."[28]

A firm with a trustworthy reputation can also avoid value destroying outcomes such as legal suits, adverse regulation, consumer boycotts, strikes, walkouts, and bad press.[29] Avoiding negative stakeholder responses can reduce expenses as well as the risks a business faces.[30] According to an expert on business ethics:

> There is a long-term cost to unethical behavior that tends to be neglected. That cost is to the trust of the people involved. Companies today—due to increasing global competition and advancing technological complexity—are much more dependent than ever upon the trust of workers, specialists, managers, suppliers,

distributors, customers, creditors, owners, local institutions, national governments, venture partners, and international agencies. People in any of those
groups who believe that they have been misgoverned by bribes, sickened by
emissions, or cheated by products tend, over time, to lose trust in the firm
responsible for those actions.[31]

One of the common criticisms of the stakeholder approach is that it leads to a
situation in which all (or most) stakeholders are equally weighted in the decision-
making process. However, this is a misconception.[32] One of the first activities
associated with a stakeholder analysis is a discussion of the priorities given to each
stakeholder. For example, in most organizations shareholders, employees and
customers would have higher management priority than financial intermediaries or
special interest groups. Indeed, it is reasonable to give priority to stakeholders
based primarily on what they contribute to the creation of value and the
achievement of the firm's goals.

Global Strategic Management

Most successful organizations eventually find that their domestic markets have
become saturated or that foreign markets offer opportunities for growth and
profitability that often are not available domestically. Many forces are leading firms
into the international arena (see Exhibit 1.6). American industrial giants like Coke,
Hasbro, McDonalds and Marriott have found tremendous opportunities for growth
and profitability by expanding into Europe and Asia. Auto giants Toyota, Honda and
Nissan have used a combination of exporting, joint ventures and international
production to expand beyond Japan and become worldwide leaders in the
automobile industry. In fact, Japanese auto manufacturers now manufacture more
automobiles in foreign countries than in Japan.[33] Kikkoman turned soy sauce into a
mainstream global product.[34] Opportunities are not limited to large firms. Some
smaller, start-up American firms have found that they can enter growing international
markets more easily than they can fight for market share in saturated U.S. markets.[35]

Falling trade barriers in European markets, a general worldwide economic
malaise, and fears of increased terrorist activity are among the most significant global
trends affecting business decision-making in international markets. Although the
process of economic unification in Europe is proceeding slowly, it is expected to lead
eventually to increased productivity and reduced costs for European businesses.

Exhibit 1.6   Forces Favoring Globalization

Saturated domestic markets
Profitability of foreign markets
Falling trade barriers
Newly industrialized countries (i.e., Korea, Taiwan, Spain) leading to increasing global competition and
    new market opportunities
Growing similarity of industrialized nations
Shift toward market economies (i.e., East Germany)
English becoming a universally spoken language
Globalization of capital markets
Availability of lower-cost resources (i.e., labor) in some foreign countries
Uniformity in technical standards
Opportunities to learn from foreign joint venture partners

Eastern Europe, despite political turmoil and a limited infrastructure, still offers substantial investment opportunities, due to low labor rates and untapped consumer markets. Latin America also offers substantial business opportunities. China is one of the fastest growing consumer markets in the world. Many American manufacturing firms are building plants in China to take advantage of low labor costs and proximity to a large, growing consumer market.

Global strategic management offers many new management challenges. The values, resources and business practices of countries vary widely, although management techniques are slowly converging.[36] Most of the larger companies described in this book have substantial international business assets. They have to deal with global issues side-by-side with domestic considerations. This book is organized in a similar fashion. Rather than breaking global strategic management out into a separate chapter, we will discuss global issues in each chapter. For example, while we are discussing business strategies we will also discuss how they can be implemented in an international context.

A Combined Approach

The strategic management process model upon which this book is based relies, to some degree, on each of the theories and ideas that have been described in these sections. With regard to the adaptation/enactment dimension, firms should adapt to forces in the external environment if it is unreasonable to try to change them, while being proactive in other areas. Also, successful strategy can emerge from the firm's planning processes, from organizational learning through trial and error, or from a combination. The resource-based view is central to the sections on internal analysis and the development of competitive advantages. The sections dealing with analysis of the external environment draw heavily from stakeholder theory, as does the material on formation of alliances. Aspects of global strategic management are integrated throughout all of the chapters.

The stakeholder perspective does not compete with the resource-based view. In fact, the two perspectives are complementary because an organization is dependent on its stakeholders for most of the resources it acquires and develops.[37] Consequently, for a firm to be successful it needs good working relationships with its stakeholders and those relationships, in turn, can be a source of competitive advantage. For example, a firm that has excellent relationships with its financial intermediaries is in a better position to obtain needed capital. Also, strong relationships with suppliers can lead to better contract terms and greater knowledge sharing.

In addition to these theories and perspectives, this book draws heavily from economic theory, especially pertaining to industrial organization economics. Much of the material on industry analysis found in Chapter 2 was developed by economists, and Michael Porter in particular. The balanced approach found in this book will provide you with a set of tools that will be applicable to a wide variety of organizational circumstances. It will give you the opportunity to integrate multiple perspectives into a comprehensive set of strategic plans.

You have now been introduced to the strategic planning process and a variety of perspectives upon which it is built. However, strategic planning processes sometimes become rigid and unimaginative. For example, some corporations give their managers strategic planning templates that need to be filled in. Such systems are unlikely to result in the meaningful changes that are necessary to success in an increasingly turbulent business environment. Strategic thinking, the topic of the next section, can help firms avoid a creative straight jacket.

STRATEGIC THINKING AND ENTREPRENEURSHIP

How do firms move beyond what is tried and proven to find successful new products and services, new ways of creating them, or new ways of doing business? Apple Computer re-invigorated itself with the iPod. IKEA broke with tradition in the furniture retailing industry by selling high volumes of high-quality furniture at discount prices and allowing customers to take it home the same day. Bill Gates once said that Microsoft is "always two years away from failure," meaning that at any time a competitor could create an operating system that would make Windows obsolete.[38]

Broadly speaking, **entrepreneurship** is the process through which individuals, groups or firms pursue opportunities to create new value.[39] It involves recognizing or creating an opportunity, assembling the resources necessary to pursue it, and then managing those resources to bring the new venture into being. Entrepreneurship can occur both within firms and independently of them. In this book we are more interested in the type of entrepreneurship that occurs within firms. This type of entrepreneurship is sometimes called strategic entrepreneurship or intrapraneurship. It is how innovation is used to create new business for the firm. Innovation and entrepreneurship are common themes in this book. Of particular importance are the section on learning and knowledge creation in Chapter 3 and the section on facilitating innovation and entrepreneurship in Chapter 7.

One of the keys to innovation and entrepreneurship is to foster strategic thinking. **Strategic thinking** is the term used to describe the innovative aspects of strategic management. A rigid strategic planning process can drive out strategic thinking. For example, some firms require their managers to establish and follow very detailed plans which do not allow for deviations. Other firms harshly penalize their managers for failure, so they are afraid to try new ideas. Effective strategic planning processes incorporate creative aspects associated with strategic thinking.

There is no consensus on the meaning of strategic thinking or exactly what it entails. However, certain characteristics are associated with the kind of thinking that is needed to stimulate innovation in the strategic planning process. These characteristics are a focus on strategic intent, a long-term perspective, consideration of the past and the present, a systems perspective, the ability to seize unanticipated opportunities, and a scientific approach.[40]

1. *Intent Focused.* Some people think of creative processes as purely random and unstructured. However, strategic thinking is not a random process. It is based on a vision of where the organization is attempting to go. This vision is sometimes called *strategic intent*. Strategic thinking leads to ideas that will help the organization achieve its vision.

2. *Long-term Oriented.* Some managers are so concerned about short-term operating details that they have a hard time focusing on where the firm is going. While it is true that efficiency often requires attention to details, it is also true that sometimes managers need to mentally step away from their day-to-day problems in order to focus on the future.

3. *Consideration of Past and Present.* Although strategic thinking is long-term oriented, it also includes learning from the past and recognizing the present. If organizations learn from the past they can avoid making the same mistakes and can capitalize on the things they have done right. This is consistent with the organizational learning perspective that strategies emerge out of a stream of decisions. Managers also need to consider the constraints of the present.

Some ideas that appear reasonable may fail because of lack of resources or poor timing.[41]

4. *Systems Perspective.* The organization sits at the center of a network of constituencies called stakeholders. Furthermore, the organizational network exists in the context of the socio-cultural, economic, technological and political/legal environment. Strategic thinking entails envisioning the whole system and how the actions a firm is taking or might take are being influenced by or influence that system. This approach helps in the generation of strategic alternatives, in their thoughtful evaluation and in anticipating the reactions of external stakeholders such as customers, competitors or government regulators to the actions a firm intends to take.

5. *Ability to Seize Opportunities.* Managers sometimes encounter unanticipated opportunities that can further the intended strategies of the firm. The strategic planning process should be flexible enough to allow managers to take advantage of these opportunities when they occur.

6. *Scientific Approach.* This may also be called "hypothesis testing." A firm should generate ideas through a creative process and then test them to see if they will work. Testing can occur through analysis, as the firm establishes criteria that are important and then weighs ideas against those criteria and an evaluation of the external environment and firm resources. Ultimately, firms have to be willing to "pull the trigger" on ideas that make it through the analysis stage and actually try them. Often with new product introductions markets are tested in a limited geography. Also, new technologies may be applied only in particular areas of the firm. The firm then collects data to assess the success of the idea. If an idea is successful it can be more broadly applied.

Strategic thinking helped Sunil B. Mittal transform his bicycle parts business into India's most profitable cellular phone company.[42] This sort of thinking also thrives in companies like Virgin Group LTD that constantly try new ideas and capitalize on the ones that work.[43] Virgin is currently involved in delivering a wide variety of products and services, including health clubs, balloon flights, gaming, airlines, credit cards, cellular phone service, motorcycle taxis, insurance and cosmetics.[44] Companies like Virgin foster an atmosphere that supports strategic thinking.

Strategic thinking happens all the time, as employees and managers think of ideas that could help the organization move towards its vision. However, firms need to be positioned to take advantage of strategic thinking when it occurs. There are several ways to foster strategic thinking. First, organizations need to have systems in place to identify and evaluate good ideas when they occur. For example, Disney periodically allows some of its employees to share ideas with top management. Also, something as simple as an easily accessible online suggestion box can help with idea collection. Second, employees and managers must be encouraged to participate in strategic thinking and rewarded when they do. Lincoln Electric, the world's largest arc welder manufacturer, has a tradition of rewarding employees handsomely for suggestions they make. Third, organizations should integrate the elements of strategic thinking directly into their strategic planning processes. For example, managers can be invited to participate in a group process of evaluating forces in the external environment, resulting in the generation and evaluation of strategic alternatives.[45] Fourth, organizations may need to provide managers and employees with training, sometimes through consultants, in how to think strategically. Finally, and perhaps most importantly, organizations have to foster a risk-taking atmosphere, in part by not harshly penalizing failures when they occur.

This chapter emphasized the importance of strategic management in modern organizations. It provided an overview of the strategic management process and a foundation for understanding the underlying theories and ideas upon which that process is based. In addition, a distinction was made between the rigid, systematic aspects of the strategic management process and strategic thinking. Organizations should incorporate aspects of strategic thinking into their planning processes to ensure that the organization remains viable now and in the longer term.

KEY POINTS SUMMARY

This chapter emphasized the important role of the strategic management process in modern organizations. Some of the most important points are:

1. The strategic management process includes the activities of internal and external analysis, establishment of strategic direction, development of strategies for the corporate and business levels of the organization, development and execution of an implementation plan, and the establishment of strategic controls.

2. The traditional process for developing strategy, sometimes called situation analysis, consists of analyzing the internal and external environments of the organization to arrive at organizational strengths, weaknesses, opportunities and threats (SWOT). The results are the basis for developing missions, goals and strategies.

3. A deterministic view of strategy argues that the key role of managers is to determine which strategy will best fit environmental, technical and human forces at a particular point in time, and then work to carry it out. However, according to the principle of enactment, organizations do not have to submit to existing forces in the environment. They can, in part, create their environments through strategic alliances with stakeholders, advertising, political lobbying and a variety of other activities.

4. The deliberate view of strategy is that managers plan to pursue an intended strategic course. On the other hand, the emergent view argues that strategy simply develops or evolves from a stream of decisions. Managers learn as they go.

5. According to the resource-based view of the firm, an organization is a bundle of resources. The most important management function is to acquire and manage resources in such a way that the organization achieves sustainable competitive advantages leading to superior performance.

6. Stakeholder theory views the organization from the perspective of the internal and external constituencies that have an interest in the organization. Competitive advantages can result from effective stakeholder management.

7. Many trends and influences are pushing firms to increase their involvement in international markets. Most large firms have substantial global investments. Even smaller, entrepreneurial firms are finding opportunities in foreign markets. Global aspects of strategic management are integrated into each chapter.

8. Strategic thinking is the term to describe the creative aspects of the strategic management process. It helps foster entrepreneurship, which is the process through which individuals, groups or firms pursue opportunities to create new value. Strategic thinking involves strategic intent, a long-term perspective, consideration of the past and the present, a total systems orientation, the ability to seize unanticipated opportunities, and a scientific approach. Organizations have to encourage strategic thinking and take advantage of it when it occurs.

REFERENCES

1   S. Hamm, "Big Blue Goes into Analysis," *Business Week* (April 27, 2009): 16; *IBM 2008 Annual Report*: 6.

2   R.E. Freeman, J.S. Harrison and A.C. Wicks, *Managing for Stakeholders: Survival Reputation and Success* (London: Yale University Press, 2007);

R.E. Freeman, *Strategic Management: A Stakeholder Approach* (Boston: Pitman Publishing, 1984).

3   A. Mackey, "The Effects of CEOs on Firm Performance," *Strategic Management Journal* 29 (2008): 1357–1367.

4   C. Tkaczyk, "Keeping Creatives Happy," *Fortune* (March 16, 2009): 40.

5   "Company Overview," http://www.google.com/corporate (April 22, 2009).

6   "Barnes & Noble, Inc. Mission Statement," http://www.missionstatements.com/fortune_500_mission_statements.html (April 22, 2009).

7   C. W. Hofer and D. E. Schendel, *Strategy Formulation: Analytical Concepts* (St. Paul: West Publishing, 1978).

8   J. Bourgeois, III, "Strategic Management and Determinism," *Academy of Management Review* 9 (1984): 586–596; L.G. Hrebiniak and W.F. Joyce, "Organizational Adaptation: Strategic Choice and Environmental Determinism," *Administrative Science Quarterly* 30 (1985): 336–349.

9   Bourgeois, "Strategic Management and Determinism," 589.

10   L. Smirchich and C. Stubbart, "Strategic Management in an Enacted World," *Academy of Management Review* 10 (1985): 724–736.

11   H. Mintzberg and A. Mc Hugh, "Strategy Formation in an Adhocracy," *Administrative Science Quarterly* 30 (1985): 160–197.

12   H. Mintzberg, "The Design School: Reconsidering the Basic Premises of Strategic Management," *Strategic Management Journal* 11 (1990): 171–196.

13   H. Mintzberg, "Learning 1, Planning 0: Reply to Igor Ansoff," *Strategic Management Journal* 12 (1991): 465.

14   C.A. Montgomery, *Resource-Based and Evolutionary Theories of the Firm* (Boston: Kluwer Academic Publishers, 1995).

15   J.B. Barney, "Firm Resources and Sustained Competitive Advantage," *Journal of Management* 17 (1991): 99–120; J.B. Barney, *Gaining and Sustaining Competitive Advantage* (Reading, Mass: Addison-Wesley, 1997); J.S. Harrison, M.A. Hitt, R.E. Hoskisson and R.D. Ireland, "Synergies and Post-Acquisition Performance: Differences Versus Similarities in Resource Allocations," *Journal of Management* 17 (1991): 173–190; J.T. Mahoney and J.R. Pandian, "The Resource-Based View

within the Conversation of Strategic Management," *Strategic Management Journal* 13 (1992): 363–380; B. Wernerfelt, "A Resource-Based View of the Firm," *Strategic Management Journal* 5 (1984): 171–180.

16   Barney, "Firm Resources and Sustained Competitive Advantage"; Mahoney and Pandian, "The Resource-Based View."

17   J.H. Dyer and N.W. Hatch, "Using Supplier Networks to Learn Faster," *MIT Sloan Management Review* Spring (2004): 57–63; J.K. Dyer and K. Nobeoka, "Creating and Managing a High-performance Knowledge-sharing Network: The Toyota case," *Strategic Management Journal* 21 (2000): 345–367.

18   T.R. Crook, D.J. Ketchen, Jr., J.G. Combs and S.Y. Todd, "Strategic Resources and Performance: A Meta-Analysis," *Strategic Management Journal* 29 (2008): 1141–1154. For a detailed review, see J.B. Barney and A.M. Arikan, "The Resource-based View: Origins and Implications," in M.A. Hitt, R.E. Freeman and J.S. Harrison, eds. *Handbook of Strategic Management* (Oxford: Blackwell Publishers, LTD, 2001): 124–188.

19   R.E. Freeman, J.S. Harrison and A.C. Wicks, *Managing for Stakeholders: Survival Reputation and Success* (London: Yale University Press, 2007); R.E. Freeman and J. McVea, "A stakeholder approach to strategic management," in Hitt, Freeman and Harrison, *Handbook of Strategic Management*: 189–207; T.M. Jones, "Instrumental Stakeholder Theory: A Synthesis of Ethics and Economics," *Academy of Management Review* 20 (1995): 404–437; T. Donaldson and L.E. Preston, "The Stakeholder Theory of the Corporation: Concepts, Evidence, and Implications," *Academy of Management Review* 20 (1995): 65–91.

20   For direct tests of the proposition that serving a broad group of stakeholders leads to higher performance, see R. Sisodia, D.B. Wolfe and J. Sheth, *Firms of Endearment: How World-Class Companies Profit from Passion and Purpose* (Upper Saddle River, NJ: Wharton School Publishing, 2007); C. Fombrun and M. Shanley, "What's In a Name? Reputation Building and Corporate Strategy," *Academy of Management Journal* 33 (1990): 233–258; A.J. Hillman and G.D. Keim, "Shareholder Value, Stakeholder Management, and Social Issues: What's the Bottom Line?" *Strategic Management Journal* 22 (2001): 125–139; L.E. Preston and H.J. Sapienza, "Stakeholder Management and Corporate Performance," *Journal of Behavioral Economics* 19 (1990): 361–375; A. Riahi-Belkaoui,

"Organizational Effectiveness, Social Performance and Economic Performance," *Research in Corporate Social Performance and Policy* 12 (1991): 143–153. For support of the more general proposition that firms that satisfy social stakeholders have higher performance, see P.C. Godfrey, C.B. Merrill and J.M. Hansen, "The Relationship Between Social Responsibility and Shareholder Value: An Empirical Test of the Risk Management Hypothesis," *Strategic Management Journal* 30 (2009): 425–445; C.E. Hull and S. Rothenberg, "Firm Performance: The Interactions of Corporate Social Performance with Innovation and Industry Differentiation," *Strategic Management Journal* 29 (2008): 781–789; M. Orlitzky, F.L. Schmidt and S.L. Rynes, "Corporate Social and Financial Performance: A Meta-analysis," *Organization Studies* 24 (2003): 403–441.

21   J.S. Harrison, D.A. Bosse and R.A. Phillips, "Managing for Stakeholders, Stakeholder Utility Functions and Competitive Advantage," *Strategic Management Journal* (2010, forthcoming); R.E. Freeman, J.S. Harrison and A.C. Wicks, *Managing for Stakeholders: Survival Reputation and Success* (London: Yale University Press, 2007).

22   D.A. Bosse, R.A. Phillips and J.S. Harrison, "Stakeholders, Reciprocity and Firm Performance," *Strategic Management Journal* 30 (2009): 447–456.

23   Sisodia, Wolfe and Sheth, *Firms of Endearment.*

24   B.R. Barringer and J.S. Harrison, "Walking a Tightrope: Creating Value Through Interorganizational Relationships," *Journal of Management* 26 (2000): 367–403; R.E. Freeman and W.M. Evan, "Corporate Governance: A Stakeholder Interpretation," *Journal of Behavioral Economics* 19 (1990): 337–359.

25   D.B. Turban and D.W. Greening, "Corporate Social Performance and Organizational Attractiveness to Prospective Employees," *Academy of Management Journal* 40 (1996): 658–672.

26   O.E. Williamson, *Markets and Hierarchies: Analysis and Antitrust Implications* (New York: The Free Press, 1975).

27   Bosse, Phillips and Harrison, "Stakeholders, Reciprocity and Firm Performance"; Y. Luo, "Procedural Fairness and Interfirm Cooperation in Strategic Alliances," *Strategic Management Journal* 29 (2008): 27–46.

28   Harrison, Bosse and Phillips, "Managing for Stakeholders, Stakeholder Utility Functions and Competitive Advantage."

29   B. Cornell and A.C. Shapiro, "Corporate Stakeholders and Corporate Finance," *Financial Management* 16 (1987): 5–14; J.S. Harrison and C.H. John, "Managing and Partnering with External Stakeholders," *Academy of Management Executive* 10 (2) (1996): 46–60; M.E. Steadman, T.W. Zimmerer and R.F. Green, "Pressures from Stakeholders Hit Japanese Companies," *Long Range Planning* 28 (6) (1995): 29–37.

30   S.B. Graves and S.A. Waddock, "Institutional Owners and Corporate Social Performance," *Academy of Management Journal* 37 (1994): 1035–1046; H. Wang, J.B. Barney and J.J. Reurer, "Stimulating Firm-specific Investment through Risk Management," *Long Range Planning* 36 (1) (2003): 49–58.

31   L.T. Hosmer, "Response to 'Do Good Ethics Always Make for Good Business,' " *Strategic Management Journal* 17 (1996): 501; L.T. Hosmer, "Strategic Planning as if Ethics Mattered," *Strategic Management Journal* 15 (1994): 17–34.

32   R. Phillips, R.E. Freeman and A.C. Wicks, "What Stakeholder Theory is Not," *Business Ethics Quarterly* 13 (2003): 479–502.

33   "Japanese Makers of Cars Produce More Overseas," *Wall Street Journal* (August 1, 2006): A2.

34   "Sauce of Success," *The Economist* (April 11, 2009): 68.

35   P. Engardio, "Smart Globalization," *Business Week* (August 27, 2001): 132–134.

36   R. Calori and B. Dufour, "Management European Style," *Academy of Management Executive* (August, 1995): 61–73.

37   J. Pfeffer and G.R. Slancik, *The External Control of Organizations: A Resource Dependence Perspective* (New York: Harper and Row, 1978).

38   G. Hamel, "The Challenge Today: Changing the Rules of the Game," *Business Strategy Review* 9 (2) (1998): 19–26.

39   J.S. Harrison, *Strategic Management of Resources and Relationships* (New York: John Wiley and Sons, 2003).

40   T. O'Shannassy, "Modern Strategic Management: Balancing Strategic Thinking and Strategic Planning for Internal and External Stakeholders," *Singapore Management Review* 25 (2003): 53–67; J.M. Liedtka, "Strategy Formulation: The Roles of Conversation and Design," in M.A. Hitt, R.E. Freeman and J.S. Harrison,

Handbook of Strategic Management (Oxford: Blackwell Publishers, LTD, 2001): 70–93; G. Hamel and C. Prahalad, *Competing for the Future* (Boston: Harvard Business School Press, 1994).

41   L. Zacharakis, G.D. Meyer and J. De Castro, "Differing Perceptions of New Venture Failure: A Matched Exploratory Study of Venture Capitalists and Entrepreneurs," *Journal of Small Business Management* (July 1999): 1–14.

42   D.G. Neeleman, "The Top Entrepreneurs," *Business Week* (January 8, 2001): 84–85.

43   G. Hamel, *Leading the Revolution* (Boston: Harvard Business School Press, 2000).

44   "Products," http://www.virgin.com/Products.aspx (April 23, 2009).

45   P.C. Nutt, "Expanding the Search for Alternatives During Strategic Decision-making," *Academy of Management Executive* 18 (4): 14–28.

2

The External Environment

STRATEGY IN FOCUS

China

China has experienced rapid economic growth of about 9% annually since the late 1970s when it began moving from a centrally-planned economy to more of a market economy. Hundreds of thousands of factories sprung up in China, making everything from refrigerators to rivets. On the foundation of a population of 1.3 billion, the country is now the fourth largest economy and the third largest trading nation. Although economic growth has helped pull millions out of poverty, China is still a developing nation, with gross domestic product per capita less than $2,000 and approximately 100 million people trying to survive on less than $1 per day.

Global economic problems hit China's economy hard, especially in its exports. In response, China's exporters redoubled their efforts in the domestic market. For instance, the Beijing-based Lenovo Group, the fourth largest PC manufacturer in the world, fired its American CEO and began to focus more on selling PCs in China. When a Russian customer cancelled an order for 50,000 televisions from the Shenzhen-based Skyworth, the company simply released them to the domestic market. Also, Dongguan Meng Qiren Fashion, which once sold all of its high-end sweaters to Polo Ralph Lauren and other Western companies, is now selling much more of its products through Chinese retailers. To spur domestic consumption, in addition to huge stimulus spending, the Chinese government engaged in programs such as giving rural consumers government-sponsored discounts on electronic products. The media showed advertisements of happy farmers buying televisions and refrigerators. China also launched a stock exchange for young growth companies, a counterpart to the Nasdaq exchange in the U.S.

In spite of a reduction in the rate of its economic growth, China's economy is still growing. Its rise over the past few decades has led China's leaders to become bolder on the world stage. This boldness is supported by a wave of nationalism among Chinese citizens who witnessed extreme economic problems in capitalist nations. Of course, China's size also means that it has a large influence on the economies of its major trading partners such as the U.S. and Japan. Also, because of the size and growth of its economy, many foreign firms have found China an attractive opportunity for investment. However, doing business in China can be tricky because of government intervention. For instance, even as Google began to enjoy increases in advertising revenues in China, the government blocked access to its YouTube service, citing offensive content.[1]

We live in an interconnected world. Economic growth in China is luring multi-nationals to make massive investments in the country. China's products are often manufactured at a lower cost than competing products produced by foreign rivals. This comparative advantage means that demand has gradually shifted from domestically produced products to Chinese products in many countries, which has reduced growth in their own gross domestic product. Also, China's thirst for basic commodities such as oil to fuel its economic growth puts pressure on world markets. Government intervention, as well as resource shortfalls, are a threat to the viability of some foreign businesses operating in the country.

Examples of global interconnectedness are abundant. Terrorism has severe repercussions for much of the global business environment. Large and highly visible business scandals have led to much closer scrutiny of accounting and business practices throughout the world. Volatile world oil prices are encouraging the development of alternative energy sources, as well as directly influencing most segments of the world economy. Trade agreements among countries dramatically alter the ability of some firms to compete in foreign markets. Each of these forces is a part of a firm's external environment.

This chapter is about the influence of the external environment on organizations and how they can adapt to or influence the environment to enhance their competitive positions.[2] Although a single organization cannot have much direct influence on its broad environment (i.e., societal and economic forces, technology trends, global politics), it can buffer itself from threats and take advantage of opportunities. Fundamental global trends and influences, which are a part of an organization's broad environment, are largely beyond the influence of any one firm. However, how companies respond to these situations can have important competitive implications.

In contrast with the largely uncontrollable elements found in an organization's broad environment, the external stakeholders that compose an organization's task environment (i.e., customers, suppliers, competitors) are subject to substantial firm influence. Organizations can create partnerships with these stakeholders or pursue a variety of other management techniques to enhance their competitive positions.[3] Exhibit 2.1, which was first presented in Chapter 1, provides an illustration of

Exhibit 2.1   The Organization and Its Environments

the broad and task environments. We will now discuss the broad environment, followed by the task environment.

THE BROAD ENVIRONMENT

Forces in the broad environment can have a tremendous impact on a firm and its task environment; however, individual firms typically have only a marginal ability to influence these forces. In rare cases, individual firms can influence trends in the broad environment, as when innovations at Intel influence technological trends in the microprocessor, microcomputer, and software industries. In general, however, it is virtually impossible for one independent firm to dramatically influence societal views on abortion, policies on trade with China, migration to the Sun Belt, the number of school-age children, or even the desirability of particular clothing styles. Consequently, although firms may be able to influence the broad environment to some degree, the emphasis in this book generally will be on analyzing and responding to this segment of the environment.

Analysis of the broad environment can help managers identify both threats and opportunities. Alternative strategies can then be devised that will help the firm respond to threats and take advantage of the opportunities. These strategic alternatives are further evaluated on the basis of information gained from analysis of the broad and task environments, as well as an analysis of internal resources and competitive advantage. Consequently, analysis of trends and influences in the broad environment is an important part of the strategic management process. The sections that follow will further demonstrate this point. The most important elements in the broad environment, as it relates to a business organization and its task environment, are sociocultural, economic, technological, and political/legal forces. Managers should evaluate these forces at the domestic and, as appropriate, global levels.

Sociocultural Forces

A few of the major sociocultural issues currently facing the United States are shown in Exhibit 2.2. Analysis of societal trends is important from at least four perspectives. First, because most of the other stakeholder groups are also members of society, some of their values and beliefs are derived from broader societal influences, which can create opportunities and threats for organizations. For example, societal interest in health and fitness has led to business opportunities in the home fitness, nutritional supplements, and low carbohydrate food industries. Similarly, concerns about smoking set the stage for regulatory and legal backlash against the tobacco companies, and new concerns about obesity may lead to a similar backlash against fast food companies.

Second, firms may reduce the risk of gaining a bad "ethical" reputation by anticipating and adjusting for sociocultural trends. In the late 1990s, Bill Gates, the founder of Microsoft, was facing rising societal concern about the extraordinary profits generated by Microsoft and by his "unimpressive philanthropic record."[4] In 1999, he donated $3.35 billion to the William Gates Foundation, which provides grants for health and human services organizations, and to the Gates Learning Foundation, which gives software, computers, and services to libraries in low income areas.[5] Now he has relinquished operating control of Microsoft to devote more time to working with his wife in philanthropic activities. In another example, the reputation of the Denny's restaurant chain suffered a significant blow when its

---

Exhibit 2.2   Major Social Issues in the United States

Influence of terrorism
Immigration laws
Role of government in health care and child care
Declining quality of education
Legality of abortion
Influence of World Wide Web
Importance and role of the military
Levels of foreign investment/ownership in the United States
Social costs of restructuring, especially layoffs
Pollution and disposal of toxic and nontoxic wastes
General increase in environmental awareness
Drug addiction
Continued migration toward the Sun Belt states
Graying of America
AIDS and other health problems
Major global issues

---

racist hiring practices become public knowledge. However, Ron Petty, Denny's CEO, introduced initiatives that turned the company into a model of multicultural sensitivity.[6] After a couple of years Denny's was listed as number one on the list of Fortune's best companies for minorities.[7]

Third, correct assessment of sociocultural trends can help businesses avoid restrictive legislation. Industries and organizations that police themselves are less likely to be the target of legislative activity. The United States Sentencing Guidelines (USSG) were a direct response to public outcry over negligence on the part of businesses in preventing white-collar crime.[8] They are a set of compulsory guidelines courts must use to determine fines and penalties when corporate illegalities are proven. Similarly, the Sarbanes-Oxley Act of 2002 was passed by Congress in response to the accounting scandals that surfaced involving Arthur Andersen, WorldCom, Enron and others. The Act, which contains eleven sections, establishes tighter rules regarding executive and director securities trading, increases executive responsibility for corporate controls and public disclosure of financial information, and increases penalties for corporate fraud.[9]

The fourth reason that analysis of sociocultural values is important is that demographic and economic changes in society can create opportunities for and threats to the revenue growth and profit prospects of an organization.[10] For example, many baby boomer couples had babies later in life than their counterparts in past generations, causing a demographic trend toward older couples with children. In the 1990s this trend led to the development of higher quality baby accessories, clothing, and supplies, as well as new business opportunities in child care, specialized education, and movies and television shows that centered on families and children. Now more of these aging baby boomers, born between 1945 and 1965, are entering their wealthy empty-nest years and retiring. Their numbers and their wealth are stimulating growth in health maintenance and leisure industries and some luxury products and services. Furthermore, the baby boomers' children have purchasing power greater than previous generations of children, stimulating demand for music, entertainment, and fashion. Demographic changes such as these can help direct organizational planning and are often at the core of any forecast of industry demand.

Not only must an organization assess the potential effects of sociocultural forces on its business, it must manage its relationship and reputation with society at large. The media acts as a watchdog for society. It is a commanding force in managing the attitudes of the general public toward organizations. Executives have nightmares about their organizations being criticized in news shows or special reports. On the other hand, a well-managed relationship with the media can have a significant positive impact on a firm's image.

Economic Forces

Economic forces can have a profound influence on organizational behavior and performance. Economic growth, interest rates, the availability of credit, inflation rates, foreign exchange rates, and foreign trade balances are among the most critical economic factors. Economic growth can also have a large impact on consumer demand for products and services. Consequently, organizations should consider forecasts of economic growth in determining when to make critical resource allocation decisions such as plant expansions. Inflation rates also can influence a variety of business decisions and outcomes. For instance, some U.S. trucking companies simply can't compete as energy prices rise. Experts estimate that for every 10-cent increase in fuel cost, approximately 1,000 trucking companies fail. Also, high energy prices reduce demand for the goods trucking companies deliver.[11]

Inflation also influences interest rates that organizations have to pay. High interest payments can constrain the strategic flexibility of firms by making new ventures and capacity expansions prohibitively expensive. Low interest rates make investment opportunities look more attractive because they are less costly to finance. In theory, the resulting increase in business investments should also help stimulate economic growth. Consequently, many governments are highly pro-active in taking actions to curb inflationary forces.

Foreign exchange rates are another major source of uncertainty. For global organizations, profit earned in a foreign country may even turn into a loss due to unfavorable exchange rates. Volatility in exchange rates makes extracting profits from particular foreign operations both difficult and risky, which discourages further investments. Foreign trade balances are also highly relevant to both domestic and global organizations because they are an indication of the nature of trade legislation that might be expected in the future. For example, when the trade surplus with European Union countries is rising, American manufacturers who export to the European Union worry about new protectionist legislation, such as high tariffs that may be enacted to reduce the trade imbalance.[12] Foreign economies are linked through more than just exchange rates and trade balances. When the U.S. economy is weak, other economies are affected because demand for their exports declines. Consequently, effective strategic analysis involves an evaluation of the entire global economy, and especially those countries in which an international firm conducts business.

The sociocultural forces discussed in the last section often interact with the economic forces. In the United States, birthrates (a sociocultural force) are low and, because of improved health care and lifestyles (another sociocultural force), more people are living longer. This demographic shift toward an older population is influencing the economic forces in society. For example, the older population means that demand for premium services are high but, simultaneously, there are shortages of young workers to fill the entry level jobs, which may drive up wage rates and lead to inflation. So, for example, a service firm tracking these trends may project that its demand will go up as it sells its services to the older customers; but its wage rates will go up as well, leading to lower unit profitability.

To assess the effect of the interdependent sociocultural and economic forces, organizations often model their business environments by proposing and evaluating different scenarios. If decision makers develop scenarios based on basic trends and uncertainties they may be able to avoid "tunnel vision" and therefore reduce the number of poor decisions they make.[13] The scenarios are often framed as "optimistic," "pessimistic," and "most likely" by applying different assumptions and interpretations of various economic and sociocultural trend data. Continuing with the previous example, the service firm may use various demand and wage rate assumptions to build several different possible future scenarios as a way of evaluating different business options. These scenarios can be updated as information becomes more certain and may be used for evaluating different courses of action, such as capacity expansions or investments in labor-saving technologies.

This brief discussion of economic forces indicates the importance of monitoring and forecasting events in the domestic and global economies. We now turn our attention to the role that technological forces play in the strategic management of organizations.

Technological Forces

Technological change creates new products, services, and, in some cases, entire new industries. It also can change the way society behaves and what society expects. The Internet, hand-held computers, direct satellite systems, and cellular telephones are technological innovations that have experienced extraordinary growth in recent years, leaving formerly well-established industries stunned, creating new industry segments, and influencing the way many people approach work and leisure. Computers and telecommunications technologies, for example, have played an essential role in creating the increasingly global marketplace.

Technology refers to human knowledge about products and services and the way they are made and delivered. Technologies typically evolve through a series of steps, and each step has its own set of implications for managers. When a new idea or technology is proven to work in the laboratory, it is called an **invention**. New inventions are made every day as corporate research laboratories, universities, and individuals invent new products, new processes, and new technologies. Only a handful of those inventions, however, are ever developed past the laboratory stage. When an invention can be replicated reliably on a meaningful scale, it is referred to as an **innovation**. Most technological innovations take the form of new products or processes, such as fax machines, airbags, and cellular phones. A **basic innovation,** such as the microprocessor, light bulb, fiber optics, or mapping of the human genome, impacts much more than one product category or one industry.

To avoid being blindsided by a new technology, organizations should monitor technological developments in industries other than their own and conduct brainstorming sessions about the possible consequences for their own products and markets. For example, recording companies might have considered the effect of digital sound transmissions via the Internet on their traditional business models before being caught off guard by new start-ups like Napster that provided those transmissions at little or no cost to the user.[14] Now Apple's iTunes dominates what has become a primary source of music sales.

To help identify trends and anticipate their timing, organizations may participate in several kinds of technological forecasting efforts. In general, organizations may monitor trends by studying research journals, government reports, and patent filings. Another more formal method of technological forecasting is to solicit the opinion of experts outside of the organization. These experts may be interviewed directly or contacted as part of a formal survey, such as a Delphi study. A third method is to develop scenarios of alternative technological futures, which capture different rates of innovation and different emerging technologies. These scenarios then become part of the larger scenario planning effort described in the previous section, which allows organizations to conduct "what-if" analyses and to develop alternative plans for responding to new innovations.

In addition to forecasting, some organizations establish strategic alliances with universities or research companies to engage in joint research projects, which allows the companies to keep abreast of new trends. For example, most of the established pharmaceutical firms have created partnerships with smaller, innovative biotechnology research firms in order to capture the next generation of biotech-driven product and process technologies. Other organizations simply donate funds to universities for research in exchange for information about findings.

With a well-thought-out plan for monitoring technological trends, an organization can better prepare itself to receive early warnings about trends that will create opportunities and threats. Now we will turn our attention to the global political and legal forces in the broad environment of organizations.

Political/Legal Forces

Political forces, both at home and abroad, are significant determinants of organizational actions. Governments and other political bodies provide and enforce the rules by which organizations operate. Even in the United States, which is considered a "free" market economy, no organization is allowed the privilege of total autonomy from government regulations. Governments can encourage new business formation through tax incentives and subsidies; they can restructure organizations, as in the case of General Motors; and they can totally close organizations that do not comply with laws, ordinances, or regulations. Government intervention in business has increased dramatically in the U.S. and other countries in recent years, although the trend towards intervention followed a period of fairly significant decline in interventionism worldwide. Organizations can also turn to governments for help, as in the case of U.S. banks and automobile manufacturers requesting an infusion of cash so that they could remain financially viable.

Alliances and treaties among governments provide an additional level of complexity for organizations with significant foreign operations. For instance, the North American Free Trade Agreement (NAFTA), which altered trade policies among North American countries and the European Union, has had a huge impact on Europe.[15] A common world currency, advocated by China, could also dramatically alter the global economy.[16]

The amount of time and effort organizations should devote to learning about regulations, complying with them, and fostering good relationships with regulatory agencies and their representatives depends, in part, on the industry. Some laws and regulations pertain to only one industry, such as nuclear energy, whereas others, such as Food and Drug Administration (FDA) and Environmental Protection Agency (EPA) regulations, apply different regulations to different industries. Other regulations cut across industry boundaries and apply to all organizations, such as those promulgated by the Occupational Safety and Health Administration (OSHA). In some industries, such as pharmaceuticals and military and defense contracting, organizations employ entire departments of analysts that are dedicated to studying regulations and ensuring compliance.

In summary, social forces, the global economy, technology and the global political/legal forces make up the broad environment, the context in which the firm and its task environment exist. Although organizations typically should attempt to adapt to trends in the broad environment, they can have a much greater influence on their task environments. The next section will discuss the task environment.

THE TASK ENVIRONMENT

The task environment consists of stakeholders with whom organizations interact on a fairly regular basis (see Exhibit 2.1). These stakeholders include domestic and international customers, suppliers, competitors, government agencies and administrators, local communities, activist groups, unions, and financial intermediaries. Michael Porter, an economist at Harvard University, assimilated years of economic research into a simple model that helps determine the influence of the first three of these stakeholders—suppliers, customers, and competitors—on competition in an industry. His model will be discussed in the next section.[17]

Competitive Forces

Michael Porter integrated the theory of industrial organization economics into a "user friendly" model of the forces that drive industry competition. **Industries** are often difficult to define, but in general they refer to a group of organizations that compete directly with each other to win orders or sales in the marketplace. Porter's model includes suppliers, customers, and industry competitors. Competitors are further divided into three types: existing competitors, potential competitors, and indirect competitors. The influence of potential competitors on industry competition is determined by the strength of entry barriers, which are the forces that discourage new firms from entering the industry. Indirect competitors sell products that can be substituted for products sold by existing competitors, such as contact lenses and corrective surgery as substitutes for glasses. According to Porter, the five forces largely determine the type and level of competition in an industry and, ultimately, the industry's profit potential.[18] These forces are illustrated in Exhibit 2.3.

An entire industry group (as opposed to a single organization) is placed in the center of the model. The way a group is defined has implications for the way substitutes and competing products/services are treated. For instance, if the entire airline industry is defined as the focal industry group, then legacy carriers like Delta and American would be considered in direct competition with regional carriers like JetBlue and Southwest, while buses and trains would be treated as substitutes. However, if the industry is defined as exclusively the legacy carriers, then Delta, American and United would be considered direct competitors, while the regional carriers would be included with other substitutes. The way an industry group is defined also has implications for analysis of customers, suppliers, and entry barriers. Consequently, it is important to define the industry group carefully prior to proceeding with an analysis of the five forces. Next we will discuss the factors that determine the strength of each of these five forces.

Customers. Although all customers are important, some have a more powerful influence on industry dynamics than others. For instance, when retail giant Home Depot announced that it would no longer buy carpet from Shaw Industries (because

Porter's Five-Forces Model of Industry Competition

Exhibit 2.3

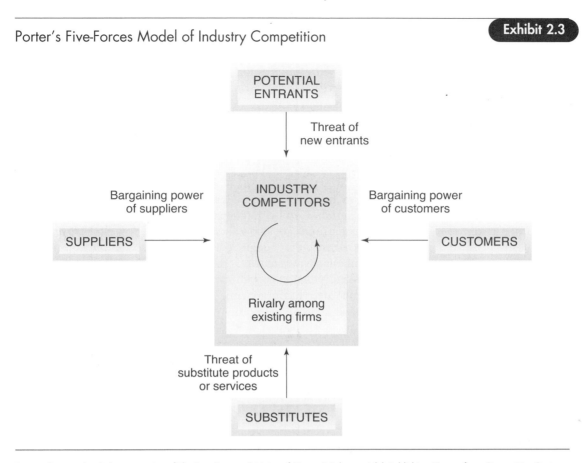

Shaw, a carpet manufacturer, was moving into retail), Shaw's stock dropped by 11% in one day.[19] According to Porter, customers tend to exhibit a powerful force on competition in an industry if the following conditions exist:

1. There are a small number of customers. In this case, losing one customer makes a big difference.
2. The customers make high-volume purchases.
3. The purchases customers make from the industry are large relative to the amount expended for items from other industries. Here customers will expend considerable effort to shop for the best price.
4. The products customers are buying are undifferentiated (also known as standard or generic). This means that customers are not concerned about which company they buy from.
5. The customers earn low profits. Customers who earn low profits are under constant pressure to keep the costs of their purchases down.
6. The customers can easily get accurate information on the selling industry's costs and demand. This gives them a real edge during negotiations.
7. The customers can easily integrate backward and become their own suppliers. Large companies sometimes buy supplier companies when they are unhappy with pricing.
8. Customers can easily switch from one seller to another.

In combination, these forces determine the bargaining power of customers—that is, the degree to which customers exercise active influence over pricing and the direction of product development efforts. Large retailers such as Wal-Mart (based in the U.S.) and Carrefour (based in France) are powerful because of high volume purchases and the ease with which they switch from one manufacturer to another for many products. In one instance, "Coca-Cola Co. said in a court ruling that it faced a 'serious risk' Wal-Mart Stores Inc. would launch a private-label rival to the Atlanta company's Powerade if Coke didn't agree to ship the sports drink directly to Wal-Mart warehouses."[20] The move outraged smaller Coke distributors who lost Wal-Mart's business.

Suppliers. Suppliers to industries provide equipment, supplies, component parts, and raw materials. The labor and capital markets from which firms draw their employees and investment funds are also a source of supply. Powerful suppliers can raise their prices and therefore reduce profitability levels in the buying industry. They also can exert influence and increase uncertainty for the buying industry by *threatening* to raise prices, reducing the quality of goods or services provided, or not delivering supplies when needed. In general, supplier power is greater under the following circumstances:

1.   Only a few suppliers are available.
2.   Few substitutes exist for the product or service that is supplied. (These first two conditions limit the ability of the buying industry to use alternative supply sources as a bargaining tool.)
3.   Suppliers are not dependent on the buying industry for a large percentage of their total sales. This means that the loss of one sale is not very important.
4.   Suppliers know that the buying industry must have the product or service that suppliers provide to manufacture their own products.
5.   Suppliers have differentiated their products, which means that the buying industry is willing to pay more for certain brands.
6.   Suppliers make it costly to switch suppliers. For example, IBM built its traditional mainframe business by making IBM mainframes incompatible with other brands, thus preventing buyers from switching.
7.   Suppliers can easily integrate forward and thus compete directly with their former buyers.

These forces combine to determine the strength of suppliers and the degree to which they can exert influence over the profits earned by firms in the industry. The laptop computer industry, for instance, is one that is particularly susceptible to the power of suppliers. Most manufacturers purchase virtually all of the laptop's components, including microprocessors, batteries, operating system software, and flat-panel displays. Consequently, the manufacturing costs, performance characteristics, and innovativeness of laptops are largely in the hands of suppliers.

Existing Competitors. In most industries, competitive moves by one firm affect other firms in the industry, which may incite retaliation or countermoves. Competitors jockey with each other for market share and for the favorable comments of investment analysts. In many industries, every new product introduction, marketing promotion, and capacity expansion has implications for the revenues, costs, and profits of other competitors. Overall profitability is most susceptible to negative pressures from competitive rivalry in industries characterized by the following:

1. Slow industry growth, which means that competitors must steal market share if they intend to grow.
2. High fixed costs, which mean that firms are under pressure to increase sales to cover their costs and earn profits.
3. Lack of product differentiation, which puts a lot of pressure on prices and often leads to price-cutting tactics.
4. A large number of competitors, which means that the total market must be divided in more ways.
5. High exit barriers, which means that firms may lose all or most of their investments in the industry when they withdraw from it. Therefore, they are more likely to remain in the industry even if profits are low.

In many industries, competition is so intense that profitability is suppressed to almost nothing, as has been the case at various times in the airline, small computer, and fast food industries.

In addition to an analysis of the level of competition in the industry, it is also useful to evaluate the strategies of industry groups. In some industries, groups of competitors are constrained by similar resource positions and follow similar strategies. The groups or clusters of similar competitors are called **strategic groups**. For example, in the steel industry, domestic steel companies are of two general types: integrated continuous mills and mini-mills. Traditionally, the two groups of competitors faced very different cost structures and competed in largely different market segments. In recent years, the integrated mills have invested in mini-mill technology and the mini-mill firms have developed new technologies to enter previously inaccessible market segments. Over time, the resource positions and strategies are converging, and the sharp differences between strategic groups are eroding.

One way to keep track of strategic groups and their behavior over time is with a strategic group map such as the one in Exhibit 2.4. A **strategic group map** is constructed by plotting industry rivals based on two or more strategic dimensions that are important to strategy in the industry. The axes of a strategic group map should describe strategy and not performance. Therefore, variables such as pricing strategy, customer service approach, level of advertising and product mix are appropriate, whereas return-on-assets and earnings-per-share are not. Furthermore, to reveal more about the industry, the dimensions should not be highly correlated with one another. Members of the same strategic group should end up in the same general location on the map.

Strategic group maps can help an organization understand the strategies of competitors. They may also highlight an area in the industry in which no firms are presently competing (an opportunity). Another helpful use is in tracking the evolution of an industry over time. If movement from one group to another is difficult, then it is likely that mobility barriers exist. Mobility barriers are similar to entry barriers, but exist between strategic groups within one industry.

Potential Competitors/Entry Barriers. Several forces determine the ease with which new competitors can enter an industry and, therefore, how many new entrants can be expected. New entrants increase competition in an industry, which may drive down prices and profits. They may add capacity, introduce new products or processes, and bring a fresh perspective and new ideas—all of which can drive

Exhibit 2.4   Strategic Group Map of Department Store and Specialty Retailing

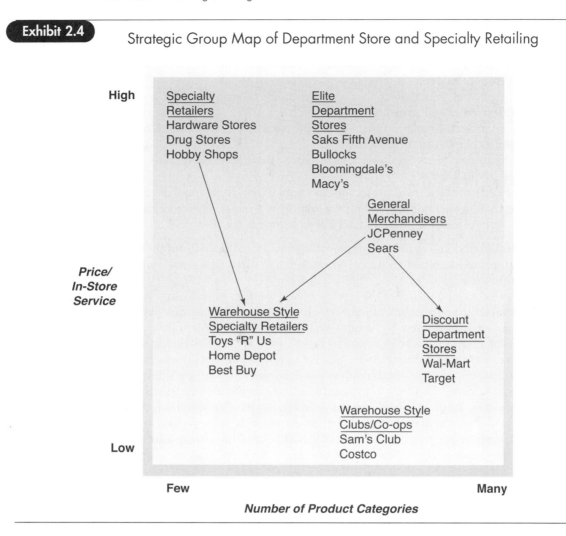

down prices, increase costs, or both. Forces that keep new entrants out, providing a level of protection for existing competitors, are called **entry barriers**.

Examples of entry barriers that are commonly found in many industries include the following:

1. Economies of scale, which occur when it is more efficient to produce a product in a larger facility at higher volume.
2. Large capital requirements, also known as start-up costs, can prevent a small competitor from entering an industry.
3. High levels of product differentiation, which means that some firms enjoy a loyal customer base, making it harder for a new firm to draw away customers.
4. High switching costs, which apply not only to suppliers, can also serve as an entry barrier protecting established firms in an industry.
5. Limited access to distribution channels, which may prevent new companies from getting their products to market.
6. Government policies and regulations that limit entry into an industry, effectively preventing new competition.

7. Existing firm possession of resources that are difficult to duplicate in the short term, such as patents, favorable locations, proprietary product technology, government subsidies, or access to scarce raw materials.
8. A past history of aggressive retaliation by industry competitors toward new entrants.

Taken together, these forces can result in high, medium, or low barriers. In industries with high entry barriers, few new firms enter the industry, which reduces competitive intensity and stabilizes profits for industry incumbents. When entry barriers are low, new firms can freely enter the industry, which increases rivalry and depletes profits. Examples of industries that are traditionally associated with high barriers to entry are aircraft manufacturing (due to technology, capital costs, and reputation) and automobile manufacturing (due to capital costs, distribution, and brand names). Medium-high barriers are associated with industries such as household appliances, cosmetics, and books. Low-entry barriers are found in most of the retailing industries.

One of the most powerful effects of the Internet has been the ability to circumvent traditional barriers to entry. For many Americans, Amazon.com is just as satisfying an outlet for buying books as the physical stores run by Barnes and Noble (and a lot quicker). Amazon.com, however, never had to face the extraordinary expense of leasing or buying land, building large bookstores in premium retail locations, stocking and maintaining inventories in remote locations, and hiring and training a workforce experienced in the nuances of book retailing. They circumvented those barriers to entry by going straight to consumers with an exclusively Internet-based strategy.

Indirect Competitors/Substitutes. If organizations provide goods or services that readily substitute for the goods and services provided by competitors in a particular industry segment, then those organizations become indirect competitors. For example, aspirin, ibuprofen, and acetaminophen are all substitute pain relievers. In the service sector, credit unions are substitutes for banks and bus travel is a substitute for airline travel. Close substitutes can place a ceiling on the price that an industry can be charged for a good or service. For example, if the price of naproxen (e.g., Aleve) pain reliever/fever reducer becomes too high, many consumers who typically prefer it may switch to aspirin, acetaminophen (e.g., Tylenol), or ibuprofen (e.g., Advil).

Other Factors. Although Porter does not explicitly address other factors in his original model, other stakeholder groups exist that can influence an industry's profitability. Special-interest groups, unions, communities and government agencies take actions that can alter the task environment and cause organizations to invest money, which can influence cost structures and profits. For example, improvements in automotive fuel efficiency and safety are largely the result of pressures from consumer groups and regulators. Also, pressure from special interest groups has resulted in many companies allocating more resources to environmental protection and better treatment of workers. Certainly, unions can have a huge impact on the way a firm operates and its ability to compete. In fact, smaller regional U.S. airline companies have traditionally enjoyed a large economic advantage against legacy carriers because of the absence of unions. These types of forces were examined at a general level in the section on the broad environment. However, it is also useful to analyze the behavior of specific groups (as opposed to broad forces) during an analysis of the task environment.

Using the Five Forces Analysis. An analysis of the five forces is useful from several perspectives. First, by understanding how the forces influence competition and profitability in an industry, a firm can better understand how to position itself relative to these forces, determine any sources of competitive advantage now and in the future, and estimate the profits that it can expect. Firm managers may also decide to alter the influence of the five forces by actions such as erecting higher entry barriers through large-scale economies or greater product differentiation, or by creating switching costs to encourage customer loyalty. Frequent-guest programs that reward customers for loyalty to one hotel company are an attempt to battle price comparisons and ease of switching. A firm may also alter its competitive environment by creating partnerships with powerful stakeholders. For example, a firm may involve a powerful customer in its research and development efforts or create a shared information system with a powerful supplier. Partnering tactics such as these will be discussed further in the next section.

An organization can also analyze the five forces within an industry prior to entry or as a basis for deciding to leave the industry. As a result of such an analysis, a firm may conclude that an industry is not attractive because of low entry barriers, powerful suppliers or buyers, close substitutes, or the number and strength of current competitors. In general, a thorough understanding of the forces within an industry can help a firm better understand the industry's overall profit potential, and those forces most likely to create opportunities and threats.

This completes our discussion of Porter's model, which we used to consider the power of several important stakeholder groups and economic forces. The next section provides additional ideas concerning how to manage relationships with external stakeholders.

Partnerships and Social Networks

In an effort to deal with the increasing complexity and competitiveness of the world economy, organizations are coming together in partnerships in increasing numbers. It is not unusual for larger firms to manage hundreds of partnerships simultaneously.[21] These partnerships come in many forms, such as joint ventures, research collaborations, consortia and many types of informal alliances.[22] Organizations interact with a large number of external stakeholders. One of the important strategic questions organizations face is deciding how to manage stakeholders and specifically, which stakeholders should become partners. Obviously, partnerships are often formed due to their direct profit potential. However, there are other important strategic reasons for forming partnerships. In general, stakeholders that are high priority for partnerships are those that have a strong influence on the outcomes of the organization. For example, Toyota has a large influence on many of its suppliers due to the large orders it makes. Or a newly appointed, aggressive government regulator may be able to dramatically alter the way a firm will operate.

Three major factors are closely associated with the capacity of a stakeholder to influence firm outcomes. First, the economic power of a stakeholder is strongly associated with its ability to influence a firm's profit potential as well as the way it operates. Analysis of the five forces can help a firm determine the economic power of customers and suppliers. Second, some stakeholders possess political power, which is the ability to influence government regulations and laws that determine the rules by which firms operate and compete.[23] Activist groups and the media are the most obvious examples of stakeholders that *may* hold political power; however, any of a firm's stakeholders may possess it. For example, a large customer with strong ties to political leaders may actually have more political power than an activist. Third, stakeholders should also be given higher priority for partnerships if they possess valuable resources that the organization needs.[24] One of the most valuable of all resources is knowledge, and often organizations come together to learn from each other.[25]

Another way to understand the factors that make a stakeholder attractive for partnerships is to think in terms of their influence on environmental uncertainty. **Environmental uncertainty** reduces a firm's ability to predict with confidence the future state of its environment, such as demand, competitor actions, new regulation, the cost of supplies, or the availability of labor. If the environment were highly predictable, the management task would be fairly simple and profits would be relatively easy to achieve. On the other hand, high levels of environmental uncertainty reduce an organization's ability to chart an effective course into the future. From this perspective, stakeholders that (1) contribute to the environmental uncertainty facing a firm or (2) are able to reduce the environmental uncertainty facing a firm, should be given higher priority for partnerships.[26] An example from the space industry demonstrates this point:

> During the 1990s, Lockheed Space Operations Company (LSOC), a division of what is now Lockheed Martin, experienced a very high level of environmental uncertainty due to changes in the way the U.S. government was managing the space program. For years, the U.S. government had been putting increasing pressure on government agencies to reduce costs. Under one of its cost initiatives, the government decided that the many contracts associated with the space shuttle and rocket operations at Kennedy Space Center should be managed by one prime contractor. The government decided to open the selection process to bidding.
>
> Executives at LSOC, who were largely responsible for the space shuttle launch operations, were concerned that they might not win the bid to manage the Center due to the political clout of Rockwell. Rockwell also had a strong presence at the Kennedy Space Center. They had built the space shuttle, which gave them specialized knowledge about its operation and maintenance. Furthermore, they had trained many of the astronauts who were now closely tied to high-level government officials (or in some cases government officials themselves). To reduce the uncertainty associated with this situation, LSOC formed a joint venture with Rockwell to run the Kennedy Space Center. The joint venture, called United Space Alliance (USA), was selected by the government from among several other contenders.

In this example, we see evidence of the three factors that had an impact on the ability of Rockwell to influence the uncertainty facing Lockheed. Although Lockheed was primarily running shuttle operations, Rockwell possessed economic power because of its own part in the process. Also, Rockwell held political power because of ties to government leaders. Finally, Rockwell's specialized knowledge about the Space Shuttle was a resource that Lockheed needed to be successful as a prime contractor at Kennedy Space Center. Once the partnership was formed, the government was left with only one reasonable bid to choose. Basically, the alliance removed uncertainty.

Firms are partnering with increasing frequency and with a broader base of stakeholders.[27] Exhibit 2.5 contains some of the more traditional techniques for managing external stakeholders, as well as several examples of partnering strategies. The first column in Exhibit 2.5 lists a few traditional stakeholder management techniques, grouped by type of external stakeholder. These techniques

Exhibit 2.5   Examples of Tactics for Managing and Partnering with External Stakeholders

Stakeholders	Traditional Management Tactics	Partnering Tactics
Customers	Customer service departments Marketing research Advertising On-site visits Product/service development Market development	Customer involvement on design teams Customer involvement in product testing Enhanced communication linkages Joint training/service programs Sharing of facilities Appointments to board of directors
Suppliers	Purchasing departments Encourage competition among suppliers Sponsor new suppliers Threat of vertical integration Long-term contracts	Supplier involvement on design teams Integration of ordering system with manufacturing Shared information systems Joint development of new products Appointments to board of directors
Competitors	Competing on the basis of differentiation, technology innovation, speed price cutting, market segmentation Intelligence systems Corporate spying and espionage*	Keiretsu* Joint ventures for R&D or market development Collective lobbying efforts Informal price leadership or collusion* Mergers (horizontal integration)
Government Agencies/ Administrators	Legal/tax departments Government relations departments Lobbying/political action committees Campaign contributions Personal gifts to politicians*	Joint or government sponsored research Joint ventures to work on social problems Joint foreign development projects Appointment of retired government officials to the board of directors
Local Communities/ Governments	Community relations offices Public relations advertising Involvement in community service/politics Donations to government/charities organizations Gifts to local government officials*	Joint urban renewal programs Cooperative training programs Development committees/boards Employment programs Joint education programs
Activist Groups	Public/political relations efforts to offset or protect them from negative publicity Financial donations	Consultation with members on sensitive issues Joint ventures for research/research consortia Appointment of group representatives to board
Unions	Avoid unions through high levels of employee satisfaction Thwarting attempts to organize Hiring of professional negotiators Public relations advertising	Mutually satisfactory (win-win) labor contracts Contract clauses that link pay to performance Joint committees on safety and other issues Labor leaders appointed to board of directors and included in major decisions
Financial Intermediaries	Financial reports/audits Finance and accounting departments High-level financial officer	Inclusion in decisions requiring financial backing Appointments to the board of directors Shared ownership of new projects

*These tactics are of questionable ethical acceptability to some internal and external stakeholders in the United States and elsewhere.

Source: Adapted from J.S. Harrison and Caron H. St. John, "Managing and Partnering with External Stakeholders," *Academy of Management Executive* (May 1996): 53. Used with permission.

are both common and essential, and they should be used where appropriate. Many of these techniques are intended to protect the organization from negative influences. However, recently the emphasis in stakeholder management has been shifting away from protecting the organization from the influence of external stakeholders toward treating stakeholders almost as if they are part of the internal organization (see the second column of Exhibit 2.5).

Efforts to partner with customers and suppliers often provide significant benefits.[28] Many firms are involving strategically important customers and suppliers in product and process design, in quality training sessions, and in online production scheduling. In fact, in recognition of the importance of excellent relationships to the quality of products and services produced, the Malcolm Baldrige National Quality Award Committee now has a separate evaluation category for "key supplier and customer partnering and communication mechanisms."[29] Toyota makes no secret of the fact that a lot of its success comes from its special relationships with its excellent suppliers. In the words of a senior executive from a company that supplies all the large automobile companies, "Toyota helped us dramatically improve our production system. We started by making one component, and as we improved, [Toyota] rewarded us with orders for more components. Toyota is our best customer."[30] These types of relationships are founded on the principle of mutual advantage. BP, the multinational petroleum company, defines **mutual advantage** as the ability "to conduct our business on a long-term and sustainable basis, founded on relationships that are mutually advantageous and capable of enduring beyond a single transaction."[31]

To combat collapsing product and process life cycles and to get a jump on new emerging technologies, competitors also are joining forces in increasing numbers. Although cooperation in price-setting, called **collusion,** is illegal in the United States and many other countries, rival organizations may still form partnerships for technological advancement, new product development, to enter new or foreign markets, or to influence government regulation through lobbying or other political tactics.[32] Goodyear and Michelin, for example, joined forces for a research and development operation and various other initiatives. They planned to share licensed technologies, set a common standard for run-flat tires (tires that run after the air is gone), and introduce a jointly developed, integrated wheel and tire system.[33]

Although firms frequently engage in specific partnerships with one or more stakeholders, they may also be involved in **social networks**, which are loosely coupled groups of autonomous firms that cooperate with each other because of mutual interests.[34] These networks are often organized around "hub firms," prominent firms with significant power, which coordinate information sharing within the network.[35] Hub firms coordinate cooperative activities among network members and also help fill structural holes, which exist when two parties in the network typically don't engage in business activities with each other. Consequently, firms that are part of social networks benefit from new business opportunities and also have access to more complete information about the environment upon which to base their strategies. Firms that manage for stakeholders, defined in Chapter 1, are in a strong position to serve as hub firms because stakeholders in the network will trust that such firms will act responsibly with regard to their own interests.[36]

This section has discussed methods that firms can use to analyze and, to some extent, manage their external environments through partnerships and other strategies. The next section will focus on external issues associated with operating in a global business environment.

GLOBAL BUSINESS ENVIRONMENTS

Over the last few decades, significant advances in transportation and communications technologies, coupled with saturated growth opportunities in home markets, have encouraged firms to venture beyond their borders. Significant changes in the global environment have opened up opportunities for organizations that are willing to take a risk and wait patiently for returns. Many of the most significant opportunities exist in developing nations like China, Russia and India. For instance, IBM is cutting jobs in the U.S. and expanding in India. IBM is focusing its investments on new software laboratories and product development, service and testing facilities. The company is hiring some of the talented Indian workers in a country that produces more people with technical degrees than any other country except the U.S. It also hopes to be able to increase its operational efficiency. In fact, IBM has told U.S. workers that they are free to apply for new positions being created in emerging markets, but that they will be paid local wages.[37]

In spite of the huge opportunities, firms that invest in emerging markets may have to deal with a host of problems, including unstable governments, inadequately trained workers, low levels of supporting technology, shortages of supplies, a weak transportation system, or an unstable currency. Firms also struggle with managing stakeholders that may have values or beliefs that are different from the values and beliefs of stakeholders found in their home countries. Consequently, it is important to carefully evaluate a foreign environment before making investments there.

Evaluating a Foreign Investment Environment

Many characteristics must be evaluated when considering a foreign country for investment. Several of them fall within the general areas of the broad environment, including the sociocultural environment, the economy, the political/legal environment and the state of technology. Other characteristics are related to specific industries and markets. Questions concerning each of these factors are listed in Exhibit 2.6, which is a useful tool for evaluating a potential country for investment.

The wrong answers to any of the questions in Exhibit 2.6 can make a country less attractive. The following are some examples that demonstrate this point: (1) an unstable government can greatly increase the risk of a total loss of investment, (2) an inefficient transportation system can increase total product costs to prohibitively high levels, (3) inadequate school systems can result in poorly skilled workers, which may not have the ability to manufacture technical products, (4) a slowly growing GNP could mean that consumer demand will be sluggish, (5) high foreign tax rates can virtually eliminate profits, and (6) if the local currency is not translatable into U.S. dollars the organization will have a tough time removing profits from the country.

Answers to the questions should also be judged based on the type of activity the organization is considering. For example, a high per capita income is favorable if the organization is only going to sell U.S. products in the foreign market (export). On the other hand, low per capita income could mean that wages are very low, which is positive if the organization is only considering foreign manufacturing or assembly. Clearly, some countries seem to foster excellence in particular industries, as the next section will demonstrate.

Examples of Questions to Ask about a Potential Foreign Market

Exhibit 2.6

Social Forces

What currently are the hot topics of debate? How well organized are special interest groups with regard to the environment, labor, and management issues? Are current policies or behaviors of the organization likely to be offensive in the new host country? What is the attitude of potential consumers toward foreign products and services? Will there be significant cultural barriers to overcome? How difficult is the language? How old is the population? What other differences could cause difficulty for the organization?

The Economy

What is the inflation rate? How large is the gross national product (GNP)? How fast is it growing? What is the income per capita? How much impact does the global economy have on the domestic economy? How high is the unemployment rate? What actions does the government take to fuel economic growth? What is the trade balance with the United States? Can the currency be exchanged for the home currency? How high are interest rates? Is the financial sector well organized? How expensive are the factors of production?

Political/Legal Environment

What is the form of government? How much influence does the government have over business? Is the government stable? What is the government's attitude toward private enterprise and U.S. firms? What is the home government's attitude toward the foreign government? How high are tax rates compared with rates in the home country? How are taxes assessed and collected? How high are import and export taxes? What is the nature of the court system? Is legal protection available through incorporation or a similar form?

Technology

Is the country technologically advanced? Do schools and universities supply qualified workers? Are the required skills available in sufficient quantity? Are suitable information systems available? Is the infrastructure sound (e.g., roads, transportation systems)? Is an appropriate site available?

Industry Specific

How large is the industry? How fast is it growing? Is it segmentable? How many competitors are there? How strong are they? What is the relative position of industry participants in relation to suppliers and customers? Are substitute products available? What is the primary basis for competition? Is it possible to reach the market through a joint venture?

Competitive Advantages of Nations

Michael Porter expanded his analyses of competitive environments to include the global economy. In his book, *The Competitive Advantage of Nations*, he developed arguments concerning why some nations produce so many stellar companies in particular industries.[38] For example, Germany is the home base for several top luxury car manufacturers and Switzerland has many leading companies in pharmaceuticals. He explains that four characteristics of countries actually create an environment that is conducive to creating globally competitive firms in certain business areas. The four characteristics are:

1. *Factor Conditions.* These are endowments enjoyed by specific nations such as uncommon raw materials or laborers with specific skills that can lead to advantages in particular industries. Other factor conditions that can lead to advantages are superior factor-producing mechanisms such as excellent schools or universities.

2. *Demand Conditions.* If buyers of a product or service in a particular country are among the most discriminating and demanding in the world, competitors in that industry have to work harder to please them.
3. *Related and Supporting Industries.* If suppliers to an industry are the very best in the world, their excellence is passed on to the buyers who use their products. Advantages can also be obtained if firms in related industries are global leaders too.
4. *Firm Strategy, Structure and Rivalry.* Sometimes the management techniques that are customary in a nation's businesses are conducive to success in particular industries. Also, particular industries may attract the most talented managers in the nation. In addition, strong competition can force competitors to excel, thus making them stronger in world markets.

These factors can indicate the potential for developing a nucleus of companies that are globally competitive. Basically, the reason companies can develop a highly competitive nucleus is that tough market environments can create world class competitors only if the competitors are also endowed with the resources they need to compete. If home markets are uncompetitive, firms will not be sufficiently motivated to produce a superior product. On the other hand, if home markets are highly competitive but the factors of production, support industries and human talent are not available, firms will likewise be incapable of producing globally competitive products. When these two conditions are met, however, an environment is created that both motivates and rewards excellence.

The logical conclusion from Porter's analysis would seem to be to locate subsidiaries in the nations with the strongest home bases in particular industries. However, he argues that this rarely happens. First, it is difficult in some cases for an "outsider," a foreign firm, to become an "insider." Second, Porter suggests that it is unlikely that the foreign subsidiary in the nation with the natural advantages will be able to influence the parent company "long distance."

Porter does, however, suggest that firms should take advantage of their own nation's natural advantages. He also recommends that some of the principles that apply to the competitive advantages of nations can be applied in any company that wants to become more competitive in the world economy. Specifically, organizations can seek out the toughest, most discriminating buyers, choose from the best suppliers in the world, seek to excel against the most outstanding global competitors, form alliances with outstanding foreign competitors and stay abreast of all research findings and innovations that are relevant to their core businesses.

KEY POINTS SUMMARY

This chapter dealt with the external environment, which consists of the broad and task environments. The following are key points from this discussion:

1. The most important elements in the broad environment, as it relates to a business organization and its task environment, are socio-cultural forces, global economic forces, technological forces, and global political/legal forces.

2. One important distinction between the task and broad environments is that the task environment is subject to a high level of organizational influence, whereas the broad environment is not.

3. The task environment includes external stakeholders such as customers, suppliers, competitors, government agencies and administrators, local communities, activist groups, unions, and financial intermediaries.

4. The five primary forces that determine the nature and level of competition in an industry include the strength of customers, the strength of suppliers, the availability of substitutes, the strength of entry barriers, and forces that determine the nature of existing competition.

5. Organizations should use partnering tactics to manage external stakeholders that have a large influence on the environmental uncertainty facing the organization. These firms may have economic or political power or they may possess critical resources. On the other hand, traditional monitoring techniques can be used to anticipate the needs of lower-priority stakeholders.

6. Important partnering tactics include joint ventures and other forms of strategic alliances, the establishment of mutually beneficial contracts, various forms of stakeholder involvement in organizational processes and decisions, and the development of political alliances to promote a favorable task environment. Firms may also participate in social networks, with hub firms coordinating the flow of information and assisting in the formation of value-creating ventures.

7. Significant changes in the global environment have created great opportunities for organizations that are willing to take a risk and wait patiently for returns.

8. Many characteristics must be evaluated when considering a foreign country for investment. Several of them fall within the general areas of the broad environment, including the sociocultural environment, the economy, the political/legal environment and the state of technology. Other characteristics are related to specific industries and markets.

9. Some nations seem to produce many highly successful companies in particular industries. Four variables that seem to explain this phenomenon are factor conditions; demand conditions; related and supporting industries; and firm strategy, structure and rivalry.

REFERENCES

1   F. Balfour and C.C. Tschang, "China's Exporters Look Homeward," *Business Week* (February 23, 2009): 26; J.E. Vascellaro and G.A. Fowler, "China Blocks Local Access to YouTube, Once Again," *Wall Street Journal* (March 25, 2009): B1; "China's New Bourse," *Business Week* (April 13, 2009): 3; "Pretend You're a Westerner," *The Economist* (February 21, 2009): 44–45; "Leaders: How China Sees the World," *The Economist* (March 21, 2009): 13; The World Bank, http://web.worldbank.org/wbsite/external/countries/eastasiapacificext/chinaextn/0,,menupk:318960~pagepk:141132~pipk:141107~thesitepk:318950,00.html (April 25, 2009).

2   M. Delmas and M.W. Toffel, "Organizational Responses to Environmental Demands: Opening the Black Box," *Strategic Management Journal* 29 (2008): 1027–1055; J.L. Murillo-Luna, C. Garcés-Ayerbe and P. Rivera-Torres, "Why Do Patterns of Environmental Response Differ? A Stakeholders' Pressure Approach," *Strategic Management Journal* 29 (2008): 1225–1240.

3   R.E. Freeman, J.S. Harrison and A.C. Wicks, *Managing for Stakeholders: Survival Reputation and Success* (London: Yale University Press, 2007).

4   D. Brittan, "Waiting for Uncle Bill," *MIT's Technology Review* 100 (3) (1997): 69.

5   A. Serwer, "Bill Gates Gets Really Generous," *Fortune* (March 1, 1999): 35.

6   F. Rice, "Denny's Changes Its Spots," *Fortune* (May 13, 1996): 133–134.

7   M. Thomas, "Advantica Tops Fortune's List of Best Companies for Minorities," *The State* (June 27, 2000): 1.

8   D.R. Dalton, M.B. Metzger and J.W. Hill, "The New U.S. Sentencing Commission Guidelines: A Wake-up Call for Corporate America," *Academy of Management Executive* (February 1994): 7–16.

9   Sarbanes-Oxley, http://www.sarbanes-oxley.com/ (August 9, 2006).

10 P. Chattopadhyay, W.H. Glick and G.P. Huber, "Organizational Actions in Response to Threats and Opportunities," *Academy of Management Journal* 44 (2001): 937–955.

11 D. Machalba, "Diesel Prices Force Small Truckers off the Road," *Wall Street Journal* (March 11, 2003): B6; C. Cooper and J. Cummings, "U.S.-Europe Battle on Iraq Heats Up," *Wall Street Journal* (March 6, 2003): A3; G.R. Simpson, "Multinational Firms are Taking Steps to Avert Antiwar Boycotts," *Wall Street Journal* (April 4, 2003): A1.

12 R.A. Melcher, "Europe, Too, Is Edgy about Imports-From America," *Business Week* (January 27, 1992): 48–49.

13 P.J.H. Schoemaker, "Scenario Planning: A Tool for Strategic Thinking," *Sloan Management Review* 36 (2) (1995): 25–40.

14 D. Clark and M. Peers, "Music Companies Fight Back, Hoping Downloads for Fees Can Prove as Popular as Free," *Wall Street Journal* (June 20, 2000): B1; L. Gomes, "Napster is Ordered to Stop the Music," *Wall Street Journal* (July 27, 2000): A3; K.T. Greenfeld, "The Digital Reckoning," *Time* (May 22, 2000): 56.

15 "The Bill That Could Break Up Europe," *The Economist* (February 28, 2009): 13.

16 "Dump the Dollar?" *Business Week* (April 6, 2009): 8.

17 M.E. Porter, *Competitive Strategy: Techniques for Analyzing Industries and Companies* (New York: The Free Press, 1980); D.F. Jennings and J.R. Lumpkin, "Insights between Environmental Scanning Activities and Porter's Generic Strategies: An Empirical Analysis," *Journal of Management* 18 (1982): 791–803.

18 This section on competitive forces draws heavily on the pioneering work of Michael Porter. See Porter, *Competitive Strategy*: 1–33.

19 "Retail," *Orlando Sentinel* (February 1, 1996): Cl.

20 C. Terhune, "Coca-Cola Filing Reveals It Feared Wal-Mart Drink," *Wall Street Journal* (June 8, 2006): B6.

21 J. Hagedoorn "A Note on International Market Leaders and Networks of Strategic Technology Partnering," *Strategic Management Journal* 16 (1995): 241–250.

22 B.R. Barringer and J.S. Harrison, "Walking a Tightrope: Creating Value Through Interorganizational Relationships," *Journal of Management* 26 (2000): 367–404.

23 R.E. Freeman and D.L. Reed, "Stockholders and Stakeholders: A New Perspective on Corporate Governance," *California Management Review* 15 (3) (1983): 88–106; R.E. Freeman, *Strategic Management: A Stakeholder Approach* (Boston: Pitman Publishing Inc., 1984).

24 J. Pfeffer and G.R. Slancik, *The External Control of Organizations: A Resource Dependence Perspective* (New York: Harper & Row, 1978).

25 J.H. Dyer and K. Nobeoka, "Creating and Managing a High-performance Knowledge-sharing Network: The Toyota Case," *Strategic Management Journal* 21 (2000): 345–367.

26 W.P. Burgers, C.W.L. Hill and W.C. Kim, "The Theory of Global Strategic Alliances: The Case of the Global Auto Industry," *Strategic Management Journal* 14 (1993); 419–432; J.S. Harrison and C.H. St. John, "Managing and Partnering with External Stakeholders," *Academy of Management Executive* (May, 1996): 50–60.

27 R.H. Shah and V. Swaminathan, "Factors Influencing Partner Selection in Strategic Alliances: The Moderating Role of Alliance Context," *Strategic Management Journal* 29 (2008): 471–494.

28 J.H. Dyer and N.W. Hatch, "Using Supplier Networks to Learn Faster," *MIT Sloan Management Review*, Spring (2004): 57–63; J.H. Dyer and H. Singh, "The Relational View: Cooperative Strategy and Sources of Interorganizational Competitive Advantage," *Academy of Management Review* 23 (1998): 660–679.

29 J.K. Liker and T.Y. Choi, "Building Deep Supplier Relationships," *Harvard Business Review* (December, 2004): 106.

30 Liker and Choi, "Building Deep Supplier Relationships."

31 "External Relationships"; BP Global, http://www.bp.com/ (August 8, 2006).

32 B.R. Barringer and J.S. Harrison, "Walking a Tightrope: Creating Value through Interorganizational Relationships," *Journal of Management* 26 (2000): 367–404.

33 C. Ansberry, "Goodyear, Michelin Hope to Raise Sales of Run-flat Tires," *Wall Street Journal* (June 23, 2000): A12.

34 C. Dhanaraj and A. Parkhe, "Orchestrating Innovation Networks," *Academy of Management Review* 31 (2006): 659–669.

35 C. Jarillo, "On Strategic Networks," *Strategic Management Journal* 9 (1988): 31–41.

36 A. Capaldo, "Network Structure and Innovation: The Leveraging of a Dual Network as a Distinctive Relational Capability," *Strategic Management Journal* 28 (2007): 585–608.

37 W.M. Bulkeley, "IBM to Cut U.S. Jobs, Expand in India," *Wall Street Journal* (March 26, 2009): B1; P. Wonacott, "IBM Seeks Bigger Footprint in India," *Wall Street Journal* (June 7, 2006): B2.

38 M.E. Porter, *The Competitive Advantage of Nations* (New York: The Free Press, 1990).

3

Organizational Resources and Competitive Advantage

STRATEGY IN FOCUS

Amazon.com

Amazon.com, Inc. opened its virtual doors on the World Wide Web in July 1995. The company seeks to be the "Earth's most customer-centric company," focusing on three primary customer groups: online retail consumers, sellers and developers. The company also generates revenue through co-branded credit cards and online advertising. In 2008 the company started shipping Kindle, a wireless reading device that offers hundreds of thousands of titles. Sales of Kindle have exceeded the company's expectations.

Amazon's focus on customer satisfaction earned it first place on *Business Week's* list of the top companies for customer service in 2009. This might seem odd for an Internet-based company because most transactions are handled without any human contact. CEO Jeffrey Bezos explains that the customer experience includes "having the lowest price, having the fastest delivery, having it reliable enough so that you don't need to contact [anyone]. Then you save customer service for those truly unusual situations. You know, 'I got my book and its missing pages 47 through 58.'"

Behind the scenes at Amazon are complex operating systems and a myriad of contractual agreements. The company runs its own fulfillment centers, warehouses, and customer service centers around the world, as well as creating outsourcing agreements with other companies to provide these services. Amazon also provides e-commerce services for other businesses that may include technology development; fulfillment services; inventory management; tax collection; payment processing; engaging third parties to perform hosting and other services; and licensing of third-party software, hardware and content.

The company takes a long-term, customer oriented approach to developing new business opportunities.

According to Bezos, "Long-term orientation interacts well with customer obsession. If we can identify a customer need and if we can further develop conviction that that need is meaningful and durable, our approach permits us to work patiently for multiple years to deliver a solution. 'Working backwards' from customer needs can be contrasted with a 'skills-forward' approach where existing skills and competencies are used to drive business opportunities. The skills-forward approach says, 'We are really good at X. What else can we do with X?' That's a useful and rewarding business approach. However, if used exclusively, the company employing it will never be driven to develop fresh skills. Eventually the existing skills will become outmoded. Working backwards from customer needs often *demands* that we acquire new competencies and exercise new muscles, never mind how uncomfortable and awkward-feeling those first steps might be. Kindle is a good example of our fundamental approach ... Amazon had never designed or built a hardware device, but rather than change the vision to accommodate our then-existing skills, we hired a number of talented (and missionary!) hardware engineers and got started learning a new institutional skill, one that we needed to better serve readers in the future."[1]

In this chapter we turn our attention inside the organization: to the organization's resources and how managers develop and use them to achieve competitive advantage. The most successful organizations, like Amazon.com, typically have managers who understand how to take full advantage of valuable resources. Mr. Bezos attributes much of Amazon's success to a competitive approach that determines where the company wants to go and then develops or acquires the resources necessary to get there.

THE STRATEGIC VALUE OF INTERNAL RESOURCES AND CAPABILITIES

Chapter 1 introduced the idea that competitive advantage may be available to firms that possess valuable resources.[2] There are several conditions that make a valuable resource a genuine source of competitive advantage.[3] In addition, other conditions must be met for the advantage to be sustainable over time.

Sustainable Competitive Advantage

Internal resources and capabilities fall into five general categories: human, physical, financial, knowledge and organizational. In general, capabilities and resources become strengths with the potential to create a competitive advantage if two conditions are met (see Exhibit 3.1):

1. The resources or capabilities are _valuable_. They allow the firm to exploit external opportunities and/or neutralize external threats. In general, value comes from the ability to use the resource to provide a good or service at a lower cost or to provide a good or service that is more desirable to the consumer. Nevertheless, value itself does not make a resource a source of competitive advantage. Additional conditions must be met.
2. The resources or capabilities are _unique_. If numerous organizations possess a particular resource or capability, then the situation is described as competitive parity–no company has the advantage. On the other hand, if only one or a small group of organizations possess a valuable resource or capability, then that resource or capability may be a source of competitive advantage.[4]

In addition, a unique and valuable resource or capability actually becomes a source of competitive advantage if the following additional conditions are met:

3. The _organization_ is suited to exploitation of the resource or capability. This means that the structure and systems of the firm are appropriate for taking advantage of the competitive advantage. For example, Xerox formed a research laboratory called PARC which, in the late 1960s and 1970s, developed an amazing assortment of technological innovations, including the personal computer, the "mouse," the laser printer, and windows-type software. However, the company did not take advantage of many of PARC's innovations because it did not have an organization in place to do so. For instance, poor communications prevented most Xerox managers from knowing what PARC was doing and a highly bureaucratic system mired a lot of the innovations in red tape.
4. The firm's managers are _aware_ of the potential of the resource or capability to lead to a competitive advantage and have taken steps to realize the advantage. Mr. Bezos, from Amazon.com, seems very aware of the resources and

Organizational Resources and Capabilities Leading to Competitive Advantage

Exhibit 3.1

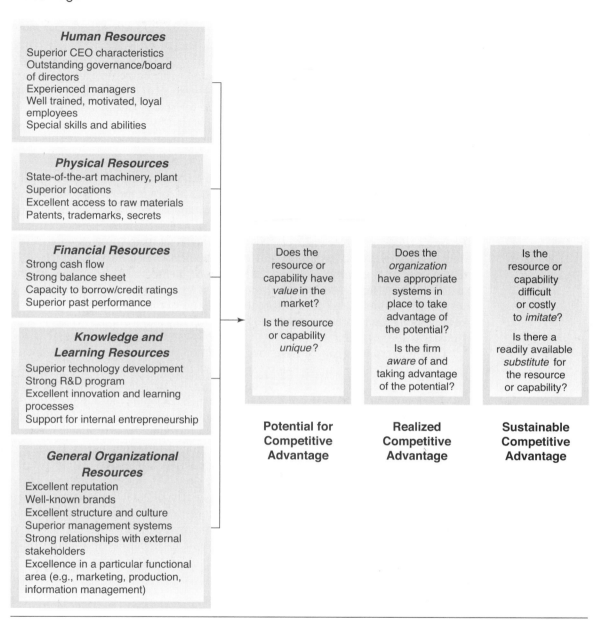

Human Resources
Superior CEO characteristics
Outstanding governance/board of directors
Experienced managers
Well trained, motivated, loyal employees
Special skills and abilities

Physical Resources
State-of-the-art machinery, plant
Superior locations
Excellent access to raw materials
Patents, trademarks, secrets

Financial Resources
Strong cash flow
Strong balance sheet
Capacity to borrow/credit ratings
Superior past performance

Knowledge and Learning Resources
Superior technology development
Strong R&D program
Excellent innovation and learning processes
Support for internal entrepreneurship

General Organizational Resources
Excellent reputation
Well-known brands
Excellent structure and culture
Superior management systems
Strong relationships with external stakeholders
Excellence in a particular functional area (e.g., marketing, production, information management)

Does the resource or capability have *value* in the market?

Is the resource or capability *unique*?

Potential for Competitive Advantage

Does the *organization* have appropriate systems in place to take advantage of the potential?

Is the firm *aware* of and taking advantage of the potential?

Realized Competitive Advantage

Is the resource or capability difficult or costly to *imitate*?

Is there a readily available *substitute* for the resource or capability?

Sustainable Competitive Advantage

---

capabilities of his organization and how to use them to maximize competitive advantage in the global marketplace.[5]

Finally, a resource or capability can be a source of sustainable competitive advantage, which is an advantage enjoyed over a long time frame, if two additional conditions are met.

5. The resources or capabilities are *difficult or expensive to imitate*. In these situations competing firms face a cost disadvantage in imitating a resource or capability. The more difficult or costly a resource or capability is, the more

valuable it is in producing a sustainable competitive advantage. In the case of a patent or a trademark that is enforceable, competing firms face an absolute cost disadvantage. This is one of the difficulties new Internet businesses encounter. The technological innovations that have spawned a flood of new E-tailers are widely available to everyone. It is difficult to create uniqueness, and even more difficult to protect it from imitation.

6.   There are *no readily available substitutes*. If other products or services can easily serve as substitutes, then the benefits associated with competitive advantage are mitigated to some extent. Substitution is another form of imitation. For example, Internet-based travel services are substituted for traditional travel agencies. In this case, the services being provided are imitated by another technology. No matter how unique and valuable the services of an agency are, it still faces pressure from online services.

If a resource or capability has all of these characteristics and it also can be applied to more than one business area, it is called a **core competency**, which may also be called a **distinctive competence**.[6] Some companies are masters at exploiting their sources of competitive advantage across different businesses. For example, Disney has a core competency in creativity that they refer to as "Imagineering." The company has extended its unique and valuable animated characters, which were created in its studios, into a multitude of businesses, including books, movies, theme parks, and television. They reversed the process by making a series of successful movies based on its theme park rides called "Pirates of the Caribbean." In another example, Sony has a core competency in micro-circuitry that it applies across a range of businesses.

Tangible resources can be seen, touched and/or quantified.[7] However, some of the most important resources can't really be identified in these terms. They are **intangible**. For many firms, the key to competitive advantage is to combine resources and develop capabilities that are hard to imitate. For example, a patent, which is tangible, may provide an organization with an advantage for a while. But the capability to quickly and accurately develop and introduce new products involves integrating the efforts of several resources: marketing (determining need), design and development engineers (creating the product, specifying raw materials), operations (arranging for raw materials and producing the product), and many others. These integrated resources and capabilities are particularly difficult for competitors to observe and imitate. Consequently, organizational knowledge and the organizational systems that create and absorb knowledge are among the most difficult resources to imitate and are therefore excellent potential sources of sustainable competitive advantage.[8]

Resource Interconnectedness

Organizational resources and capabilities across five organizational areas will be described in the sections that follow. As mentioned previously, they are human resources, physical resources, financial resources, knowledge and learning resources, and general organizational resources. In reality, these resources are highly inter-connected. For instance, a firm with strong financial resources can hire better human resources, develop better physical resources, put more money into knowledge and learning resources, and invest more in relationships with stakeholders, a part of the category of general organizational resources. In addition, excellent knowledge and learning resources can result in technology development to improve physical resources, management of financial resources, the skill levels of human resources

Organizational Resource Interconnectedness

Exhibit 3.2

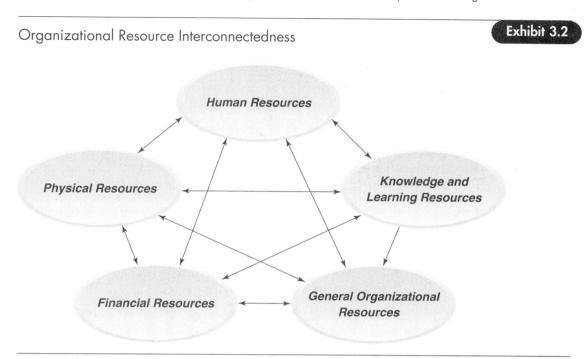

and the strength of a firm's reputation. It is possible to find these sorts of relationships among all of the resource categories, as Figure 3.2 illustrates.

The implication of resource interconnectedness for managers is that none of the resource areas can be neglected. If one of them becomes weak it can influence all of the other resource areas. In these situations a firm will eventually wear down. Strategic managers have the task of constantly balancing needs in the various resource areas and determining if weakness in one of them is stifling progress towards the attainment of organizational objectives. Human resources will be the first area of discussion.

HUMAN RESOURCES

Examples of internal stakeholders include managers, employees, owners and—if the organization is a public corporation or if a private company decides to appoint one—a board of directors. Many of the other resources a firm might possess are easy to duplicate, but each human is unique. Consequently, employees and the way they are recruited and managed can be important sources of competitive advantage.

> Few employers spend as much time cultivating their workforce as Procter & Gamble. The consumer-products company expects to get 400,000 applications for entry-level management positions this year. It will hire less than half of 1% of them . . . Careful vetting, training and career development pay off. P&G boasts 23 brands with at least $1 billion in annual sales and is market leader in everything from detergent to diapers to razors. True, the company's renowned marketing skills and deep pockets help. But another important edge is personnel management—bringing in and promoting creative thinkers.[9]

Many executives and human resource professionals believe that management of human resources will become more difficult in the future, but will bring a bigger pay-off than ever before. For instance, in the U.S., in addition to being both specialized and mobile, the workforce is becoming more diverse demographically, ethnically and geographically.[10] These trends affect job design and reward systems, and increase the difficulty of molding an effective organizational culture. A possible upside to this difficulty, however, is that firms that conquer these challenges are in a stronger competitive position.[11]

Companies vary significantly with regard to how they acquire, train and reward their employees.[12] For example, companies like Starbucks seek to attract the very finest employees by giving them higher-than-industry pay and excellent benefits. Even part-time employees get tuition benefits after a year, a practice that is well above the norm for employee treatment in the restaurant industry.[13] Firms that treat their employees well are investing in the future because employee retention is likely to be higher. Furthermore, they may expect higher levels of productivity due to higher motivation levels and commitment among their employees. Some programs, such as educational benefits, provide immediate advantages to the firm because employees bring new ideas and improved skills to the workplace.

Potential employees may be drawn to firms that have a reputation for excellent employee treatment.[14] *Fortune* publishes a list each year of the best U.S. companies to work for. Topping the list in 2009 was NetApp, the Sunnyvale, California based data storage and management company, with $3.3 billion in sales.[15] The company has an egalitarian culture. Employees say that the company feels more like a start-up company than a corporation with over 7,000 employees. Hourly employees make an average of $88,525 per year and some of the unusual benefits they receive include five paid days for volunteer work, adoption aid, and coverage for unusual medical conditions like autism. The company has been growing at two to three times the industry average for data storage companies.

BP, one of Britain's biggest companies and one of the largest petrochemical groups in the world, is very deliberate about the way it treats its employees. The company has specified six values that guide decisions:

Human capability and technology: to nurture human capability and invest to ensure that the right technology, skills, behaviours and intellectual property are available for the pursuit of the board goals.

Employee treatment: to treat employees fairly and with respect and dignity.

Employee expectations: to make clear the expectations the group has of each employee in line with the group's general principles of delegation. Each employee will be given open and constructive feedback to aid his or her continuing development and performance.

Inclusion: to enable employees to feel included as part of a meritocratic organization of people from diverse backgrounds.

Merit and diversity: to recruit, select, develop and advance its employees on merit, irrespective of age, gender, nationality, physical challenge, race, religious belief, sexual orientation or identity.

Remuneration: to reward employees in a manner that reflects their role in the group and their contribution to the achievement of targets.[16]

Effective training programs can also be a source of competitive advantage. JetBlue, a small but growing U.S. airline with highly acclaimed customer service, created JetBlue University for employee training.[17] USAA, an insurance and financial services company that focuses on military families, cross-trained its call center representatives so that they can answer questions about investments as well as insurance. This meant that the company did not have to expand its call center staff, even in the wake of Hurricane Ike and the stock market crisis. Not only did the company save money, but it also earned a number two ranking in *Business Week's* list of customer service champions.[18]

Of course, managers can also be a source of competitive advantage.[19] Research has shown that top managers can have a significant impact on the strategies and performance of their organizations.[20] Jeffrey Bezos is an excellent example of how a top manager can influence performance. The highest ranking officer in a large organization can be called by a number of titles, but the most common is **chief executive officer**, or CEO. The CEO has primary responsibility for setting the strategic direction of the firm, although larger organizations are typically led by several high ranking officers such as chief operating officers and vice presidents who form the top management team. The most important responsibilities of the CEO and other top management team members are associated with strategic leadership, which is the topic of Chapter 4.

Boards of directors also can be a valuable resource to organizations. As we will discuss in the next chapter, they play an important role governing the behavior of top managers. However, board members can also play other important strategic roles, such as providing advice to managers with regard to strategies and strategic direction. If a board of directors is composed of highly successful executives from a range of different industries, they will be able to provide a broader perspective to top management. Also, directors can provide social network ties which act as linkages to external stakeholders.[21] Social network ties can help organizations create strategic alliances. Two studies, in fact, discovered higher performance in companies with boards that participated more actively in organizational decisions, compared to companies with "caretaker" boards.[22] Consequently, an effective board of directors can be a source of competitive advantage.

This section has discussed how the human resources of an organization can be sources of competitive advantage. An effective internal analysis can help identify these sources and this information is then used in strategy development. For instance, a firm that is weak in recruitment or training may need to create a strategy that overcomes these weaknesses in order to achieve its broader objectives. Alternatively, a firm with very well trained and loyal employees may have more flexibility with regard to the types of strategies it can consider. Also, a strong board with directors from many industries can provide excellent advice in determining the strategies and direction of the organization. The next section discusses physical resources.

PHYSICAL RESOURCES

Physical resources are tangible, such as machinery, plants, buildings, and products. Resource locations also fall into the physical resource category. Caterpillar, the world leader in earth mover manufacturing, is one example of a company that used physical resources to create competitive advantage:

> Caterpillar has enjoyed amazing financial performance in recent years. However, in the mid-80s the company was facing high costs, old factories and enormous international competition. "The Japanese were killing us," recalled Jim Owens. Their problems with the unions received a lot of media attention. Less well known are the physical resource strategies they followed to turn the company around.
>
> Cat moved much of its manufacturing base into nonunion regions in the Southern U.S. They built 20 smaller, more specialized factories to feed

components into their large assembly operations. Their total investment in manufacturing was $1.8 billion, including robots, modern tools and the elimination of bottlenecks that were reducing efficiency. A factory in Brazil adopted a manufacturing system similar to Toyota's with multiple lines that quadrupled capacity while only doubling employment. A factory in the U.S. that used to spend three days on a bulldozer now finishes it in one day. Of course, they have also taken maximum advantage of their strong dealer network.[23]

Machinery and plants, because they are tangible and thus able to be imitated, tend not to be sources of sustainable competitive advantage. It is important to distinguish here between technology development and the resulting physical resources. A firm may have a core competency in technology development that leads to state-of-the-art machinery and plants. The ability of the firm to develop technologies can be a source of sustainable competitive advantage; however, the machinery and plants probably cannot. They are imitated too quickly. Basically, a firm with a competency in technology development will continue to improve its machinery and plants, so that by the time something they have created is imitated by competitors, the firm has something newer and better. The same sort of logic applies to products; however, products are a little different because they can be protected for several years by patents.

Locations also can be a source of competitive advantage. Organizations tend to cluster by industry so that they can take maximum advantage of the resources available in those areas.[24] Competitive clusters exist in computer technology (Silicon Valley), high-tech automobiles (southern Germany) and entertainment (Hollywood). Clusters are also prevalent throughout the world in service industries such as lodging, restaurants and retail establishments. Clustering may lead to higher performance because of improved production that comes from the availability of specialized raw materials or human resources in an area. For example, Japanese auto parts suppliers tend to locate near firms that assemble the automobiles and they also tend to prefer areas with high concentrations of manufacturing.[25]

Clustering may also lead to demand advantages because consumers are drawn to areas with a larger variety from which to choose. Hotels, for instance, tend to cluster in particular areas because they realize that travelers prefer a choice of accommodations in an area. In fact, researchers studied the lodging industry in the U.S. and discovered that hotels that are located near luxury hotels have higher performance, in essence enjoying the consumer preference those hotels have created without paying for creating it.[26]

The ability of competitors to imitate a firm's locations depends on the industry and on the competitive situation. There are certain cost benefits associated with being an early entrant in a location that later becomes popular. The pioneers in Silicon Valley, for instance, were able to obtain land and human resources at much lower prices than later entrants. The cost advantages associated with the land can remain for a long time; however, human resource costs will increase for all firms in the area. In some cases, firms are protected from imitation of their locations because there are simply no more locations available.

FINANCIAL RESOURCES

Financial resources also can be a source of advantage, although they rarely qualify as "unique" or "difficult to imitate." Nevertheless, strong cash flow, low levels of debt, a strong credit rating, access to low interest capital, and a reputation for

Commonly Used Financial Ratios

Exhibit 3.3

Ratio	Calculation	What It Measures
Profitability Ratios		
Gross profit margin	$\dfrac{\text{Sales} - \text{COGS}}{\text{Sales}} \times 100$	Efficiency of operations and product pricing
Net profit margin	$\dfrac{\text{Net profit after tax}}{\text{Sales}} \times 100$	Efficiency after all expenses are considered
Return-on-assets (ROA)	$\dfrac{\text{Net profit after tax}}{\text{Total assets}} \times 100$	Productivity of assets
Return-on-equity (ROE)	$\dfrac{\text{Net profit after tax}}{\text{Stockholders' equity}} \times 100$	Earnings power of equity
Liquidity Ratios		
Current ratio	$\dfrac{\text{Current assets}}{\text{Current liabilities}}$	Short-run debt-paying ability
Quick ratio	$\dfrac{\text{Current assets} - \text{inventories}}{\text{Current liabilities}}$	Short-term liquidity
Leverage Ratios		
Debt-to-equity	$\dfrac{\text{Total liabilities}}{\text{Stockholders' equity}}$	The relative amount of debt and equity financing (common measure of financial risk)
Total debt to total assets (debt ratio)	$\dfrac{\text{Total liabilities}}{\text{Total assets}}$	Percentage of assets financed through borrowing (also a common risk measure)
Activity Ratios		
Asset turnover	$\dfrac{\text{Sales}}{\text{Total assets}}$	Efficiency of asset utilization
Inventory turnover	$\dfrac{\text{COGS}}{\text{Average inventory}}$	Management's ability to control investment in inventory
Average collection period	$\dfrac{\text{Receivables} \times 365 \text{ days}}{\text{Annual credit sales}}$	Effectiveness of collection and credit policies
Accounts receivable turnover	$\dfrac{\text{Annual credit sales}}{\text{Receivables}}$	Effectiveness of collection and credit policies

creditworthiness are powerful strengths that can serve as a source of strategic flexibility. Firms that are in a strong financial position can be more responsive to new opportunities and new threats, and are under less pressure from stakeholders than their competitors who suffer financial constraints. NetApp, cited earlier in this chapter as an example of a great company to work for, had $2 billion in cash in 2009 to help it ride out the financial slump. Consequently, it did not need to cut back on employees or the benefits it provides to them.[27]

Among other things, financial analysis is used to indicate the ability of the firm to finance growth. For example, managers of a firm that has very high leverage (long-term debt) may have to be less ambitious in their strategies for taking advantage of opportunities. On the other hand, an organization with a strong balance sheet is well poised to pursue a wide range of opportunities. Strong financial resources are often hard to imitate in the short term. Financial analysis is also an important strategic tool used by managers in assessing their performance, and identifying strengths, weaknesses, and trends. In general, financial analysis involves making two essential comparisons: (1) a comparison of the firm to its competitors, to determine relative financial strengths and weaknesses, and (2) a comparison of the firm to itself over time, to show trends. Some of the most common ratios used in financial analysis are found in Exhibit 3.3.

Firms often attempt to compare their expenses, investments, sources of income, and resulting profitability to competitors as a way of assessing the success of their strategies. A firm may observe that competitors are making more aggressive investments in R&D or paying higher wages to employees, which may heighten competitive intensity in the future. The findings from a competitor comparison must always be weighed against the goals of the firm. For example, a firm's investment in inventories may be higher than that of competitors for one of three reasons: (1) it is not as effective at managing inventories as competitors, which would be a cause for concern, (2) higher levels of inventories support its particular strategy (e.g. fast delivery and guaranteed availability), or (3) the items in inventory or accounting conventions are different, making a meaningless "apples and oranges" comparison.

Firms also track their own expenses and sources of income over time as a way of identifying trends. Poor financial trends are sometimes symptoms of greater problems. For example, a firm may discover that administrative costs are increasing at a faster rate than sales. This could be an indication of diseconomies of scale or the need for tighter controls on overhead costs, or, on the contrary, part of a deliberate attempt by the firm to position itself now for future sales growth.

KNOWLEDGE AND LEARNING RESOURCES

More than 50% of the gross domestic product in many developed economies, including the U.S., is based on intangible skills and intellectual assets.[28] For this reason, our generation might be said to be living in a "knowledge economy." Organizational learning is closely connected to the other resource areas. It requires well trained and skilled human resources and it leads to better products and services and ways of producing them. The products and services, as well as the technologies that support them, lead to brand image and organizational reputation. All of these things are related to financial success, and continuous investments of time and other resources are required to continue the development of organizational learning processes.

Knowledge can be divided into two types: codified and tacit.[29] Codified knowledge can be communicated with precision through written means. It includes things like formulas, designs, and computer code. Tacit knowledge, on the other hand, is difficult to describe with words. For instance, creative processes are hard to describe. You would have to experience them to know how they work. Tacit knowledge can be a valuable source of competitive advantage because it is very difficult to imitate. Codified knowledge is closely related to the concept of tangible resources that was described earlier in this chapter, whereas tacit knowledge tends to be associated with intangible resources and capabilities.

Organizational learning involves (1) knowledge creation, (2) knowledge retention, (3) knowledge sharing and (4) knowledge utilization.[30] Knowledge creation requires effective research and development programs, as well as a climate that encourages discovery. Much of the knowledge that is created in an organization does no good because it is not recorded or stored. Although information management systems that handle large volumes of data at low cost have made it efficient to record and store knowledge, companies have to be deliberate in doing so.

Once knowledge is created and stored, it has to be shared. Knowledge has to be available to the employees and managers that can make use of it. Lockheed Martin, the U.S.-based aerospace company, sends out monthly newsletters to its employees regarding innovations and developments in key areas. Many companies have developed database-management systems to organize ideas generated from employees so that they can be systematically retrieved in the future.

Knowledge sharing is more difficult across international borders. For example, researchers studied the ability of French food retailers to transfer knowledge about their operations to Polish companies over a ten year period.

> We discovered that the retailers experienced great difficulty in reproducing their model in Poland because knowledge transfer was impeded by the difference between the management of the French retailers and the behavior model of their Polish recruits. Both models were imbedded in quite dissimilar home country administrative heritages. The resulting blockage threatened the growth potential of French hypermarkets, which relied on the rapid training of large numbers of store management and staff.[31]

Effective sharing of knowledge in an international context requires consideration of local cultures and contexts. For instance, labor laws, regulations and local customs can make programs and systems that work in one context inoperable in another. Such difficulties were experienced by a German multinational when it attempted to implement a "lean" production program in both the U.S. and Germany. The program worked well in the heavily regulated German environment, but failed in the U.S.[32] Also important are a willingness among the recipients of the knowledge to acquire it, open and frequent communications among participants, a mandate to actually use the information in the business, and lots of time.[33]

Knowledge-creation systems are hard to imitate because they tend to be more tacit than codified. Furthermore, because they are so closely connected to the other resource areas, they can be powerful sources of sustainable competitive advantage. If a firm has a strong knowledge-creation system it is also likely to have valuable general organizational resources.

GENERAL ORGANIZATIONAL RESOURCES

Organizational reputation and a well-known corporate brand are also hard to imitate. Coca-Cola, IBM and Microsoft recently topped *Business Week's* annual ranking of the most valuable brands, with Google moving into the top ten for the first time.[34] What goes with the brand equity that these companies have is the ability to set themselves above the competition, either in the prices they can obtain or quantities sold or both. Michael Eisner, past CEO of Disney, once said:

> We are fundamentally an operating company, operating the Disney Brand all over the world, maintaining it, improving it, promoting and advertising it with taste. Our time must be spent insuring that the Brand never slides, that we

innovate the Brand, nurture the Brand, experiment and play with it, but never diminish it. Others will try to change it, from outside and from within. We must resist. We are not a fad! The Disney name and products survive fads![35]

Unique configurations of stakeholder relationships, another general organizational resource, can also be very difficult, if not impossible, to imitate.[36] For example, Microsoft has developed a strong web of formal and informal relationships with some of its largest customers. While it may be possible for a company to create a product that is superior to one of Microsoft's products, it would be very difficult for that company to break into the unique configuration of relationships within which Microsoft operates. This type of advantage is also found in some of the more successful .com companies, such as Yahoo. Early entrants were able to establish critical relationships with hundreds of other companies, making it very difficult for new competitors to establish a competitive foothold. Many companies could not establish a strong network and failed.

A firm may also have a competitive advantage because of the way it is structured internally. Nokia describes its structure as flat and networked.[37] A flat structure has few levels in it, which means that high level managers are not far removed from customers and that there are fewer levels to pass through with new ideas. A networked structure has a lot of work teams and groups, which facilitates knowledge sharing.

Related to a firm's structure are its management systems. Firms may have excellent systems for managing and rewarding managers or for communicating between and across levels. These systems too can be sources of competitive advantage. Excellent management systems can result in strengths in any of the functional areas of a firm. For instance, a firm may have an outstanding accounting system, financial control system, financial analysis system, production system, marketing system, delivery system, or competitor intelligence system. Human resource systems were already discussed in a previous section. Value chain analysis, which will be described in the next section, can help a firm identify its functional strengths and weaknesses.

An organization's culture, the system of shared values that guides employees, is another important component of the internal environment. It also provides a context within which the organization establishes its strategic direction and formulates and implements particular strategies.[38] Organization culture often reflects the values and leadership styles of the firm's executives and managers and is, to a great degree, a result of the past human resource management practices, such as recruitment, training, and rewards.

An organization's culture can be its greatest strength or its greatest weakness. Some organizations have succeeded in creating cultures that are completely consistent with what the organization is trying to accomplish—high performance cultures. At Nucor Steel, the company's stated commitment to a low cost strategy is supported by a culture that expects efficiency and tight fiscal policy. At Johnson & Johnson, the company's commitment to customers as its primary stakeholder is reflected in policy statements and adopted by employees. In other organizations, poor morale and a cynical attitude toward customers often undermine organizational performance.

This concludes our discussion of the five organizational resource areas. Because they are interconnected, none of them can be neglected; however, some of the areas have more potential for creating sustainable competitive advantage. Resources and capabilities that are hard to imitate, such as an organization's knowledge creation system or its reputation, tend to have the highest potential. Also, the resources and capabilities that lead to competitive advantage are different in each industry and can also change over time. For example, researchers discovered that high-performing film studios during the period from 1936 to 1950 possessed superior property-based resources such as exclusive long-term contracts with stars and theaters. However, during the period from 1951 to 1965 knowledge-based resources in the form of production and coordinative talent and budgets were associated with high performance. They attributed these findings to the capabilities needed to deal with increasing uncertainty in the film industry.[39] Their study also demonstrates that organizational resources only result in a competitive advantage if they are uniquely valuable in the external environment.

RESOURCE ANALYSIS AND THE DEVELOPMENT OF STRATEGY

In evaluating the resources and capabilities of the organization, it is important to consider all of the various activities of the business and understand the role they play in building advantage and implementing strategies. Strategy should be based on what the organization does well relative to competitors *or* on the capabilities or resources the firm *wants to develop* that will create a competitive advantage in the future. Consistent with the discussion of strategic thinking found in Chapter 1, organizational constraints should be considered but should not place absolute limits on strategy. Instead, long-term organizational success often depends on developing new competencies. This was demonstrated by Amazon's creation of the Kindle wireless reading device.

Organizations can determine the potential for competitive advantage by asking the questions found in Exhibit 3.1 for each of its resources and capabilities. Is the resource or capability valuable in helping the firm overcome weaknesses or exploiting strengths? Is it unique? Does the firm have the appropriate systems in place to realize the competitive advantage and is it aware of the opportunity? Is the resource or capability hard to imitate or substitute? These questions should be asked in the context of the firm's industry and the broad environment. In addition, value chain analysis can serve as a supplement to the approach described in this chapter.

Value Chain Analysis

Michael Porter developed a framework, called the value chain, which allows systematic study of the various value-adding activities of a business (see Exhibit 3.4).[40] Value chain analysis may be used to identify key resources and processes that represent strengths, areas that need improvement, and opportunities to develop a competitive advantage.

The **value chain** divides organizational processes into distinct activities that create value for the customer. The primary activities include inbound logistics, operations, outbound logistics, marketing and sales, and service. **Inbound logistics** includes supply chain activities associated with acquiring inputs that are used in the product—warehousing, materials handling, and inventory control. **Operations** refers to transforming inputs into the final product through activities such as machining, assembly, molding, testing, and printing. **Outbound logistics** are activities related to storing and physically distributing the final product to customers, such as finished goods warehousing, order processing, and transportation. **Marketing and sales** include processes through which customers can purchase the product

Exhibit 3.4   The Value Chain Including Support Activities

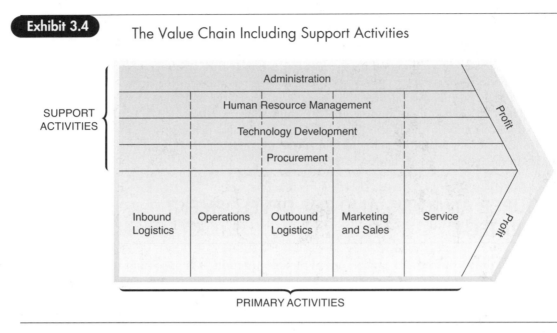

and through which they are induced to do so, such as advertising, distribution of catalogs, direct sales, distribution channeling, promotion and pricing. Finally, **service** refers to providing service to enhance or maintain product value, such as repairing, supplying parts, or installation.

Organizations also engage in activities that support these primary functions. These activities are placed above the primary activities in Exhibit 3.4. **Procurement** refers to the processes and activities involved in purchasing inputs and not to the inputs themselves or to the way they are handled once they are delivered. **Technology development** refers to product and process development processes and to organizational learning processes, which result in improved products and services and in improvements in the way organizational functions are performed. **Human resource management** includes human-based activities such as recruiting, hiring, training, performance evaluation, employee development, and compensation. Finally, **administration** consists of general management activities such as planning and accounting.

The dotted lines connecting the support activities with the primary activities demonstrate that they can be associated with each of the primary activities as well as support the complete chain. For example, technology developments are generally manifested in the products, services, and processes in the primary value-adding activities. Profit, which is on the right hand side of Exhibit 3.4, indicates that firms can achieve higher profit margins through the development of competencies and superior resources based on their value chain activities.

Once a firm's primary and support activities are well described and documented, they are compared to the activities of close competitors. Based on this analysis, an organization can develop a competitive advantage (1) in any of the primary or support activities *or* (2) in the way they are combined *or* (3) in the way internal activities are linked to the external environment. The cumulative effect of value chain activities and the way they are linked inside the firm and with the external environment determine organizational strengths, weaknesses, and performance relative to competitors.

A thorough profile of the strengths and weaknesses of the major value-adding activities requires in-depth study of the specific actions, resources, and capabilities at the functional level. For example, an evaluation of marketing's value adding performance and potential would consider the number and type of target customers, product positioning, product line mix, product line breadth, pricing strategies, promotion practices, and distribution channels. Each aspect would be characterized as a strength or weakness and then evaluated for its fit with current and future strategic plans. By identifying the specific strengths and weaknesses within each category of value-adding activities, plans can be developed for correcting or avoiding weaknesses, and for cultivating and building strengths. A detailed framework for profiling organizational strengths and weaknesses is shown in the case analysis appendix at the end of this book.

KEY POINTS SUMMARY

This chapter described internal resources and capabilities and the way they are used to achieve competitive advantage through the development of strategies that take advantage of strengths or overcome weaknesses. The following are some of the most important points that were made:

1. Resources and capabilities that have the potential to lead to competitive advantage have market value and are unique. For a firm to realize this potential it must have systems in place to take advantage of the resource or capability, must be aware of the potential and must be taking actions to realize it. If the resource or capability is also difficult to imitate or substitute the competitive advantage may be sustainable.

2. Resources and capabilities fall into the areas of human, physical, financial, knowledge and learning, and general organizational. All of the resource areas are highly interconnected, so a firm cannot afford to neglect any of the areas.

3. Resources fall into the general categories of tangible and intangible. Tangible resources can be seen, touched and/or quantified. Intangible resources are hard to identify in these terms. Intangible resources are much more difficult to imitate and thus have high potential for competitive advantage. Tacit knowledge is closely associated with the creation of intangible resources and capabilities, whereas codified knowledge, which can be described in words, is related to tangible resources.

4. Human resources hold excellent potential for sustainable competitive advantage. Possible sources of advantage include excellent human resources, superior top managers or an excellent system of corporate governance. Directors can provide advice to top managers and help the firm acquire resources through its stakeholder network.

5. Physical resources such as plants, machinery and products tend to be easy to imitate, so they hold less potential for sustainable competitive advantage. Locations can be good sources of competitive advantage in some situations and industries.

6. Strong cash flow, low levels of debt, a strong credit rating, access to low interest capital, and a reputation for creditworthiness are powerful strengths that can help firms be more responsive to new opportunities and new threats. Financial analysis can help a firm identify financial strengths and weaknesses and determine its ability to fund growth strategies.

7. Organizational learning is closely connected to the other resource areas. It involves (1) knowledge creation, (2) knowledge retention, (3) knowledge sharing and (4) knowledge utilization. Transfer of organizational knowledge is much more difficult across international boundaries.

8. A firm's general organizational resources include its reputation and brand names; relationships with external stakeholders; and its organizational structure, management systems and culture, in addition to particular strengths in one or more of the functional areas. These resources are hard to imitate and therefore firms that have strong general organizational resources tend to be highly competitive.

9. Strategy should be based on what the organization does well relative to competitors *or* on the capabilities or resources the firm wants to develop that will create a competitive advantage in the future.

10. The value chain may be used in determining the strengths and weaknesses of the different value-adding activities of the business, and may be useful in identifying sources of competitive advantage.

REFERENCES

1   H. Green, "How Amazon Aims to Keep You Clicking," *Business Week* (March 2, 2009): 34–40; "Amazon.com 2008 Annual Report," http://phx. corporate-ir.net/phoenix.zhtml?c=97664andp= irol-reportsAnnual (April 27, 2009).

2   T.R. Crook, D.J. Ketchen, Jr., J.G. Combs and S.Y. Todd, "Strategic Resources and Performance: A Meta-Analysis," *Strategic Management Journal* 29 (2008): 1141–1154.

3   S.L. Newbert, "Value, Rareness, Competitive Advantage, and Performance: A Conceptual Level Empirical Investigation of the Resource-based View of the Firm," *Strategic Management Journal* 29 (2008): 745–768.

4   J.B. Barney, "Firm Resources and Sustained Competitive Advantage," *Journal of Management* 17 (1991): 99–120; J.B. Barney, *Gaining and Sustaining Competitive Advantage* (Reading, MA: Addison-Wesley, 1997).

5   J.B. Barney, "Looking Inside for Competitive Advantage," *Academy of Management Executive* (November, 1995): 49–61.

6   Barney, "Looking Inside for Competitive Advantage."

7   M.A. Hitt, R.D. Ireland, R.E. Hoskisson and J.S. Harrison, *Competing for Advantage*, 2nd ed. (Mason, Ohio: Thomson Higher Education, 2008).

8   S. Berman, J. Down and C.W.L. Hill, "Tacit Knowledge as a Source of Competitive Advantage in the National Basketball Association," *Academy of Management Journal* 45 (2002): 13–32.

9   W.C. Rapplege, "Human Capital Management: The Next Competitive Advantage," *Across the Board* 36 (September, 1999): 39–48.

10 M. Herbst, "A Narrowing Window for Foreign Workers?" *Business Week* (March 16, 2009): 50.

11 J.J. Hughes, "Views of the Future," in R.L. Wolkoff, ed., *Next-Generation Manufacturing: A Framework for Action* (Bethlehem, PA: The Agility Forum, 1997).

12 R.W. Griffith, P.W. Hom and S. Gaertner, "A Meta-analysis of Correlates of Employee Turnover: Update, Moderator Tests and Research Implications for the New Millennium," *Journal of Management* 26 (2000): 463–488.

13 "100 Best Companies to Work For," http://www. cnnmoney.com/magazines/fortune (August 8, 2006).

14 D.B. Turban and D.W. Greening, "Corporate Social Performance and Organizational Attractiveness to Prospective Employees," *Academy of Management Journal* 40 (1996): 658–672.

15 R. Levering and M. Moskowitz, "And the Winners Are . . ." *Fortune* (February 2, 2009): 67–68.

16 "People and Capability," http://www.bp.com (August 8, 2006).

17 S. Finkelstein and D.C. Hambrick, *Strategic Leadership: Top Executives and Their Effects on Organizations* (Minneapolis: West Publishing Company, 1996): Chapter 2.

18 J. McGregor, "When Service Means Survival," *Business Week* (March 2, 2009): 26–30.

19 T.R. Holcomb, R.M. Holmes, Jr., and B. Connelly, "Making the Most of What You Have: Managerial Ability as a Source of Resource Value Creation," *Strategic Management Journal* 30 (2009): 457–485.

20 A. Mackey, "The Effects of CEOs on Firm Performance," *Strategic Management Journal* 29 (2008): 1357–1367.

21 M.A. Carpenter and J.D. Westphal, "The Strategic Context of External Network Ties: Examining the Impact of Director Appointments on Board Involvement in Strategic Decision Making," *Academy of Management Journal* 44 (2001): 639–660.

22 W.Q. Judge, Jr., and C. Zeithaml, "Institutional and Strategic Choice Perspectives on Board Involvement in the Strategic Decision Process," *Academy*

of *Management Journal* 35 (1992): 766–794; J.A. Pearce II and Shaker A. Zahra, "The Relative Power of CEOs and Boards of Directors: Associations with Corporate Performance," *Strategic Management Journal* 12 (1991): 135–153.

23   J. Muller, "Surviving Globalism," *Forbes* (February 27, 2006): 44–47.

24   L. Canina, C.A. Enz and J.S. Harrison, "Agglomeration Effects and Strategic Orientations: Evidence from the U.S. Lodging Industry," *Academy of Management Journal* 48 (2005): 565–581; R. Pouder and C.H. St. John, "Hot Spots and Blind Spots: Geographical Clusters of Firms and Innovation," *Academy of Management Review* 21: 1192–1225; M.E. Porter, "Clusters and the New Economics of Competition," *Harvard Business Review* (November-December, 1998): 77–90.

25   D. Smith and R. Florida, "Agglomeration and Industry Location: An Econometric Analysis of Japanese-affiliated Manufacturing Establishments in Automotive-related Industries," *Journal of Urban Economics* 36 (1994): 23–41.

26   L. Canina, C.A. Enz and J.S. Harrison, "Agglomeration Effects and Strategic Orientations: Evidence from the U.S. Lodging Industry," *Academy of Management Journal* 48 (2005): 565–581.

27   R. Levering and M. Moskowitz, "And the Winners Are . . ." *Fortune* (February 2, 2009): 67–68.

28   G.G. Dess and G.T. Lumpkin, "Emerging Issues in Strategy Process Research," in M.A. Hitt, R.E. Freeman, and J.S. Harrison, eds. *Blackwell Handbook of Strategic Management* (Oxford, U.K.: Blackwell Publishers LTD, 2001): 3–34.

29   D.J. Teece, *Managing Intellectual Capital* (New York: Oxford University Press, 2000).

30   D.M. DeCarolis and D.L. Deeds, "The Impact of Stocks and Flows of Organizational Knowledge on Firm Performance," *Strategic Management Journal* 20 (1999): 954–968.

31   M. Hurt and S. Hurt, "Transfer of Managerial Practices by French Food retailers to Operations in Poland," *Academy of Management Executive* 19 (2) (2005): 36.

32   D. Friel, "Transfering a Lean Production Concept from Germany to the United States: The Impact of Labor Laws and Training Systems," *Academy of Management Executive* 19 (2) (2005): 50–58.

33   R.C. May, S.M. Puffer and D.J. McCarthy, "Transferring Management Knowledge to Russia: A Culturally Based Approach," *Academy of Management Executive* 19 (2) (2005): 24–35.

34   B. Helm, "Best Global Brands," *Business Week* (September 29, 2008): 52–54.

35   *Walt Disney Company 1995 Annual Report*: 6–7.

36   J.H. Dyer, "Specialized Computer Networks as a Source of Competitive Advantage: Evidence from the Auto Industry," *Strategic Management Journal* 17 (1996): 271–291.

37   "The Nokia Way and Values," http://www.nokia.com/nokia (April 16, 2003).

38   R.D. Ireland and M.A. Hitt, "Achieving and Maintaining Strategic Competitiveness: The Role of Strategic Leadership," *Academy of Management Executive* 19 (4) (2005): 63–77.

39   D. Miller and J. Shamsie, "The Resource-Based View of the Firm in Two Environments: The Hollywood Film Studios from 1936 to 1965," *Academy of Management Journal* 39 (1996): 519–543.

40   M.E. Porter, *Competitive Advantage: Creating and Sustaining Superior Performance* (New York: The Free Press, 1985): Chapter 2.

4

Strategic Leadership and Strategic Direction

Colgate-Palmolive

The personal care and oral care consumer markets may not typically be thought of as highly attractive investment opportunities. In fact, these businesses are not growing rapidly, at least in the United States and competition is fierce. Consider, for example, the intensity of the rivalry for the top spot in toothpaste, with Colgate going head-to-head with Procter & Gamble's Crest. Nevertheless, after five years of cutting costs, raising prices, and flooding third world markets with its products to offset slow U.S. growth, Colgate-Palmolive has the highest worldwide market shares in some of its product categories and enjoyed strong sales and profits even during the recent economic downturn. In fact, the company increased its dividend by 10% during the height of the economic crisis. The company sells its consumer products in over 200 countries.

Leading the company is Ian M. Cook, Chairman and Chief Executive Officer. He joined the company in the United Kingdom in 1976 and held a number of senior management roles around the world before his appointment as CEO in 2005. The company is also governed by a nine member Board of Directors, eight of which are independent. "The Board believes that an independent director should be free of any relationship with Colgate or its senior management that may in fact or appearance impair the director's ability to make independent judgments, or compromise the director's objectivity and loyalty to stockholders ..." The only exception is Mr. Cook, who serves as Chairman.

Colgate-Palmolive managers and employees are guided by three fundamental values—Caring, Global Teamwork and Continuous Improvement. According to top management, "They are the foundation for our business strategy and are reflected in every aspect of our work life."

Caring

The Company cares about people: Colgate people, customers, shareholders and business partners. Colgate is committed to act with compassion, integrity and honesty in all situations, to listen with respect to others and to value differences. The Company is also committed to protect the global environment and to enhance the communities where Colgate people live and work.

Global Teamwork

All Colgate people are part of a global team, committed to working together across countries and throughout the world. Only by sharing ideas, technologies and talents can the Company achieve and sustain profitable growth.

Continuous Improvement

Colgate is committed to getting better every day in all it does, as individuals and as teams. By better understanding consumers' and customers' expectations and continuously working to innovate and improve products, services and processes, Colgate will "become the best."[1]

High performing companies tend to have an organizational identity that is understood by both internal and external stakeholders. On the inside, well-established values can provide guidance to managers at all levels as they make strategic decisions.[2] For example, the values of Colgate-Palmolive encourage managers and employees to treat stakeholders well, foster teamwork at the global level and continuously strive for improvement. In addition, these values are communicated to external stakeholders through the decisions and actions of the firm. Firms that treat stakeholders well may find it easier to sell their products, establish profitable contracts, create alliances, and enjoy other benefits that have been discussed in previous chapters. Values are a part of a broader concept called strategic direction. **Strategic direction** can be defined in terms of a firm's vision of where it is heading, the businesses in which it is involved, and its purpose.

The best performing companies also tend to have highly effective leaders. In particular, the CEO can have a large impact on the performance of the firm.[3] These leaders are responsible for establishing strategic direction. They also perform a variety of other roles that help the firm to achieve its goals and purpose. This chapter will begin with a discussion of strategic leadership, followed by a more in-depth exploration of strategic direction.

STRATEGIC LEADERSHIP

The traditional view of leaders in organizations is that they set direction, make the important decisions, and rally the followers (usually employees). According to Peter Senge, this traditional view is particularly common in the West where leaders are often equated with heroes.[4] There are many examples of visionary decision makers in recent years. Steven Jobs of Apple Computer, Bill Gates of Microsoft and Jeff Bezos of Amazon.com are just a few of the CEOs who are widely viewed as visionary leaders. It is common for organizations to incorporate stories about their great leaders in the myths and rituals that form the organizational culture.[5]

In the traditional model of leadership, the CEO decides where to go and then, through a combination of persuasion and edict, directs others in the process of implementation.[6] For many organizational scholars, the traditional view of the CEO and upper management as brilliant, charismatic leaders with employees who are "good soldiers" is no longer valid in many organization settings. Turbulent global competitive environments and multi-business organizations make the top management task far more complex than it used to be. Also, varied situations may require different leadership approaches, suggesting that leaders may need to vary their style and methods to fit circumstances.[7]

Primary Leadership Responsibilities

Perhaps the most important role of the CEO is to harness the energy, talents and creativity of the individuals that make up the organization.[8] In this capacity, the CEO has four primary responsibilities. First, he or she must create or design the organization's purpose, vision, and core values. Second, the CEO must oversee the creation of policies, strategies, and structure that translate purpose, vision, and core values into business decisions.

Third, the CEO should create an environment for organizational learning by serving as a coach, teacher and facilitator.[9] A learning environment is created by helping organizational members question their assumptions about the business and its environment: what customers want, what competitors are likely to do, which technology choices work best, and how to solve a problem. For learning to take place, members must understand that the organization is an interdependent network of people and activities. Furthermore, learning requires that members keep their work focused on creating patterns of behavior that are consistent with strategy rather than reacting haphazardly to problems. Leaders play the essential role in creating an environment where employees question assumptions, understand interdependency, see the strategic significance of their actions, and are empowered to lead themselves.[10]

Finally, CEOs and other managers must serve as stewards for their organizations in the sense that they care about the organization and the society in which it operates. Organizational leaders should feel and convey a passion for the organization, its contribution to society, and its purpose. They should feel that "they are part of changing the way businesses operate, not from a vague philanthropic urge, but from a conviction that their efforts will produce more productive organizations, capable of achieving higher levels of organization success and personal satisfaction than more traditional organizations."[11]

Effective Strategic Leaders

Two competing perspectives exist regarding effective leadership. The first is that effective leaders have a set of traits or abilities that apply to practically every setting. Dale Carnegie's famous 1936 book titled *How to Win Friends and Influence People* outlined methods for handling people so that they will like you, agree with you and change in ways that you would like them to change.[12] Since that time many scholars and practitioners have espoused their own theories of what makes leaders effective. One of the more popular recent contributions was by Jim Collins in a book titled *Good to Great*.[13]

According to Collins, not all managers have the ability to become effective strategic leaders. Leadership skills fall into a hierarchy in which managers must master lower-level skills such as becoming a capable individual before they can move on to the higher-level skills:

Capable Individual: A manager must have a set of basic skills that make him or her capable of achieving success in an organizational setting.

Team Player: A manager must be able to work effectively with other people in teams.

Organizer: A manager must have an ability to organize people and resources so as to accomplish organizational objectives.

Effective Leader: A manager must be able to articulate a clear strategic intent and motivate followers to carry it out.

Transformational Leader: These executives possess all of the skills associated with the other levels and also have an unwavering commitment to lead their companies to greatness.

Another interesting leadership perspective was contributed by Daniel Goleman, who conducted research into the relationship between emotional intelligence and leadership effectiveness. He concluded that, in addition to basic intelligence and technical expertise, successful leaders exhibit high levels of emotional intelligence, which he divided into five areas.[14] Self-awareness is defined as the ability of a leader to understand his/her own moods and emotions as well as their impact on others. Self-regulation is the ability to regulate impulses and think before acting. Motivation describes the personal drive to achieve, optimism, and passion. Empathy is the ability to understand the emotional make-up of other people. Finally, social skill pertains to the ability to manage relationships for particular purposes.

One of Goleman's key points is that the capabilities associated with emotional intelligence can be learned over time. He also argued that leadership styles are not inherently ingrained in the individual, but can be changed to suit the situation. He believes that leaders should exhibit many styles and should seek to expand their repertory of leadership behaviors.[15] For example, in a crisis or situation requiring fast action, a leader may find it necessary to exhibit a coercive, "do what I tell you" or "do what I do, now" style. These styles, while negative if applied consistently over the long run, may be required in some circumstances. Coaching and consensus-building styles are appropriate when attempting to improve employee performance, improve communication, stimulate creativity, and get valuable input from employees.

Goleman's argument regarding flexible leadership styles hints at the second of the major leadership perspectives, which suggests that different leadership characteristics are appropriate in different settings. In fact, some scholars have tried to establish guidelines for what types of leaders are needed in particular situations.[16] For instance, some research suggests that strategies focused on cost reduction are best implemented by managers with production/operations backgrounds because of the internal focus on efficiency and engineering. The research also suggests that strategies focused on developing differences that customers will value need to be managed by marketing and R&D-trained executives because of the innovation and market awareness that are needed.[17] There is also some tentative evidence that strategic change or innovation in organizations is more likely to occur with managers that are younger (both in age and in time in the organization) but well educated.[18] Growth strategies may be best implemented by managers with greater sales and marketing experience, willingness to take risks, and tolerance for ambiguity. However, those same characteristics may be undesirable in an executive managing the activities of a turnaround strategy.[19] Finally, when radical restructuring is required, a less biased outsider may be needed.[20]

The reality is that effective leadership is probably a combination of basic traits and situational traits. It would be hard to argue that the emotional skills of empathy and motivation would be disadvantageous in any situation. On the other hand, it is probably also true that people with different skill sets or experience will be more prone to success in particular situations.

Top Management Teams

While the CEO is the most important leader in most corporations, he or she typically shares leadership responsibilities with a select group of other high-ranking leaders, called the **top management team**. For instance, Colgate-Palmolive's top management team consists of the CEO, a chief operating officer, a chief financial officer, and a senior vice president who serves as general counsel and secretary. Also, the company has a few dozen vice presidents with varying responsibilities, with ten of them holding an additional designation as corporate officer.[21] An essential element of firm success is having a top management team with outstanding management and decision-making skills.[22]

Because of the complexity of environmental forces and the need to manage relationships with a diverse group of stakeholders, top management teams need a variety of strengths, capabilities, and knowledge.[23] A **heterogeneous top management team** is made up of mangers with a wide variety of functional backgrounds, education and experience. Members of a heterogeneous top management team benefit from discussing issues from a wide variety of perspectives. These discussions can improve the quality of firm decisions.[24] Heterogeneity is also positively associated with innovation and strategic change.[25] Nevertheless, in spite of these advantages, heterogeneity can also make implementing a strategy more difficult, in part because of communication difficulties resulting from managers who have very different perspectives and cognitive skills.[26]

Corporate Governance and Agency

The board of directors is another important part of the leadership structure in a corporation. **Corporate governance** examines the relationships between boards of directors, top managers, and various stakeholder groups, with an emphasis on the stockholders of the corporation. Of particular interest are the responsibilities of each of these groups to each other and how those responsibilities influence behavior. According to Sir Adrian Cadbury, previous chairman of Cadbury Schweppes PLC and a greatly admired expert on corporate governance:

> Corporate governance is concerned with holding the balance between economic and social goals and between individual and communal goals. The corporate governance framework is there to encourage the efficient use of resources and equally to require accountability for the stewardship of those resources. The aim is to align as nearly as possible the interests of individuals, corporations and society.[27]

Most larger companies, and smaller companies needing funds for growth, have issued stock. Therefore, their owners are the shareholders. If all of the stock is owned by a few individuals, often within the same family, the company is referred to as closely-held or private. On the other hand, in larger, publicly owned companies, the interests of shareholders are protected by a board of directors, who are elected by the voting shareholders. The board of directors is responsible for hiring, firing, supervising, advising and compensating top managers within the firm. Boards typically also reserve the right to approve or reject major strategic decisions such as the development of a new line of business, mergers, acquisitions, or entrance into foreign markets.

Companies often appoint subsets of the board of directors into working committees so that they are better able to focus on the issues at hand.[28] For example, China Mobile LTD of Hong Kong, one of the 200 largest companies in the world, has an audit committee, a nomination committee, a remuneration committee, and an information disclosure committee. They have also enhanced internal controls and reporting procedures. These actions have earned the company worldwide recognition.[29]

As soon as ownership and management are separated, as is the case in most public organizations, the potential for conflicts of interest exists. From an agency theory perspective, top managers are **agents** for the owners of the firm—they have a fiduciary duty to act in the owners' best interests.[30] When managers attempt to maximize their own self-interests at the expense of shareholders, an **agency problem** exists. Some examples of possible agency problems are shown in Exhibit 4.1.

One of the most important responsibilities of boards is to monitor top managers and prevent agency problems.[31] For example, boards need sufficient power to both monitor and discipline CEOs and other top executives. This power comes, in part, from their ability to determine their compensation. In some cases they even need to be fired, as in the case of Novell, Inc., the computer software company, whose board removed both its CEO and its chief financial officer due to poor performance.[32]

Exhibit 4.1   Evidence of Agency Problems

The following are a few commonly mentioned problems that may be evidence of agency conflicts:

High Salaries
It is in the best interests of CEOs to draw a high salary; however, these high salaries reduce the amount of earnings available to the shareholders. CEO compensation packages for the largest U.S. companies typically reach into the millions of dollars annually.

Current Expenses versus Future Investments
Since research and development expenditures reduce current earnings and often do not provide financial benefits for many years, CEOs who are compensated based on profitability levels have a built-in incentive not to approve research projects.

Status and Growth
Some power-hungry or status-conscious top managers may expand the size of their empires at the expense of organizational shareholders. For example, a few years ago Harding Lawrence led Braniff Airways to financial ruin through overzealous growth.

CEO Duality
CEO duality means that the CEO is also the chair of the board of directors. As chair, the CEO is in a strong position to ensure that personal interests are served even if the other stakeholders' interests are not.

Highly vigilant boards are widely regarded as the best defense against conflicts of interest.[33] Even so, some business experts believe that many boards are negligent in their fiduciary duties associated with reprimanding or replacing top managers who are not acting in the best interests of shareholders and they point to increasing incidence of shareholder suits and other actions against boards of directors as evidence of that concern.[34] For example, Exxon Mobile shareholders, unhappy with a massive pay package given to its outgoing chairman, passed a resolution opposed by management that would require a majority vote to elect a board member.[35] In a more subtle move, over 30% of shareholders "withheld" their votes for 10 of 11 directors of Home Depot, the largest home improvement retailer in the United States[36]

In addition, big investors are putting lots of pressure on board members and directly on CEOs to initiate organizational changes that will lead to more accountability and higher performance.[37] A proxy fight is one form this pressure can take. In one common type of proxy fight, one or a group of shareholders sends a document to all shareholders recommending that management be replaced. Even a threat of a proxy fight can stimulate change, as in the case of Tribune Co., owner of the *Los Angeles Times* and dozens of other media businesses:

> Putting aside the public rancor of the past few months, Tribune Co. management and the Chandler family, the company's biggest shareholder, have returned to the bargaining table to try and resolve their differences about the future of the newspaper and broadcasting concern, people familiar with the matter say. The talks follow a bitter falling-out between the family and Tribune management that became public in June, when the Chandler family called for Tribune to be either broken up or sold. Calling the company's strategy "disastrous," the family threatened a proxy fight to replace Tribune's management. Tribune's board rebuffed the family and defended the company's management. The new discussions . . . partly focus on restructuring two complex partnerships jointly owned by the family and Tribune.[38]

One highly publicized method that companies have used to increase the ability of their boards to monitor the actions of top management has been to include a majority of non-employee directors (outsiders) on their board. These types of boards are called "independent." For instance, BP directors "are required by the board governance principles to be independent in character and free from any business or other relationship that could materially interfere with the exercise of their judgment."[39] Similar rules are found in the Colgate-Palmolive example at the beginning of this chapter.

Inclusion of outsiders may not be a potent force in reducing agency problems if external board members are personal friends of the CEO or other top managers. These types of relationships often limit the objectivity of outsiders. For example, Michael D. Eisner had close personal relationships with many of the directors on Disney's board, a situation that gave him almost unquestioned authority and brought him and the company criticism.[40] Also, there is little research evidence that board independence leads to higher performance in companies under normal circumstances.[41] Nevertheless, there is evidence that institutional investors will pay a premium for good corporate governance practices, including mostly outside directors, formal evaluation processes, and compensation of directors through stock options.[42] Also, the composition of the board of directors seems to make a difference in crisis situations such as bankruptcies or during takeovers.[43]

Incentive compensation is another mechanism boards use to encourage CEOs and other high-level executives to act in a responsible manner with regard to shareholders' interests. For example, firms may provide CEOs with stock or stock options, which are contracts that allow a CEO to purchase stock at a future time at a price that will be attractive if the company performs well. Frequently such non-cash compensation is greater than the cash portion of a CEO's total annual compensation.

Governments are providing stricter regulations regarding corporate governance, partially as a response to major scandals like Enron and World-Com, in which top executives were involved in corrupt practices that resulted in huge losses to shareholders and other stakeholders. One example is the U.S. Sarbanes-Oxley Act of 2002. Sarbanes-Oxley provides requirements regarding independence of corporate auditors and the creation and disclosure of financial controls. It also requires that financial records be kept for at least five years and that the CEO and chief financial officer personally certify the corporation's financial reports.[44]

Thus far this chapter has examined strategic leadership, including a discussion of the responsibilities of strategic leaders, the principles of effective leadership, top management teams and corporate governance. One of the most important responsibilities of a strategic leader is to establish strategic direction, the topic of the next section.

STRATEGIC DIRECTION

Strategic direction typically is established and communicated through tools such as a mission, vision, business definition, values statement, sustainability statement and/or a code of ethics. However, it is important to distinguish between these written statements and the actual strategic direction of a firm. Some firms don't have a physical mission statement, but they still have a strategic direction, although it may not be well defined or communicated. Other firms may have written statements that reflect strategic direction, but they don't seem to follow them. Neither of these situations is optimal. A well-crafted strategic direction that is successfully communicated internally and integrated into the planning processes of the firm can provide direction to employees and managers as they make decisions and take actions. It can also help a firm establish a solid reputation with external stakeholders such as customers, suppliers and the communities in which it operates. This section presents concepts and tools that aid organizations in creating strategic direction.

Influences on Strategic Direction

Strategic direction results from influences both inside and outside the firm (see Exhibit 4.2). The CEO has the primary responsibility of creating, communicating and implementing strategic direction. Some CEOs are particularly good at doing this. For example, Sam Walton had a vision of making Wal-Mart the largest retailer in the United States. He would travel all over the country visiting Wal-Mart stores, rallying the associates in each store, talking to customers to make sure they were being treated right, and generally instilling his vision of what Wal-Mart should be. Other legendary leaders include Akio Morita of Sony, Jack Welch at General Electric, and Steve Jobs at Apple.

Other members of the top management team and board of directors typically are consulted during the creation or revision of a firm's strategic direction. Employees would typically only have input in smaller organizations, although their feedback on existing strategic direction can be useful to any organization when missions, visions, or values statements are being revised.

The external environment also can have a large influence on strategic direction. Recently, societal trends have caused organizations to adopt statements and create programs regarding the way they treat stakeholders, communities and the environment. Public outcry has led to more deliberate attempts to define corporate values and codes of ethics and conduct. Pressure from the financial community and business leaders has led to a high priority on shareholder returns. Firms also may imitate competitors. For instance, if a major competitor creates a statement

---

Exhibit 4.2   Influences on Strategic Direction

on "sustainability," managers may feel compelled to do likewise for fear of being singled out by the media or other stakeholder groups if they do not.

History is another important influence on an organization's strategic direction. The global conglomerate Philips attributes its emphasis on sustainability to its history and the influence of its founders Anton and Gerard Philips. Toyota's history also has a strong influence on its current direction (see Exhibit 4.3).

Like Toyota, organizations should learn from their past experiences and the feedback they receive from stakeholders. For example, customer demand for products and services is a form of feedback. The reactions of competitors are also feedback, as are financial performance and the response of the financial community. However, sometimes firms don't learn from their past. Past successes can create strong **structural inertia**, the term for forces at work to maintain the status quo.[45] These forces can include systems, structures, processes, culture, sunk costs, internal politics, and barriers to entry and exit. Anything that favors the "status quo" has the potential to cause inertia.

Structural inertia is also related to human nature. Most humans desire a certain amount of predictability in their work. In other words, they have learned to cope with their organizational environment—they are comfortable. They may also fear that changes will reduce their own power or position in the organization or that they will no longer be considered competent. If the forces favoring inertia are strong and

---

The Influence of History on Present-day Toyota

Exhibit 4.3

Since its establishment and right up to the present day, Toyota has always overcome the numerous challenges it has encountered. Toyota compiled what it learned through these actual experiences, both in good times and hard, in "The Toyota Way 2001."

One of Toyota's most difficult challenges was the unprecedented worldwide recession set off by the 1973 oil crisis. Compared to the previous period, Toyota Motor Company Ltd. (TMC) accounts for the fiscal term ending in May 1974 showed that sales were down by 14% and operating profits by 83%. Facing this harsh reality, a project team began to focus on building a system that generates profits even when the production rate is 80%. In September 1974, committee members gathered from various divisions set a six-month cost improvement objective of 10,000 yen per car, starting with Toyota's top mass-produced car, the Corolla.

After implementing changes in processes in divisions beyond manufacturing and in parts, even down to individual bolts, a goal achievement rate of 128% was accomplished. This defied the conventional common sense of focusing only on manufacturing improvements and brought about the groundbreaking concept to incorporate all divisions, including design and engineering, in the kaizen process. Thorough cost reviews were then conducted model by model for both passenger and commercial cars, and by the end of the June-November 1974 fiscal term, the cost improvement effect reached 5 billion yen.

The scope of the improvement activities soon expanded further. Parts manufacturers were encouraged by Toyota to establish an "80% production rate" as their purchasing objective and to aim for Toyota's Quality Performance Award, which was established in September 1969. Improvement themes were specially tailored to each supplier, and the factories proceeded to carry out the necessary changes.

In September 1977, then TMC Executive Vice President Shoichiro Toyoda (current Honorary Chairman), spoke to the companies that won the Toyota Quality Performance Award. "Our efforts for the Quality Performance Award to improve Toyota were enabled by all the companies working together as a team," he said. "By doing so, tangible and intangible merits, such as consensus among top executives and employees, started to appear and contributed greatly to the strengthening of the entire Toyota Group."

Toyoda's words are just as relevant today as they were back then. Under difficult conditions, it is as important as ever for all associates to form one team through mutual collaboration and work towards a stronger business organization.

Source: http://www.toyota.co.jp/en/history; visited on April 14, 2009

if the organization has been successful in the past, people will be highly resistant to any major shift in missions or strategies. Inertia based on past successes was one of the main reasons for the decline of the railroads as a form of passenger transportation in the United States. They continued to pursue the same strategies until it was simply too late.[46] Similarly, resistance to change had a strong detrimental effect on the U.S. automobile industry, which allowed Japanese and other foreign rivals to acquire much of their worldwide market share. Structural inertia, then, is another potential threat to the survival and prosperity of an organization.

Organizational Mission and Vision Statements

One of the most common means to communicate strategic direction is a written mission statement. An organization's mission, whether written down or just apparent from the organization's pattern of decisions and actions over time, provides an important vehicle for communicating ideals and a sense of direction and purpose to internal and external stakeholders. It can also help guide organizational managers in resource allocation decisions. Sometimes there is confusion between the terms "mission" and "vision." In general, an organizational mission is what the organization is, whereas a vision is a forward looking view of what the organization wants to become. As examples of this distinction, the mission and vision statements for the Bank of India are as follows:

> **Our Mission**   "to provide superior, proactive banking services to niche markets globally, while providing cost-effective, responsive services to others in our role as a development bank, and in so doing, meet the requirements of our stakeholders."

> **Our Vision**   "to become the bank of choice for corporates, medium businesses and upmarket retail customers and to provide cost effective developmental banking for small business, mass market and rural markets."[47]

Vision statements are not always separated from mission statements. Frequently, they are embedded in the formal mission statement. In fact, a written mission statement may include a vision, business definition, values and/or statements about an organization's purpose.

The labels a firm uses for its written documents are not nearly as important as including in them all of the essential elements of strategic direction. In one form or another, a firm should define what it is and what it is trying to become, including a definition of its business and what it strives to do for its key stakeholders. PepsiCo's mission statement is short, yet it summarizes these things fairly well:

> Our mission is to be the world's premier consumer products company focused on convenient foods and beverages. We seek to produce financial rewards to investors as we provide opportunities for growth and enrichment to our employees, our business partners and the communities in which we operate. And in everything we do, we strive for honesty, fairness and integrity.[48]

Other PepsiCo corporate documents expand and clarify the meaning of this mission statement.

As an organization is first established, its mission may be as simple as "provide software services to the local business community" and its vision may just be to survive. The mission and vision are often informal and seldom written down. As organizations succeed in their business environments, opportunities arise that allow the organization to grow in revenues and number of employees, and encourage it to expand into new product and market areas. As organizations take advantage of such opportunities, they are also increasing the scope of their business definitions by serving the needs of a much broader group of stakeholders. More formal written statements are useful at this point to guide internal decisions and help the organization meet the needs of its stakeholders. If used properly, an organization's mission and vision should provide a screen for evaluating opportunities and proposals and making decisions.

Many organizations prominently display their mission and vision statements or print them on identification cards or key chains for their employees. If top managers are not deliberate in the process of communicating missions and visions to internal stakeholders, they will have no positive effect on their behavior.

In addition to providing direction for internal stakeholders, organizations often prepare written mission statements as a way of communicating with the public. For example, mission statements are frequently included in annual financial reports, press releases, or letters to various stakeholders. Since they are public relations tools, they should be carefully crafted and concise enough so that people will actually read them. However, creating a mission or vision statement should not be an exercise in slogan writing. Some managers worry more about writing a catchy, short phrase that can be printed on a business card than about managing with purpose. Mission and vision statements should have real meaning and accurately reflect the true direction of the organization.

For an organization's mission to be a management tool, it must be grounded in the realities of the business. One of the first steps in creating a clear sense of mission is to fully understand the nature of the business in which the organization participates. This step, defining the business, will now be discussed.

Business Definition

A clear business definition is the starting point of all strategic planning and management.[49] It provides a framework for evaluating the effects of planned change, and for planning the steps needed to move the organization forward. When defining the business, the question, "What is our business?" should be answered from three perspectives: (1) Who is being satisfied? (2) What is being satisfied? (3) How are customer needs satisfied?[50] The first question refers to the markets that the organization serves, the second question deals with the specific functions provided to the customers identified in question 1, and the third question refers to the resources and capabilities that the firm uses to provide the functions identified in question 2. In actuality, most business definitions also identify specific product groups and/or services provided by the organization. In this regard, a fourth question, which is an extension of the third question, can be stated as, "What are our products and services?" This approach is, admittedly, marketing oriented. Its greatest strength is that it focuses on the customer, a very important external stakeholder for most firms.

The scope of an organization is the breadth of its activities across markets, functions, resource conversion processes, and products. Some large organizations, such as General Electric and Nestle, have a very broad scope. General Electric, for instance, has businesses in areas that are as unrelated to each other as aerospace, large consumer appliances, entertainment and financial services. This strategy is called **unrelated diversification**. Other firms may be broad in scope but have products and services that are closely related to the core competency of the company, a strategy referred to as **related diversification**. For example, Johnson & Johnson is involved in numerous product groups, but they all relate to the company's emphasis on health.

Firms may also move forward or backward in their industrial supply chains. A supply chain begins with raw materials and ends with final consumption of a good or service. For instance, notebook paper begins in trees, then paper pulp, then paper, which is packaged and shipped through wholesalers and distributors to various retail outlets, where it is purchased by consumers. If a company becomes involved in additional business activities in its industry supply chain, forwards toward the final consumer or backwards toward raw materials, it is pursuing **vertical integration**. These concepts—related diversification, unrelated diversification, and vertical integration—will be better defined and evaluated in Chapter 6. At this point we are only concerned with using them to help define a firm's businesses.

Peter Drucker suggested that the business definition question should be stated not only as "What is our business?" but also as "What will it be?" and "What should it be?"[51] The second question refers to the direction that the organization is heading at the current time. In other words, where will the organization end up if it continues in its current course? The third question, "What should it be?" allows for modifications to the existing strategy to move the organization in an appropriate direction. Consequently, the aspect of a business definition is closely related to an organization's vision.

Defining a firm's businesses now and determining where a firm wants to go in the future are essential to determining strategic direction. A business definition helps answer the "What?" question regarding firm operations, but it does not completely answer the "Why?" question. Also essential to strategic direction is defining a firm's values, purpose and ethics. These topics will be addressed in the next section.

ORGANIZATIONAL VALUES AND PURPOSE

In the first chapter we defined business ethics in terms of moral obligations to individuals, stakeholders and to a broader society. We suggested that the **values** of an organization define what matters when making decisions and what is rewarded and reinforced. They are a practical application of business ethics. For instance, if an organization puts a lot of value on treating stakeholders with respect, then presumably managers and employees who exhibit this sort of behavior will be acknowledged and rewarded. At least, in organizations that really stand by their values this sort of behavior will be rewarded.

Values help a firm define its purpose, which is sometimes called an enterprise strategy.[52] **Enterprise strategy** is the term that is used to join ethical and strategic thinking about an organization. It answers the fundamental question, "What do we stand for?" It helps to define the way stakeholders are treated and the value they are given in the decisions a firm makes. In this case the term "stakeholder" is used broadly to include society and its expectations. An enterprise strategy may contain statements concerning a desire to maximize shareholder value, satisfy the interests of all or a subset of other stakeholders, protect the environment or increase the common good of society.[53] Researchers have found that organizational mission statements containing the elements of an enterprise strategy are more likely to be found in high-performing than low-performing corporations.[54]

One of the interesting and ongoing debates pertaining to business values regards an organization's emphasis on profits versus its emphasis on satisfying stakeholders. As was discussed in Chapter 1, some scholars believe that an emphasis on satisfying a broad group of stakeholders is irresponsible because it reduces profits that should be returned to shareholders. Clearly, firms can go too far in allocating value back to stakeholders; however, at this point substantial support has been provided for a stakeholder perspective on strategic management. Chapter 1 introduced the concept and provided research support that firms that balance the interests of a broad group of stakeholders may be more successful in achieving their business objectives. Chapter 2, the external analysis chapter, provided examples of ways that firms can partner with their stakeholders in order to reduce business uncertainties and enhance their competitiveness. In Chapter 3, on internal analysis, strong stakeholder relationships were cited as a possible source of sustainable competitive advantage. The point is that profits and stakeholder interests do not have to be in conflict and, in fact, that a stakeholder perspective on strategic management can enhance a firm's ability to create profits. An interesting article from the *Financial Times* supports the idea that an obsession with profits is unhealthy:

> Jack Welch, who is regarded as the father of the "shareholder value" movement that has dominated the corporate world for more than 20 years, has said that it was "a dumb idea" for executives to focus so heavily on quarterly profits and share price gains. The former General Electric chief told the Financial Times the emphasis executives and investors had put on shareholder value—which began gaining popularity after a speech he made in 1981—was misplaced.
>
> Mr. Welch, whose record at GE encouraged other executives to replicate its consistent returns, said managers and investors should not set share price increases as their overarching goal. He added that short-term profits should be allied with an increase in the long-term value of a company. "On the face of it, shareholder value is the dumbest idea in the world," he said. "Shareholder value is a result, not a strategy . . . Your main constituencies are your employees, your customers and your products."[55]

Most organizations will not have a written document called an "enterprise strategy." Instead, the enterprise strategy is incorporated into the corporate mission or vision statement directly, or it may be contained in several documents, in addition to the mission or vision, such as a values statement, a statement of corporate social responsibility or corporate citizenship, or a code of ethics. One of the most famous of these types of statements was produced by Johnson & Johnson, the world's largest health care product manufacturer, in 1943. It was created by founder General Robert Wood Johnson and outlines the company's responsibilities to its customers, employees, communities and stockholders (see Exhibit 4.4). Over the years, the Credo has had a large impact on business decisions at Johnson & Johnson:

> The values that guide our decision making are spelled out in Our Credo. Put simply, Our Credo challenges us to put the needs and well-being of the people we serve *first*.
>
> Robert Wood Johnson, former chairman from 1932 to 1963 and a member of the Company's founding family, crafted Our Credo himself in 1943, just before Johnson & Johnson became a publicly traded company. This was long before anyone ever heard the term "corporate social responsibility." Our Credo is more than just a moral compass. We believe it's a recipe for business success. The fact that Johnson & Johnson is one of only a handful of companies that have flourished through more than a century of change is proof of that.[56]

Corporate values statements have become increasingly popular in recent years, partially as a response to highly publicized corporate scandals and stakeholder legal suits. Johnson & Johnson's Credo is a statement of values. As another example, SAFRAN Group, the French aerospace giant, has carefully defined seven values that guide firm actions and decisions (see Exhibit 4.5).

Exhibit 4.4　　Johnson & Johnson's Credo

We believe our first responsibility is to the doctors, nurses and patients, to mothers and fathers and all others who use our products and services. In meeting their needs everything we do must be of high quality. We must constantly strive to reduce our costs in order to maintain reasonable prices. Customers' orders must be serviced promptly and accurately. Our suppliers and distributors must have an opportunity to make a fair profit.

We are responsible to our employees, the men and women who work with us throughout the world. Everyone must be considered as an individual. We must respect their dignity and recognize their merit. They must have a sense of security in their jobs. Compensation must be fair and adequate, and working conditions clean, orderly and safe. We must be mindful of ways to help our employees fulfill their family responsibilities. Employees must feel free to make suggestions and complaints. There must be equal opportunity for employment, development and advancement for those qualified. We must provide competent management, and their actions must be just and ethical.

We are responsible to the communities in which we live and work and to the world community as well. We must be good citizens—support good works and charities and bear our fair share of taxes. We must encourage civic improvements and better health and education. We must maintain in good order the property we are privileged to use, protecting the environment and natural resources.

Our final responsibility is to our stockholders. Business must make a sound profit. We must experiment with new ideas. Research must be carried on, innovative programs developed and mistakes paid for. New equipment must be purchased, new facilities provided and new products launched. Reserves must be created to provide for adverse times. When we operate according to these principles, the stockholders should realize a fair return.

Source: http://www.jnj.com/our_company/our_credo/index.htm (August 11, 2006).

Values statements and other outward manifestations of enterprise strategy can help organizations resolve **ethical dilemmas**, which occur when the values of different stakeholders of the organization are in conflict over a particular issue. For example, a firm may be trying to decide whether to close an unprofitable plant. The union, employees and surrounding community would be expected to resist the closing, but financiers and shareholders may favor it. Frequently there is not a legal dimension to these dilemmas, but rather an issue of trust or good faith. Organizational ethics help to determine whether issues of trust, good faith and moral obligation are raised when decisions are being deliberated and the degree to which they influence the final outcome. This is not to say that plants should never be closed. However, a firm that practices good stakeholder management would be expected to consult with union representatives, employees and community leaders first to gain their perspectives on how the plant might be changed so as to make it profitable or, if it is closed, how to minimize the negative impact.

There are also ethical dilemmas which are related to the gray areas surrounding legal behavior: the definitions of what society views as right and wrong. In some cases, they are part of an obvious organizational crisis such as a plant closing, product recall, or environmental or safety accident. However, employees face decisions every day that have ethical implications: whether to tell a customer the truth that their order will be shipped late, whether to exaggerate a travel expense claim for a particularly inconvenient business trip, whether to ship a marginal product as first quality in order to meet the daily output quota. Although some of these decisions concern personal honesty more than business practice, the organization's ethics help determine how employees deal with them.

One of the reasons organizations sometimes fall into patterns of poor ethical behavior is that people often do not personalize ethical issues. It is as if the "organization" is responsible, and the individuals are not. Even individuals who

SAFRAN Group Core Values

Exhibit 4.5

Focus on customers

Customer satisfaction is our primary objective and guiding principle. We must continually focus on: listening to our customers, anticipating and understanding their requirements, and meeting them by being available and responsive; contributing to their success through targeted initiatives and personalized support.

Meeting our commitments

Meeting our commitments implies the ability to mobilize our energies to meet or exceed expectations. All employees must meet their commitments to customers and partners, whether internal or external, in compliance with the Group's ethics standards.

Innovation

We are a high-technology group, and our innovative and entrepreneurial mindset applies to all aspects of our business—products, services, support functions, etc.—at every level of the enterprise. This dynamic value is based on continuous improvement, calling on everybody's creative instincts and the inspiration and satisfaction of meeting challenges.

Responsiveness

It is imperative that we anticipate market requirements, and provide a quick response under all circumstances. Responsiveness depends on a streamlined corporate organization and straightforward employee behavior. Being responsive also means being mobile, making a proactive commitment to necessary reforms, and knowing how to adapt to change.

The power of Teamwork

SAFRAN fosters a team spirit, based on solidarity and sharing knowledge, both inside the Group and with our partners in France and around the world. The power of teamwork is the watchword behind our corporate continuous improvement initiative, Action V.

People development and recognition

This core value means providing the conditions for everybody to succeed, and recognizing results. Collective performance depends on the quality of each individual. We let the world know that we nurture the development of our human potential.

Corporate citizenship

Acknowledged for the excellence of our products and services, SAFRAN fosters and shares progress across the board, covering economic, social and cultural aspects. For example, we are committed to the development of a culture of prevention, to manage all health, safety and environmental risks entailed by our businesses. We make a proactive contribution to social solidarity and unity through our policy of integrating disadvantaged persons and promoting diversity within the enterprise.

Source: http://www.safran-group.com/; Visited on April 17, 2009.

see themselves as very ethical in their personal lives may pass through an ethical dilemma without recognizing it as one, or will view the dilemma as ultimately someone else's problem. For many ethical dilemmas, one person is not physically capable of correcting the problem alone.[57] If strong guiding values are not reinforced in an organization, then decision makers may not know what to do in the event of a crisis, such as a finding that a product is dangerous in some circumstances to the customers who buy it. If organizational ethics emphasize the safety of customers, then the decision is easy. This sounds self-evident, but unfortunately it is not. The case of Manville is illustrative of this point:

> Nearly sixty years ago, employees and managers of Manville (then Johns-Manville) started to receive information that asbestos inhalation was associated with various forms of lung disease. Manville chose to ignore this information

and suppress research findings. The company even went so far as to conceal chest X-rays from employees in their asbestos operations. When confronted about this tactic, a Manville lawyer was quoted as saying that they would let their employees work until they dropped dead, all in the interest of saving money. Eventually, this neglect of research findings and their own employees led to financial ruin for Manville.[58]

In addition to values statements, many organizations create codes of ethics to help communicate the values of the corporation to employees and other stakeholders. Codes of ethics are also a part of the organization's enterprise strategy. Whirlpool Corp., the global manufacturer of major home appliances, has adopted a sixteen page code of ethics based on the following preamble:

> BUSINESS WITH INTEGRITY   "We will pursue our business with honor, fairness, and respect for the individual and the public at large . . . ever mindful that there is no right way to do a wrong thing."[59]

Values statements and codes of ethics are helpful in defining a firm's enterprise strategy, but they do not ensure compliance. Enron had an inspiring code of ethics. One of the most difficult tasks associated with strategic direction is ensuring that statements about ethics and values are translated into organizational actions. The key is to create and sustain an ethical climate in which managers and other employees behave ethically as a matter of routine.[60]

High-level managers, especially the CEO, have a great deal of influence on the ethics of an organization. Managers who work with a CEO quickly identify his or her value system and communicate it to lower-level managers and employees. The CEO may also discuss organizational values in speeches, news releases, and memos. To the extent that the CEO controls the rewards systems, managers who make decisions that are consistent with the values of the CEO are likely to be rewarded, thus reinforcing what is expected. Many of the people who strongly disagree with the new values will leave the organization voluntarily. Or, if their own behavior pattern is inconsistent with the new rules of the game, they will be "forced out" through poor performance evaluations, missed promotions, and/ or low salary increases. Thus, over a period of time, the example and actions of the CEO are reflected in most of the major decisions that are made by the organization.[61]

Besides top management leadership and rewards systems, organizations can establish systems and programs to ensure ethical compliance. United Technologies, a highly diversified global technology company, has a very explicit set of guidelines for dealing with customers, suppliers, employees, shareholders, competitors and worldwide communities, as well as a comprehensive system for ensuring compliance. Employees are encouraged to report violations to their supervisors or a Vice President for Business Practices, and toll free numbers make such reporting easy to do. Also, retribution against employees for making reports of violations is specifically prohibited.

Research findings suggest that ethical compliance programs can have a positive impact in ensuring that organizational members do not step too far out of the boundaries the firm and society has established.[62] However, "integrity programs" that communicate and reinforce values have an even longer lasting influence.[63] For instance, Johnson and Johnson conducts regular surveys to assess how well it is living up to its Credo.

Dealing with values and ethics is a difficult task in organizations that compete within a single domestic economy. However, the difficulty level increases for global organizations because value systems are highly divergent across international boundaries. For example, a survey of over three thousand female seniors attending hundreds of universities and colleges in Tokyo revealed that they not only expected sexism in the work place, but don't seem to mind it. "More than 91% said they would not mind being treated as 'office flowers.' Nearly 25% considered that to be a woman's role. Over 66% said acting like an office flower would make the atmosphere more pleasant."[64] This attitude concerning the role of women is inconsistent with the values found in many countries.

Effective stakeholder management implies that an organization will be sensitive to the environment, safety, diversity and other issues that are of concern to society, while still maintaining a focus on business objectives and the satisfaction of key stakeholders such as shareholders, customers and employees. Fortunately, there is research evidence that firms that are good citizens also tend to be high performers. In fact, the evidence supports causality in both directions: high performance allows firms to be more socially responsible *and* social responsibility leads to high performance.[65]

Social responsibility contains four major components: (1) economic responsibilities such as the obligation to be productive and profitable and meet the consumer needs of society; (2) a legal responsibility to achieve economic goals within the confines of established laws; (3) moral obligations to abide by unwritten codes, norms, and values implicitly derived from society; and (4) discretionary responsibilities that are volitional or philanthropic in nature.[66] Chiquita Brands International, Inc., a leading international marketer and distributor of high-quality fresh produce, has defined its corporate social responsibility in the following terms:

> Our Core Values–Integrity, Respect, Opportunity and Responsibility–guide our daily decisions, and our Code of Conduct clearly defines our standards for corporate responsibility. In addition to strict legal compliance, we define corporate responsibility to include social responsibilities, such as respect for the environment and the communities where we do business, the health and safety of our workers, labor rights and food safety. We see a clear link between our Core Values and our company's vision, mission and sustainable growth strategy.[67]

This statement includes the concept of sustainability, which has recently become very important to the strategic direction of many organizations. **Sustainable development** can be defined as business growth that does not deplete the natural environment or damage society in any way. In fact, most organizations define their sustainability practices in terms of what they are doing to advance technology, environmental protection, and the communities and societies in which they operate. John Chambers, CEO of the networking products giant Cisco Systems, embedded the concept of sustainability into a fairly comprehensive statement of Cisco's enterprise strategy. His statement serves as a fitting conclusion to this section on ethics and values:

> At Cisco we believe that corporations have a responsibility to consider the broader effects of operations on the communities in which they do business and on the world in general. We at Cisco are passionate about not only maximizing return on investment to our shareholders, but also about the integrity and health of the company as well as the global community ... Cisco is dedicated to the success of our customers, our employees, and the communities in which we conduct business.

> - We act responsibly in delivering networking products and services worldwide.

- Our policies aim to improve the energy efficiency of our products, enhance the accessibility of the workplace for people with disabilities, and improve our stewardship of the environment.
- We have employee services that encourage work-life balance, a flexible work environment, and career development.
- Our inclusive culture promotes better decision making and creates a workforce that mirrors our customers.
- We expect our employees and those conducting business on behalf of Cisco to be aligned with our values of collaboration, openness, integrity, and generosity.

These actions foster our own success and create financial and social benefits for our shareholders and for the global community.[68]

KEY POINTS SUMMARY

This chapter examined strategic leadership and strategic direction. The following are some of the most important points that were made:

1. The traditional view of the CEO and upper management as brilliant, charismatic leaders with employees who are "good soldiers" is no longer valid in many organization settings. Turbulent global competitive environments and multi-business organizations make the top management task far more complex than it used to be. Also, varied situations may require different leadership approaches, suggesting that leaders may need to vary their style and methods to fit circumstances.

2. The CEO has four primary leadership responsibilities: (1) create or design the organization's purpose, vision, and core values; (2) oversee the creation of policies, strategies, and structure that translate purpose, vision, and core values into business decisions; (3) create an environment for organizational learning by serving as a coach, teacher and facilitator; and (4) serve as a steward for the organization.

3. The CEO typically shares leadership responsibilities with other high-ranking leaders, called the top management team. A heterogeneous top management team is made up of mangers with a wide variety of functional backgrounds, education and experience. Heterogeneity can improve strategic decisions, but can also make strategy implementation difficult.

4. Corporate governance examines the relationships between boards of directors, top managers, and various stakeholder groups, with an emphasis on the stockholders of the corporation.

5. When top managers, as agents for the owners of the firm, attempt to maximize their own self-interests at the expense of shareholders, an agency problem exists.

6. One of the most important responsibilities of boards is to monitor top managers and prevent agency problems. Highly vigilant boards are widely regarded as the best defense against conflicts of interest. One highly publicized method that companies have used to increase the ability of their boards to monitor the actions of top management has been to include a majority of non-employee directors (outsiders) on their board. Incentive compensation is another mechanism boards use to encourage CEOs and other high-level executives to act in a responsible manner with regard to shareholder interests.

7. Strategic direction is defined in terms of a firm's vision of where it is heading, the businesses in which it is involved, and its purpose. It is established and communicated through tools such as mission, vision and values statements; business definitions; and codes of ethics. High-performing companies tend to have an organizational identity that is understood by both internal and external stakeholders.

8. Strategic direction is influenced by internal and external stakeholders, the broad environment

and a firm's history. Structural inertia, which includes all the forces at work to maintain the status quo, can limit the ability of a firm to learn from its mistakes, especially if the firm has been successful in the past.

9. When defining the business, the question, "What is our business?" should be answered from three perspectives: (1) Who is being satisfied? (2) What is being satisfied? (3) How are customer needs satisfied? In actuality, most business definitions also answer a fourth question, "What are our products and services?" The scope of an organization is the breadth of its activities across markets, functions, resource conversion processes, and products.

10. Enterprise strategy is a statement of the purpose and values of the firm, especially regarding the way stakeholders are treated. Organizations communicate their enterprise strategy through their mission or vision statements, or in documents such as a value statement, a statement of corporate social responsibility or corporate citizenship, or a code of ethics.

11. Social responsibilities include (1) economic responsibilities, (2) legal responsibilities, (3) moral obligations and (4) discretionary responsibilities. Sustainable development is business growth that does not deplete the natural environment or damage society in any way.

REFERENCES

1 M. Boyle, "Still the King of Dental Care," *Business Week* (April 6, 2009): 48; "Corporate Governance," http://www.colgate.com/app/Colgate/US/Corp/Governance/HomePage.cvsp (April 13, 2009).

2 G.G. Dess, "Consensus on Strategy Formulation and Organizational Performance: Competitors in a Fragmented Industry," *Strategic Management Journal* 8 (1987): 259–277; L.J. Bourgeois, "Performance and Consensus," *Strategic Management Journal* 1 (1980): 227–248; L.G. Hrebiniak and C.C. Snow, "Top Management Agreement and Organizational Performance," *Human Relations* 35 (1982): 1139–1158.

3 A. Mackey, "The Effects of CEOs on Firm Performance," *Strategic Management Journal* 29 (2008): 1357–1367.

4 P. Senge, "The Leader's New Work: Building Learning Organizations," *Sloan Management Review* 32 (1) (1990): 7–24.

5 E.H. Schein, *Organization Culture and Leadership* (San Francisco: Jossey-Bass, 1985).

6 Nutt, "Selecting Tactics to Implement Strategic Plans," *Strategic Management Journal*, 10 (1989): 145–161.

7 D. Goleman, "Leadership That Gets Results," *Harvard Business Review* (March-April, 2000): 78.

8 Senge, "The Leader's New Work"; C.C. Manz and H. Sims, "SuperLeadership," *Organization Dynamics*, 17 (4) (1991): 8–36.

9 Senge, "The Leader's New Work."

10 Senge, "The Leader's New Work"; Manz and Sims, "SuperLeadership."

11 Senge, "The Leader's New Work," 13.

12 D. Carnegie, *How to Win Friends and Influence People* (New York: Simon and Schuster, 1936).

13 J. Collins, *Good to Great: Why Some Companies Make the Leap ... and Others Don't* (New York: Harper Business, 2001).

14 D. Goleman, "What Makes a Leader?" *Harvard Business Review* (Nov/Dec, 1998): 93–102.

15 D. Goleman, "Leadership That Gets Results," *Harvard Business Review* (March-April, 2000): 78.

16 A few representative studies are J.G. Michel and D.C. Hambrick, "Diversification Posture and Top Management Team Characteristics," *Academy of Management Journal* 35 (1992): 9–37; S.F. Slater, "The Influence of Style on Business Unit Performance," *Journal of Management* 15 (1989): 441–455; A.S. Thomas, R.J. Litschert and K. Ramaswamy, "The Performance Impact of Strategy-Manager Coalignment: An Empirical Examination," *Strategic Management Journal* 12 (1991): 509–522.

17 V. Govindarajan, "Implementing Competitive Strategies at the Business Unit Level: Implications of Matching Managers to Strategies," *Strategic Management Journal* 10 (1989): 251–269.

18 K.A. Bantel and S.E. Jackson, "Top Management and Innovations in Banking: Does the Composition of the Top Team Make a Difference?" *Strategic Management Journal* 10 (1989): 107–124; C.M. Grimm and K.G. Smith, "Management and Organizational Change: A Note on the Railroad Industry," *Strategic Management Journal* 12 (1991): 557–562; M.F. Wiersema and K.A. Bantel, "Top Management Team Demography and Corporate Strategic Change," *Academy of Management Journal* 35 (1992): 91–121.

19 A.K. Gupta and V. Govindarajan, "Business Unit Strategy, Managerial Characteristics, and Business Unit Effectiveness at Strategy Implementation," *Academy of Management Journal* 27 (1984): 25–41.

20 B. Brenner, "Tough Times, Tough Bosses: Corporate America Calls in a New, Cold-eyed Breed of CEO," *Business Week* (November 25, 1991): 174–180.

21 "Executive Management Team," http://www.colgate.com/app/Colgate/US/Corp/Governance/ExecutiveManagementTeam (April 13, 2009).

22 I. Goll, R. Sambharya and L. Tucci, "Top Management Team Composition, Corporate Ideology, and Firm Performance," *Management International Review* 41 (2) (2001): 109–129.

23 C. Pegels, Y. Song and B. Yang, "Management Heterogeneity, Competitive Interaction Groups and Firm Performance," *Strategic Management Journal* 21 (2000): 911–923.

24 D. Knight, C.L. Pearce, K.G. Smith, J.D. Olian, H.P. Sims, K.A. Smith and P. Flood, "Top Management Team Diversity, Group Process and Strategic Consensus," *Strategic Management Journal* 20 (1999): 446–465.

25 W.B. Werther, "Strategic Change and Leader-follower Alignment," *Organizational Dynamics* 32 (2003): 32–45; S. Wally and M. Becerra, "Top Management Team Characteristics and Strategic Changes in International Diversification: The Case of U.S. Multinationals in the European Community," *Group & Organization Management* 26 (2001): 165–188; W. Boeker, "Strategic Change: The Influence of Managerial Characteristics and Organizational Growth," *Academy of Management Journal* 40 (1997): 152–170.

26 S. Barsade, A. Ward, J. Turner and J. Sonnenfeld, "To Your Heart's Content: A Model of Affective Diversity in Top Management Teams," *Administrative Science Quarterly* 45 (2000): 802–836; C.C. Miller, L.M. Burke and W.H. Glick, "Cognitive Diversity among Upper-echelon Executives:

Implications for Strategic Decision Processes," *Strategic Management Journal* 19 (1998): 39–58.

27 World Bank, "Global Corporate Governance Forum," http://www.o2.com/o2_glossary.asp (August 9, 2006).

28 R.M. Ferry, "Boardrooms Yesterday, Today and Tomorrow." *Chief Executive* (March, 1999): 44–48.

29 "Corporate Governance," http://chinamobileltd.com (August 8, 2006).

30 M.C. Jensen and W. Meckling, "Theory of the Firm: Managerial Behavior, Agency Costs and Capital Structure," *Journal of Financial Economics* 3 (1976): 305–360.

31 C.W.L. Hill and T.M. Jones, "Stakeholder-agency Theory," *Journal of Management Studies* 29 (1992): 131–154.

32 R. Tomsho, "Novell CEO, Finance Chief are Replaced Amid Overhaul," *Wall Street Journal* (June 23, 2006): B5.

33 E. Fama and M.C. Jensen, "Separation of Ownership and Control," *Journal of Law and Economics* 26 (1983): 301–325.

34 I.F. Kesner and R.B. Johnson, "Crisis in the Boardroom: Fact and Fiction," *Academy of Management Executive* (February, 1990): 23–35.

35 J. Ball, "Exxon Shareholders Vote Their Unhappiness," *Wall Street Journal* (June 1, 2006): A8.

36 C. Terhune and J.S. Lublin, "Home Depot Vote Shows Measure of 'Pay Rage,'" *Wall Street Journal* (June 2, 2006): A2.

37 M. Magnet, "Directors, Wake Up!" *Fortune* (June 15, 1992): 86–92.

38 S. Ellison, "Tribune and Chandlers Return to Bargaining Table," *Wall Street Journal* (August 4, 2006): A13.

39 "Board Independence," http://www.bp.com (April 14, 2009).

40 "Delaware Court of Chancery Finds Disney Directors Not Liable for Approval of an Employment Agreement Providing $140 Million in Termination Payments," *Harvard Law Review* 119 (2006): 923–930.

41 For a review, see S. Chatterjee and J.S. Harrison, "Corporate Governance," in M.A. Hitt, R.E. Freeman, and J.S. Harrison, eds. *Blackwell Handbook of Strategic Management* (Oxford, U.K.: Blackwell Publishers LTD, 2001): 543–563.

42   S. Webb, "Good Corporate Governance Will Spur Investor Premiums, According to Survey," *Wall Street Journal* (June 19, 2000): B6.

43   S. Chatterjee, J.S. Harrison, and D. Bergh, "Failed Takeover Attempts, Organizational Governance and Refocusing," *Strategic Management Journal* 24 (2003): 87–96.

44   M. Osheroff, "SOX as Opportunity," *Strategic Finance* (April, 2006): 19–20.

45   D. Dobosz-Bourne and A.D. Jankowicz, "Reframing Resistance to Change," *International Journal of Human Resource Management* 17 (2006): 2021–2040; J. Betton and G.G. Dess, "The Application of Population Ecology Models to the Study of Organizations," *Academy of Management Review* 10 (1985): 750–757.

46   T. Levitt, "Marketing Myopia," *Harvard Business Review* (July/August, 1960): 45–60.

47   "Mission," http://www.bankofindia.com/mission.aspx (April 14, 2009).

48   "Our Mission and Vision," http://www.pepsico.com/Company/Our-Mission-and-Vision.aspx (April 14, 2009).

49   D.F. Abell, *Defining the Business: The Starting Point of Strategic Planning* (Englewood Cliffs, New Jersey: Prentice Hall, 1980): 169.

50   Abell, *Defining the Business*, 169.

51   P. Drucker, *Management—Tasks, Responsibilities, Practices* (New York: Harper and Row, 1974): 74–94.

52   R.E. Freeman, J.S. Harrison and A.C. Wicks, *Managing for Stakeholders: Survival Reputation and Success* (London: Yale University Press, 2007); L.T. Hosmer, "Strategic Planning as if Ethics Mattered," *Strategic Management Journal* 15 (1994): 17–34.

53   R.E. Freeman and D.R. Gilbert, Jr., *Corporate Strategy and the Search for Ethics* (Englewood Cliffs, New Jersey: Prentice Hall, 1988).

54   J.A. Pearce, II and F. David, "Corporate Mission Statements: The Bottom Line," *Academy of Management Executive* (May, 1987): 109–115.

55   F. Guerrera, "Welch Denounces Corporate Obsessions," *Financial Times* (March 13, 2009): 1.

56   "Credo," http://www.jnj.com/our_company/our_credo/index.htm (April 17, 2009).

57   B. McCoy, "The Parable of the Sadhu," *Harvard Business Review* (September/October, 1983): 103–108.

58   S.W. Gellerman, "Why 'Good' Managers Make Bad Ethical Choices," *Harvard Business Review* (July/August, 1986): 85–90.

59   "Code of Ethics," http://www.whirlpoolcorp.com/shared/content/responsibility/code-of-ethics.pdf (April 17, 2009).

60   T. Thomas, J.R. Schermerhorn, Jr., and J.W. Dienhart, "Strategic Leadership of Ethical Behavior in Business," *Academy of Management Executive* 18 (2) (2004): 56–68.

61   E.H. Schein, *Organizational Culture and Leadership* (San Francisco: Jossey-Bass, 1985); E.H. Schein, "The Role of the Founder in Creating Organizational Culture," *Organizational Dynamics* (Summer, 1983): 14; P. Selznik, *Leadership in Administration* (Evanston, Illinois: Row, Peterson, 1957).

62   L.K. Treviño and M.E. Brown, "Managing to be Ethical: Debunking Five Business Ethics Myths," *Academy of Management Executive* 18 (2) (2004): 69–83.

63   T. Thomas, J.R. Schermerhorn, Jr., and J.W. Dienhart, "Strategic Leadership of Ethical Behavior in Business," *Academy of Management Executive* 18 (2) (2004): 56–68.

64   E. Thronton, "Japan: Sexism OK With Most Coeds," *Business Week* (August 24, 1992): 13.

65   For summaries and meta-analyses of the proposition that firms that satisfy social stakeholders have higher performance, P.C. Godfrey, C.B. Merrill and J.M. Hansen, "The Relationship Between Social Responsibility and Shareholder Value: An Empirical Test of the Risk Management Hypothesis," *Strategic Management Journal* 30 (2009): 425–445; C.E. Hull and S. Rothenberg, "Firm Performance: The Interactions of Corporate Social Performance with Innovation and Industry Differentiation," *Strategic Management Journal* 29 (2008): 781–789; M. Orlitzky, F.L. Schmidt and S.L. Rynes. "Corporate Social and Financial Performance: A Meta-analysis," *Organization Studies* 24 (2003): 403–441.

66   A.B. Carroll, "A Three Dimensional Model of Corporate Social Performance," *Academy of Management Review* 4 (1979): 497–505.

67   *Chiquita Brands International, Inc. 2005 Annual Report*: 21.

68   J. Chambers, "From the President and CEO," in *Corporate Citizenship Report* (San Jose, CA: Cisco Systems): 1.

5

Business-Level Strategies

WAL-MART

An obsession with cost helped Wal-Mart become the largest retailer in the world. The company developed a highly efficient distribution system using large, strategically placed warehouses and technology. The size of the company provided economies of scale and Wal-Mart put pressure on its suppliers to drop their prices so that the savings could be passed on to the consumer. Employees, called "associates," were treated with respect, although the company kept wages low to support its low-cost strategy.

When Sam Walton, Wal-Mart's visionary founder, handed the reins over to David Glass in 1988, Glass continued to guide the company in a cost leadership approach. Prior to his appointment as CEO, Glass was famous for persuading Walton to invest in some highly effective inventory management technology that became central to Wal-Mart's emphasis on keeping costs low. Under the leadership of Glass, the company continued to invest billions in cost-saving technologies. However, by the time Glass stepped down in 2000, external stakeholders such as environmentalists and unions had helped to create an image for Wal-Mart as an "evil empire." It was not hard to do. Wal-Mart's size meant that its products left a large "footprint" on the environment and its employment practices and resistance to unionization were easy targets.

Lee Scott, the new CEO, worked to transform Wal-Mart's image, in part, through a sustainability initiative that includes external environmental reporting and projects such as reusable grocery bags. He also moved the company from a "boots" culture to a "suits" culture, in part by firing seasoned managers who resisted his plan. He led the refurbishment of stores to compete more effectively with competitors like Target, and Wal-Mart began offering products that appeal to more discriminating tastes. In 2006 Scott began to move the company back toward its low-cost roots, which put Wal-Mart in an excellent position to gain market share during the ensuing economic downturn.

Given his successes at Wal-Mart, Scott surprised many people by announcing his retirement in November of 2008. Mike Duke, his successor, was previously head of international operations. At the time of his appointment, Duke was expected to continue in the direction set by his predecessor, including expanding Wal-Mart's presence in China and Russia to offset slow growth in the United States[1]

Business-level strategy defines an organization's approach to growth and competition in its chosen business segments. Wal-Mart's retail businesses—which include standard Wal-Mart stores, superstores that sell groceries as well as non-food items, smaller markets and warehouse stores—tend to follow a similar cost leadership approach. However, some diversified firms, such as General Electric, develop different business-level strategies for each of the segments in which they compete. The strategies may vary widely from business to business because they are shaped by competitive forces as well as the resources possessed by each unit of the firm.

As demonstrated in the Wal-Mart example, business-level strategies have potential weaknesses as well as strengths. For instance, Wal-Mart's obsession with low costs put the company at odds with environmental groups and unions, and tended to repel higher income people with more discriminating tastes. Addressing these issues runs the risk of moving the company away from its low-cost approach, which is a primary source of competitive advantage for Wal-Mart. Tradeoffs such as these make the job of a business-level manager both interesting and challenging.

Within single business firms, and within each business unit of a multi-business firm, business-level managers must decide how to position the business to achieve its growth and profit targets. Some of the major strategic management responsibilities of business-level managers are listed in Exhibit 5.1. They include establishing the overall direction of the business unit, ongoing analysis of the changing business situation, selecting strategies for satisfying customers and dealing with competition, and managing resources to support firm strategies and produce competitive advantages. These responsibilities and the methods for carrying them out are similar in for-profit and nonprofit organizations.[2] This chapter focuses on selecting business-level strategies that help firms develop distinctive competencies that lead to competitive advantages.

Exhibit 5.1	Major Business-Level Strategic Management Responsibilities
Major Responsibilities	Key Issues
Direction setting	Establishment and communication of mission, vision, ethics, and long-term goals of a single business unit
	Creation and communication of shorter-term goals and objectives
Analysis of business situation	Compilation and assessment of information from stakeholders and other sources
	Identification of strengths, weaknesses, opportunities, threats, sources of sustainable competitive advantage
Selection of strategy	Selection of a generic approach to competition—cost leadership, differentiation, best cost. Also, the extent to which the firm will focus on particular customer segments.
	Determination of competitive tactics, including growth strategy and level of aggressiveness.
Management of resources	Acquisition of resources or development of competencies leading to a sustainable competitive advantage
	Development of functional strategies and an appropriate management structure to support business strategy

There are many ways to classify business-level strategies. One helpful way to divide them is to distinguish between a firm's basic approach to satisfying its customers and the tactics it uses when dealing with competitors. **Generic strategies** are concerned with how the firm intends to position itself to create value for its customers in ways that are different from those of competitors. **Competitive tactics** refer to the competitive *actions* firms take to grow and to increase the strength of or to protect their competitive positions. They are necessary because competitive environments are in a constant state of change. Firms that do not develop tactics for dealing with dynamic competitive environments are unlikely to succeed over the long run simply because they will no longer be viable in the new competitive setting that emerges. These two types of business-level strategies obviously are connected, but they are not the same thing. A firm can pursue any of the generic strategies in combination with any of the competitive tactics.

GENERIC BUSINESS-LEVEL STRATEGIES

The objective of a generic business-level strategy is to establish a competitive position that distinguishes the organization from competitors and creates value for customers.[3] In general, firms pursue competitive advantage by offering (1) products or services that are different from those of competitors, where those differences are valued by customers (e.g., novel designs, higher quality, unique features); (2) products or services that are standard, but produced at lower cost and usually offered at a lower price; or (3) a combination of the first two options, a hybrid competitive strategy called "best cost." The objective is to offer products and/or services that serve customer needs in ways that competitors do not, thus creating a strong **value proposition** for customers and superior financial returns for the firm. Any number of firms might be pursuing the same broad strategy, but each firm would tend to pursue it in different ways, and with varying degrees of success. The generic strategy types of differentiation, low-cost leadership, and best cost will now be described in detail.

Differentiation

In differentiation strategies, the emphasis is on creating value through sustainable uniqueness. Uniqueness can be achieved through product innovations, superior quality, or superior service, which is then sustained and leveraged through creative advertising, brand-building, and strong supply chain relationships. Another requirement for a successful differentiation strategy is that customers must be willing to pay more for the uniqueness of a product or service than the firm paid to create it. Apple is a clear example of a firm following a differentiation strategy. Over the past few years, the company has offered novel new products and services in computers, digital music players, cell phones, and online music delivery. The company has consistently demonstrated the ability to develop creative, novel products and services and command a price premium across multiple business units. Other examples of firms with clear differentiation strategies are BMW through its styling and performance, IBM with its high-quality service and emphasis on helping clients improve their performance, and Nintendo with its continuous game updates and innovations such as the Wii gaming system.[4]

Although cost may not be their primary focus, firms pursuing differentiation strategies cannot ignore their cost positions. When costs are too high relative to competitors, a firm may not be able to recover enough of the additional costs through higher prices. Therefore, a differentiator must carefully manage costs across its entire production process from idea inception to delivery, but particularly in those areas that are not directly related to the sources of differentiation. A differentiation strategy will lead to higher firm performance only if buyers value the attributes that make a product or service unique enough to pay a higher price for it or if they choose to buy from that firm preferentially.

Consequently, the major risks associated with a differentiation strategy center on the difference between added costs and incremental price. One risk is that customers will sacrifice some of the features, services, or image possessed by a unique product or service because it costs too much. Another risk is that customers will no longer perceive an attribute as differentiating. For example, customers may come to a point at which they are so familiar with a product that brand image is no longer important.

If a firm is successful at differentiation of its products or services, it is likely to become the target of the imitative efforts of competitors. As competitors imitate, the formerly differentiating features will become commonplace and no longer the basis for a differentiation claim. Rivalry in an industry can make it very difficult to sustain a competitive advantage from any one innovation for very long. For example, competitors are able to obtain detailed information on 70% of all new products within one year after development.[5] Consequently, staying ahead of the competition in product development requires *constant* innovation. As one business writer put it, "For outstanding performance, a company has to beat the competition. The trouble is the competition has heard the same message."[6]

Low-Cost Leadership

Firms pursuing cost leadership set out to become the lowest cost providers of a good or service. Examples include Nucor, a very successful steel company, and Big Lots, the largest closeout retailer in the United States Wal-Mart, featured in the introduction to this chapter, is also pursuing cost leadership. In the frozen dinner market, ConAgra has positioned its Banquet dinners as the low-cost leader. When the company raised its prices, which meant that many retailers were selling the dinners for more than one dollar, consumer demand dropped significantly. According to CEO Gary Rodkin, "The key component for Banquet dinners—the key attribute—is you've got to be at $1. Everything else pales by comparison."[7] The company took action to reduce both its prices and its costs.

Generally, low-cost leadership allows a firm to compete by lowering prices when needed without becoming unprofitable. When demand for products and services exceeds the available industry supply, a low-cost leader will be able to price its products at the commodity or average industry price and reap larger profits than competitors. When there is an excess of supply, competitors will drop prices to win customers—and the low-cost leader will be able to secure a small profit even when competitors are losing money. Consequently, low-cost leaders may be better positioned for economic downturns than companies pursuing other types of strategies. Evidence of this is found in the success of Wal-Mart during the huge economic downturn that began in 2008.[8]

To fully appreciate the significance of the low-cost leadership strategy, it is important to understand the factors that underlie cost structures in firms. Firms pursuing a low-cost strategy will typically employ one or more of the following factors to create their low-cost positions: (1) high capacity utilization, (2) economies of scale, (3) technological advances or (4) learning/experience effects.[9]

For instance, Tata Motors combined economies of scale with technological advances to produce its Nano microcar.[10] These factors will now be explained. Whether the firm is specifically pursuing low-cost leadership or some other competitive strategy, these cost characteristics of industries have important implications for the profits that can be derived from any strategy.

High Capacity Utilization. When customer demand is high and the firm's capacity (floor space, employees, equipment) is fully utilized, fixed costs are spread over more units, which lowers unit costs. This concept is just as relevant for hospitals, retail stores, and software developers as it is for manufacturing plants. If and when customer demand falls off, the fixed costs are spread over fewer units (e.g., customers, products, transactions, patients), so that costs associated with each unit increase. This basic concept suggests that a firm capable of maintaining higher levels of capacity utilization, either through better demand forecasting, conservative capacity expansion policies or aggressive pricing to generate purchases or transactions, will be able to maintain a lower cost structure than a competitor of equal size and capability. Failure to maintain a sufficient level of capacity utilization will often undermine all other efforts to control or lower costs.

Economies of Scale. The second major factor with the potential to lead to cost advantages is economies of scale. Economies of scale are often confused with increases in the "throughput" of a manufacturing plant or other facility. As described above, increases in capacity utilization that spread fixed expenses can lead to lower unit costs. However, true economies of scale are cost advantages associated with larger-sized facilities rather than with increased volume through an existing facility. For example, the cost of constructing a 200-bed hospital should not be twice the cost of building a 100-bed hospital, all other things held equal, so the initial fixed cost per unit of capacity will be lower.

Other scale economies are also evident in many industries. Continuing with the previous example, the administrator of the larger hospital will not generally receive double the salary of the manager of the smaller facility. Also, activities such as X-ray and blood analysis laboratories, purchasing and central supply typically do not require twice as much time, twice as much equipment, or twice as many employees. In addition, the purchasing manager of the larger hospital may be able to negotiate better volume discounts on supplies and equipment. In summary, the larger hospital may be able to achieve per patient savings in fixed costs, indirect labor costs, and supply costs. If per-unit costs are not lower in the larger plant, then the company has *not* achieved economies of scale. In fact, **diseconomies of scale** occur when a firm builds facilities that are so large that the sheer administrative costs and confusion associated with the added bureaucracy overwhelm any potential cost savings.

Technological Advances. Firms often invest in research and development leading to cost-saving technologies.[11] Companies that make investments in cost-saving technologies are often trading an increase in fixed costs for a reduction in variable costs. While investments of this type are typically associated with the factory floor, it is just as common for investments to be made in office and service automation. For example, the automated distribution system at Wal-Mart, the automated ordering and warehouse system at Lands' End, Internet banking services provided by most banks, and the reservation systems maintained by the major airlines all represent investments in technology that serve to lower overall costs and provide a degree of information and control that was previously impossible.

Experience Effects. A final factor that influences cost structures is **experience effects,** which may also be referred to as learning effects. When an employee learns to do a job more efficiently with repetition (gains experience), then learning is taking place. The time required to complete a task will decrease as a predictable function of the number of times the task is repeated. In theory, the time required to complete the task may be expected to fall by the same percentage each time cumulative production doubles. For example, a firm might see a 10% reduction in the time required to manufacture its products between the first and second unit of product, another 10% reduction between the second and fourth units, and another 10% reduction between the fourth and eighth unit.

Clearly, dramatic time savings are achieved early in the life of a product, process, or service. However, with maturity, tangible cost savings from experience are harder to achieve because companies that survive to reach maturity have often exploited many of the learning opportunities. Experience effects do not just happen. They only occur when management creates an environment that is favorable to both learning and change, and then rewards employees for their productivity improvements.

Experience effects relate to indirect labor as well as direct production labor. For example, with experience a sales person becomes more efficient at identifying prospective clients and preparing sales presentations, and a purchasing manager becomes more efficient at negotiating supply agreements. In modern organizations, experience effects related to indirect labor are even more important than direct labor learning effects because direct labor often represents less than 15% of total product costs. Much of the downsizing of middle management that we are seeing in industry today is an attempt to combine experience effects with economic gains from technologies (computer systems) to achieve a higher level of organization efficiency and effectiveness with fewer people.

Learning effects can be described by an experience curve such as the one found in Exhibit 5.2.[12] Following from the logic of this curve, the market share leader should enjoy a cost advantage relative to competitors because of the extra learning and experience that has occurred by producing the additional output. This concept has led many firms to fierce competitive pricing in order to obtain the highest market share and thus move right on the curve as far as possible.

Exhibit 5.2   A Typical Experience Curve

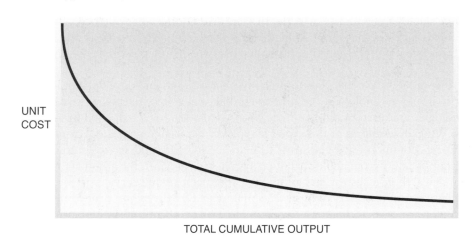

As the curve flattens, however, it becomes increasingly difficult to gain cost advantages from learning and experience effects. The same sort of phenomenon exists with respect to economies of scale.

Companies that are able to achieve high capacity utilization, economies of scale, economies of technology and/or experience effects may have lowest cost, but do not have to charge the lowest price. In other words, a *cost* leader does not have to be a *price* leader. If a firm is able to achieve the lowest cost, but charge a price that is the same as that of competitors, it will enjoy higher profits as a result. However, this approach entails some risk because there is no price incentive for customers to select their product over another. If customers are lured away to other brands, the loss of sales could reduce capacity utilization, lower learning and experience effects or undermine scale benefits. As is the case with all strategies, the success of the low-cost leadership strategy is a function of supply and demand in the marketplace, the needs and preferences of customers, the capabilities and actions of competitors, and the effectiveness of the firm's strategy execution.

There are several risks associated with too strong of a focus on a low-cost strategy. First, firms pursuing cost leadership may not detect required product or marketing changes because of a preoccupation with cost reduction. Second, these firms run the risk of making large investments in plants or equipment only to see them become obsolete because of technological breakthroughs by competitors. Their large investments make them reluctant to keep up with changes that are not compatible with their technologies. Third, efforts to seek low-costs may just go too far—with important elements of safety, quality, and service undermined.

Best Cost

Many firms have been successful in pursuing cost leadership and differentiation simultaneously. In some situations, the two strategies can detract from each other if they divide the attention of management and work against each other. In fact, in most organizations, it is common for marketing and sales, both of whom are close to customers, to advocate forms of differentiation at the same time that operations and finance are advocating investments in cost reduction and high levels of capacity utilization. Without an overarching strategy that guides the decision making, different groups pursuing different paths can create inconsistent and inadequate strategy execution.[13]

However, in today's intensely competitive global market place, some of the most successful organizations in the world have successfully combined pursuit of both low-cost leadership and differentiation in the eyes of customers. As Toyota has demonstrated and analysis has proved, the highest levels of product quality and reliability can be complementary with low cost.[14] Technological investments often allow firms to lower their costs while improving their performance on features that differentiate the company's products or services in the eyes of customers. Internet banking services and debit/ATM cards improve access and availability of teller services while reducing direct labor costs. A well-designed Web site can provide more detailed, easy-to-access information to customers at much lower cost than staffing teams of service operators. Over time, the profits generated from the successful pursuit of one element of strategy (i.e., low cost) allow investment in other elements such as differentiating features. Consequently, this strategy is called "best cost," implying that it provides the most reasonable trade-off between low cost and differentiating features.[15]

Some strategy scholars have argued that a combination of differentiation and low costs may be necessary to create a sustainable competitive advantage: "The immediate effect of differentiation will be to increase unit costs. However, if costs fall with increasing volume, the long-run effect may be to reduce unit costs."[16] Rather than envisioning differentiation and low-cost leadership as two ends of a spectrum, it may be better to think of both as foundation accomplishments that must be reinforced and improved over time as part of the iterative, on-going strategic management process. Successful differentiation makes the product more attractive to the market, which leads to volume increases. Then, as volume increases, management has the opportunity to employ the cost drivers noted earlier (capacity utilization, economies of scale, learning, automation) to drive down unit costs. Earnings that come from lower costs can then be reinvested into new forms of differentiation and cost efficiency. Jack Welch, former CEO of General Electric, described it this way:

> We're playing in a game where we'll show up and we'll be selling an engine against another engine competitor. Now, to get the deal, *you've got to have performance and all the other things*, but you'd better have low-cost. And as you go around the world, and you want to sell turbines to developing countries, you'd better have a low-cost base. Because in the end, you could have performance, you can have quality, but you'd better have cost (italics added).[17]

A best-cost strategy can be understood in terms of supply and demand economics. For example, assume that three organizations manufacture hunting knives. The first firm pursues a low-cost strategy. It is able to produce a knife for $10 and sell 100,000 a year at $20, for a total profit of $1 million. On the other hand, the second firm uses a differentiation strategy. It produces a premium product with features that the market finds attractive. The premium product costs $40 to make. The firm can sell 50,000 at $60. The total profit is also $1 million, although the unit volume is half that of the low-price competitor. Both companies seem to be successful; however, they are each achieving success using a different generic strategy.

However, assume that a third company can create a very good product, through a variety of product and process technological advances, for $20. Further suppose that this product is almost as appealing as the product of the second firm. If the firm can sell 75,000 at $50, the total profit will be over $2 million and consumers will believe they are getting a great deal (saving $10). This is the essence of a best-cost strategy—finding a level of differentiation that will bring a premium price while doing so at a reasonable cost.

Of course, pursuit of a best-cost strategy requires a careful balance of differentiation and cost leadership. Akio Toyoda, president of Toyota, is convinced that the company may have gone too far in the direction of differentiation at the expense of low-cost. His predecessor Katsuaki Watanabe led the company to change the way it designed its cars and factories. The strategy resulted in a lot of technological advances, but also added significant costs. Now Toyoda wants to put more emphasis on reducing costs.[18] The result should be a company that is more balanced in its approach between differentiation and low-cost leadership.

Focus

Another element of a firm's generic strategy is the extent to which it attempts to serve the needs and wants of a particular segment of its market. This is called a **focus strategy**. A firm like Toyota has diversified its product line such that it is apparent that the company is pursuing a very broad consumer market. Contrast Toyota's approach with that of Porsche, which focuses on a very specific group of consumers. The amount of focus a firm pursues is important to guiding specific decisions regarding how the firm will execute its generic business-level strategy.

A focus strategy defines specific customers a firm attempts to serve, but it does not define how they will be served. Therefore, a firm that focuses will do so in combination with one of the other three approaches. This being said, there are actually three types of focus strategies: focus through differentiation, focus through low-cost leadership and focus through best cost. For example, a firm might focus on older consumers through a cost leadership strategy, on foreign tourists through a differentiation strategy, or on vegetarians through a best-cost strategy.

COMPETITIVE TACTICS

The generic business-level strategies discussed in the last section are used to describe a firm's approach to satisfying the needs and wants of its customers. This section examines the tactics firms engage in as they participate in give-and-take competition with rivals. As illustrated in Chapter 2, the environments in which firms compete are constantly changing and firms that do not address changes are in danger of losing their competitiveness.

A famous economist named Joseph Schumpeter explained that leading firms will inevitably decline because competitors continuously pursue creative opportunities and eventually one of these opportunities will result in a superior product or service. Schumpeter called this process "creative destruction."[19] This idea can be applied to any resource that provides a competitive advantage for a firm. Even if the resource cannot be imitated, which suggests that it may be a source of sustainable competitive advantage, eventually the environment will change such that the resource will lose its value. No advantage is sustainable forever. Consider, for example, how Gilead Sciences changed the market for HIV drugs. It was one of the first companies to develop once-a-day pills that replaced mixtures of medications that were sometimes even administered intravenously. The previous market leaders in HIV drugs lost their edge because of this innovation. Gilead's HIV drugs now have an 80% market share for new patients diagnosed with HIV in the United States[20]

A number of competitive tactics describe the actions firms take as they deal with the dynamics of a competitive environment. These tactics can be divided into growth strategies, offensive tactics, defensive tactics, collaborative tactics, political tactics and avoidance tactics. Firms may also stress strategic flexibility in the tactics they pursue. This section discusses each of these tactics in turn.

Growth Strategies

One set of competitive tactics deals with the methods firms use to grow, or **growth strategies**. These methods, outlined in Exhibit 5.3, can be divided into internal and external growth strategies. In Chapter 4, we defined a firm's scope as the breadth of its activities across markets, functions, resource conversion processes, and products. Firms may select growth strategies that enhance their competitive positions in current businesses. An internal growth strategy such as market penetration is aimed exclusively at increasing a firm's market share in an existing business. Similarly, the external growth strategy of horizontal integration increases market share immediately. However, growth strategies may also cause a firm to expand the scope of its activities into new businesses, which is called diversification. Growth strategies used for the purpose of diversification are discussed further in Chapter 6.

Exhibit 5.3	Common Growth Strategies

Internal Growth Strategies

Market penetration	Increase market share in current business segments through advertising, promotions or stepped-up sales effort. May also involve finding new ways for existing customers to use products
Market development	Identify new market segments for existing products
Product/service development	Modify existing products (or services) or develop new products (or services) that appeal to new or existing customers
Vertical integration	Increase business activities by moving forward (toward ultimate consumers) or backward (toward suppliers and raw materials producers) on the industry supply chain; may also be achieved through external growth in the form of a joint venture or acquisition

External Growth Strategies

Alliances/joint ventures	Create business relationships with other firms to achieve a stronger competitive position through development of new products or processes, joint manufacturing, opening new market opportunities or increasing political influence
Acquisitions	Purchase of a company to enhance competitive position through obtaining new customers, entering new markets, acquiring new technology, obtaining valuable and rare resources, cutting costs or for other strategic reasons
Horizontal integration	Acquisition of company in the same line of business usually in an effort to reduce costs and/or increase market power

Offensive Tactics

Offensive tactics reduce the ability of rivals to compete. They include aggressive competition and pursuing first-mover advantages.

Aggressive Competition. Some firms use their abundant resource positions to overwhelm their rivals by rendering their countermoves ineffective.[21] For instance, Walt Disney uses the most advanced technologies and the most talented performers and production people when they create a movie that is intended to be a blockbuster. They then roll it out with an amazing amount of advertising and promotional campaigns using their own media as well as their theme parks and company stores. Similarly, Microsoft employs many of the most talented people in the software industry to develop new products and then uses its powerful distribution network to launch them.

For an aggressive strategy to work, the firm must have a vast supply of valuable resources, at least some of which are unique. In addition, if those resources are also hard to imitate the firm may be able to sustain its aggressive approach to competition for a longer period of time. Disney's success with aggressive tactics is made possible because the company has a powerful and unique brand and a network of complementary companies that reinforce each other's actions. Other resources can also provide a strong base for aggressive tactics, including a strong financial position, possession of uniquely valuable resources such as trademarks or patents, strong stakeholder relationships, or valuable locations. For firms that possess sufficient resources, engaging rivals with a larger number of competitive moves tends to increase firm performance.[22]

First-Mover Advantages. Firms may also enjoy competitive advantages by being first-movers in their industries. For instance, Intel has a strong research program that keeps the company at the forefront of its industry in producing advanced microprocessors for computers. However, firms do not need to be in high-tech industries to enjoy first-mover advantages. For instance, Domino's Pizza enjoyed advantages from being the first to offer a 30-minute delivery guarantee, a giant pizza called the "Big Foot," direct mail coupons, and then handy magnets with the phone number of local Domino's locations.[23]

Significant resources need to be invested in research and in developing new products and services for a first-mover advantage to be viable. Consistent with the principle of creative destruction, there is a fairly high risk that an industry leader may be overtaken by the aggressive moves of companies in second place.[24] Furthermore, early imitators, or "second-movers" may also enjoy high performance.[25] Firms that rapidly imitate competitor innovations may enjoy many of the same benefits of a first-mover without bearing all of the research and development costs.

Defensive Tactics

Some competitive tactics are not intended to overwhelm competitors, but to prevent them from engaging in particular competitive behaviors in the first place.

Threat of Retaliation. Firms may threaten severe retaliation in an effort to prevent competitors from taking actions that may be damaging to their own competitive positions. For this tactic to work, the threatening organization must have sufficient resources to carry on with a competitive battle if it occurs. Firms with a lot of financial liquidity, such as a high cash balance, excess production capacity, or new technologies that can alter the competitive landscape are in a particularly strong position to threaten retaliation.[26]

Multipoint competition, in which firms compete in multiple markets, makes retaliation even more effective as a competitive tactic. A firm can threaten to do something in one market if its competitor does something in a different market. An industry that involves a lot of companies that are multipoint competitors is likely to be characterized by mutual forbearance, and thus limited rivalry. Limited rivalry can lead profit margins to be higher, whereas lack of multimarket competition can lead to more rivalry and thus lower profit margins in the industry.[27]

Barriers to Imitation. Imitation is a very common competitive countermove because a "follower" organization can simply learn from the leader. However, some firms attempt to create barriers to this sort of imitation. Many of the barriers firms might erect to prevent imitation are similar to the barriers to entry discussed in Chapter 2, except that barriers to imitation are intended to prevent the imitation of cost savings or sources of differentiation, whereas entry barriers are intended to keep firms from entering the industry in the first place. This difference is significant because many of the sources of entry barriers are possessed by most firms in an industry. For instance, the large competitors in the brewing industry all enjoy economies of scale. On the other hand, a barrier to imitation needs to be possessed only by the firm that is trying to prevent imitation by other industry competitors.

Common barriers to imitation include strong brand names or trademarks, patents, technological secrets, unique locations, exclusive contracts or special relationships with suppliers or customers, or even economies of scale, so long as other competitors do not enjoy the same advantages. A firm may also deter imitation through offering a lot of new services, large investments in advertising, or even withholding information about how profitable a new product or service is so that competitors are not eager to imitate it. [28] As discussed in Chapter 3, intangible assets frequently are the most difficult to imitate. Consequently, a state-of-the-art research and development process is more difficult to imitate than a particular product or service. A high-performing organizational culture likewise is hard to imitate.

Collaborative Tactics

One of the recurring themes in modern strategic management is that organizational collaborations with stakeholders are valuable to obtaining competitive advantages.[29] Collaborations can take a variety of forms, including joint ventures (to be discussed in depth in Chapter 6), organizational alliances, industry consortia, research groups or trade unions.[30] Also, firms may participate in **innovation networks,** which are loosely coupled groups of firms that cooperate with each other and share information. These firms tend to be organized around a hub firm that helps to coordinate their activities and flows of information.[31]

Collaborations can be used offensively or defensively. For instance, a firm may use its participation in a joint venture to develop a cutting edge product or to battle a large competitor. For example, Sony and Google formed a partnership to challenge Amazon in the digital books market.[32] Participation in an exclusive alliance may prevent a rival from enjoying a particular advantage such as the ability to obtain knowledge created in the alliance. Sometimes a leading firm will select a particular group of firms for an alliance specifically to hurt other firms or to put them out of business. For instance, a joint venture between Hilton, Hyatt, Marriott, Six Continents and Starwood to sell hotel rooms at a discount puts other competitors at a competitive disadvantage.[33] Collaborative relationships can be difficult to imitate, thus providing a potential source of sustainable competitive advantage.

Political Tactics

As mentioned in Chapter 2, political tactics include organizational activities that have as one of their objectives the creation of a friendlier political climate for the firm. A firm may want to change the "rules of the game" by influencing laws and regulations that affect how they conduct business. For instance, a U.S. district court judge ruled that Visa and MasterCard could no longer prevent their member banks from issuing rival credit cards such as American Express and Discover.[34]

Political lobbying and campaign contributions are two of the most widely used political tactics. Firms may also become involved in community service in an effort to create a good relationship with local government organizations or other stakeholders with whom the firm interacts. Most larger firms have public relations offices and officers. Many do public relations advertising or publish sustainability or social responsibility reports that are intended to paint the firm in a favorable light.

Individual firm lobbying efforts may not be as effective as joint efforts.[35] Many firms have joined together in various forms of collaboration such as trades associations, chambers of commerce and labor or industry panels. Firms become involved in these sorts of collaborations to obtain legitimacy in the eyes of the people who are making decisions that could influence their business, which enables them to gain acceptance and influence those decisions.[36] Trade associations also perform information management and monitoring for their members. Firms may also engage in industry and labor panels to facilitate their negotiations with unions and activist groups.

Avoidance (Blue Ocean) Tactics

The tactics described so far may require significant resources and include a great deal of managerial attention. However, firms may also avoid confrontation by focusing on a niche in the market in which most other firms do not compete. This tactic is similar in concept to the focus strategy discussed previously. A niche can be defined as a particular geographic area or as a segment of the product/market that does not appeal to most competitors because of its limited potential for growth. For instance, in the lodging industry, the chain hotels tend to cluster in areas with a high level of tourist traffic. However, many independent hotels and resorts find success by locating in areas that do not appeal to the chains. Similarly, there are large numbers of firms that exist simply because they have found a way to appeal to small segments of the population with custom-tailored products and services.

Another way to avoid competition is to create a new market space for your products and services, or what Chan Kim and Renée Mauborgne call a "blue ocean."[37] A **blue ocean strategy** utilizes a best-cost generic strategy, a combination of cost leadership and differentiation, but it is an attempt to do so in a completely unique way. An early example of a blue ocean strategy was the Ford Model T. In the early 20th Century automobiles were being built custom-made by hundreds of manufacturers. Henry Ford introduced a mass-produced automobile, made of high-quality components, that would be affordable to a large percentage of American consumers. Similarly, Barnes & Noble and Borders reinvented the concept of a bookstore by adding areas to read and to enjoy refreshments within their stores. At the time of this innovation, the typical bookstore frowned on reading books within the store, worried perhaps that such reading would discourage a purchase.[38]

Strategic Flexibility

Tactics associated with strategic flexibility allow a firm to manage the amount of risk it faces while earning a high return.[39] Firms pursuing such tactics can move their resources out of markets that are less-than-desirable in a minimum of time and with as little loss as possible. One way to remain strategically flexible is to avoid investments that have significant exit barriers. Exit barriers discourage a firm from turning away from the investment because of the loss that will be sustained by doing so. Significant exit barriers frequently are associated with large capital investments, such as construction of factories that have limited uses. Firms may also create exit barriers because of a long pattern of smaller investments that have accumulated over the years. These may include lost synergies from stakeholder relationships that have been built over time, loss of a market position or loss of customers.

Firms may retain strategic flexibility by reducing investments that are likely to lead to high exit barriers. For instance, many companies in service industries such as lodging and airlines lease many of their assets. A hotel chain may even build a hotel and then sell it to another company while retaining the name and the operating contract. Similarly, several airline companies now lease many of their jets. Another tactic that increases strategic flexibility is subcontracting. Companies are able to subcontract practically all of their activities, including research and development, manufacturing, payroll services, marketing and sales, service, and even management. However, firms should be careful not to subcontract activities that are associated with the rare and inimitable resources that are a source of competitive advantage. And, as a practical matter, all of the activities associated with strategic flexibility reduce a firm's control over its own business processes as well as the profit potential from activities in which it does not engage.

Interdependence of Generic and Competitive Strategies

While it has been useful to discuss each of the generic strategies and competitive tactics independently, they obviously are highly interdependent. A firm may use aggressive competition to support its generic strategy of differentiation. Alternatively, a firm may use the tactic of strategic flexibility to keep its costs low as part of a low-cost leadership strategy. Note also that many of the competitive tactics can be used simultaneously. For example, a firm may engage in a collaboration that prevents imitation and also increases political power. Similarly, a first-mover tactic can be part of an overall strategy of aggressive competition. There is nothing wrong with these interdependencies. In fact, firms should think in terms of how competitive tactics can be used to carry out their generic business-level strategies and achieve competitive advantage.

Growth strategies are also linked to other elements of a firm's business-level strategy. As companies pursue growth strategies that involve them in new market segments, they often find they must change their competitive tactics to fit the characteristics of that segment. For example, a company that makes and sells ice cream through its own ice cream shops should consider changes to its competitive tactics if it decides to sell its ice cream in large volume to grocery stores. The production, packaging, distribution, and marketing would be very different in the new segment, as would the nature of competitive rivalry. The growth strategy, then, introduces fundamental questions about the priorities underlying the competitive strategy. For companies that are pursuing international expansion, these issues are particularly acute, as discussed in more detail in the next section.

STRATEGIES IN AN INTERNATIONAL CONTEXT

Firms should develop their core competitive strategies in their home environments before launching them into other countries. Once the basics are mastered in the home country, then a firm can adapt its core strategy to a particular international environment. Then, after a firm is involved successfully in a variety of international contexts, it can work on integrating strategies across countries to maximize the potential for efficiency through economies of scale and sharing of resources and knowledge.[40]

International Growth Tactics

Firms can apply a variety of expansion tactics as they pursue global opportunities. Among the most common are:

1. *Exporting*. Transferring goods to other countries for sale through wholesalers or a foreign company.
2. *Licensing*. Selling the right to produce and/or sell a brand name product in a foreign market.
3. *Franchising*. This is the services counterpart to a licensing strategy. A foreign firm buys the legal right to use the name and operating methods of a U.S. firm in its home country.
4. *Joint Venture*. Cooperative agreement among two or more companies to pursue common business objectives in foreign countries.
5. *Greenfield Venture*. Creation of a wholly owned foreign subsidiary.[41]

Among the most important criteria when deciding on an option for international growth are cost, financial risk, profit potential, and control. To some extent, moving down the list of alternatives from 1 to 5 entails greater cost and greater financial risk but also greater profit potential and greater control. In a very general sense, these alternatives represent a tradeoff between cost and financial risk on the one hand, and profit and control on the other. Of course, this is a generalization. Some of the options, such as joint venture, are hard to judge on the basis of these four criteria because the exact nature of the agreement can vary so widely from venture to venture.

Business-Level Strategies in Multiple International Markets

Organizations that are involved in multiple international markets may have advantages available to them in pursuing their business-level strategies. For example, firms that seek to improve their competitive position through cost leadership may choose to purchase materials or components from lower-cost international suppliers, subcontract the assembly or manufacture of their products to international companies with lower labor and overhead costs, or purchase finished products from international companies for branding and resale in the home country. In addition to the cost advantages derived on the supply side, companies may pursue international markets as a way to increase their volume and secure cost advantages associated with volume and scale. Finally, some companies may choose to form strategic alliances or joint ventures with international partners to gain access to cost-saving technology or knowledge.[42]

International strategies, if managed properly, may also help a company advance its competitive strategy of differentiation. Some of the options available include (1) licensing new advanced technology from abroad, (2) distributing high-value imported products at a premium price into the domestic market, or (3) growing an international brand for a premium domestic product by selling into high-end international markets.

One of the key issues facing top managers as their organizations pursue international strategies is determining the degree to which products and services must be customized to meet unique customer demands. If customers in nations and regions of the world have different needs or make purchase decisions in very different ways, then it will make sense to create products and services that serve those specific needs. This approach, called a **multidomestic** approach, involves custom tailoring products and services around individual market needs and may involve conducting the design, assembly, and marketing on a country-by-country or region-by-region basis. Most food products, some furniture items and home appliances, and some music and book publishing are conducted on this basis. On the other hand, some products appeal to the global marketplace, which means one product design can be marketed in the same fashion throughout the world. This **global** approach[43] is typical of steel and other commodity materials, personal and mainframe computers, athletic shoes, and some high-end automobiles.

Bausch & Lomb successfully used a multidomestic approach or strategy when it pursued different product designs in each region of the world:

> The key to global success for Bausch & Lomb is to "Think globally, act locally," by letting country managers make their own decisions. This strategy was applied in Bausch & Lomb's Ray Ban division. In Europe, Ray Bans tend to

be flashier and costlier than in the U.S. In Asia the company redesigned them to better suit the Asian face and sales took off. This strategy has paid off. Ray Ban commands an awesome 40% of the world market for premium-priced sunglasses.[44]

Cummins Engine has followed a multidomestic approach in its participation in India and China. Cummins conducts R&D within each nation, identifies unique partners that assist with marketing, manufactures products locally, cultivates local management talent, and establishes local supply arrangements.[45] Multidomestic strategies are intuitively appealing from a stakeholder point of view, since they emphasize the satisfaction of segmented customer needs. However, customization may add more costs to the products or services than can be successfully recaptured through higher prices. A few years ago, a well-known marketing scholar, Theodore Levitt argued that:

> ... well managed companies have moved from emphasis on customizing items to offering globally standardized products that are advanced, functional, reliable—and low-priced. Multinational companies that concentrated on idiosyncratic consumer preferences have become befuddled and unable to take in the forest because of the trees. Only global companies will achieve long-term success by concentrating on what everyone wants rather than worrying about the details of what everyone thinks they might like.[46]

A global strategy makes most sense when (1) there is a global market for a product or service, (2) there are economic efficiencies associated with a global strategy, (3) there are no external constraints such as government regulations that will prevent a global strategy from being implemented, and (4) there are no absolute internal constraints either.[47] BMW, for example, manufactures a number of its automobile lines in a plant in Spartanburg, South Carolina, and ships them all over the world.

Some organizations are now pursuing a hybrid **transnational** approach that combines the efficiencies of the global strategy with the local responsiveness of the multidomestic strategy.[48] For example, Honda pursues a strategy they call "glocalization" which is essentially a transnational strategy. In one year the company opened a motorcycle plant in India, an automobile plant in the United Kingdom and an automobile plant in Alabama in the United States. Although the company emphasizes low-cost production through economies of scale, each of these operations was built to better serve the local markets.[49]

Another example is Nestle. Nestle is the leader in hundreds of products categories worldwide, including Stouffer's frozen dinners, Perrier and Pellegrino water, Nescafe coffee, Friskies cat food, Carnation milk, Buitoni pasta and After Eight chocolate mints. The company pursues a transnational strategy that attempts to achieve low costs through global integration while responding to local preferences. At the largest Kit-Kat manufacturing plant in the world in York, England, Nestle invested $11 million in robots for the production line, installed a new $1.6 million automated packaging machine, and cut staff from 60 to 28. Interestingly, Kit Kat's formula is different for every region of the world—sometimes coarser, sweeter, smaller, or fruit-flavored. Each product is developed after extensive market research on local tastes and over 20 types are made at the cost-efficient York plant.[50]

This completes our discussion of business-level strategies, and the specific issues associated with international expansion. The final section of this chapter provides a discussion of how industry life cycles can be used to frame the changes in market and competitive conditions that influence strategies. In general, most industries and products move through predictable stages although the rate of change and the intensity of the forces will be different in different industries.

CHANGES IN STRATEGY OVER TIME

As we have noted throughout this book, strategic management is an iterative, on-going process of managing a firm over time. The typical changes that industries and products undergo over time can be described in terms of life cycles stages: origination or introduction, growth, maturity, and then, in some cases, decline. Study of life cycle concepts can help an organization understand the dynamic nature of strategy. As an industry, a product, and even an organization move through the stages of the life cycle, different strategies and organizational resources are needed to compete effectively.

An **industry life cycle** portrays how sales volume for a class of products or an entire industry changes over its lifetime. For managers involved in strategy formulation and implementation, it is useful to have an understanding of the typical competitive and strategy changes that often accompany the different life cycle stages. There have been several completely new industries spawned in the last 40 years including personal computers and online retailing, to name just a few. In general, industries originate as a result of a new innovation or a new societal need. Understanding industry life cycles not only helps an organization understand demand, but can also help the organization formulate strategies.[51]

During the **origination or introduction stage** of a new industry, a product or service that is as yet unknown to the world is introduced. Often the first products are high-priced and appeal to a very specific high-end customer group. During the **growth stage**, more customers begin purchasing the product or service. The increase in demand will attract new competitors. After a prolonged period of time—sometimes years, sometimes decades—sales growth eventually begins to level off, which signals the **maturity** stage of the life cycle. This slowing of growth can lead to a competitive "shake out" of weaker producers, resulting in fewer competitors. During the **commodity or decline stage**, the demand curve can take many shapes. The traditional curve, representing decline, is labeled C in Exhibit 5.4. However, if the product becomes a commodity, which means that it is used in many other products or becomes a basic part of life for some consumers, demand may just level off, as in B, or may gradually increase over an extended time period, represented by A.[52]

The strategies of the firms in the industry will evolve as the industry evolves. During the **introduction stage**, as demand for the new type of product gradually builds, organizations that have entered early are primarily concerned with survival—producing the product at low enough cost and selling it at a high enough price so that they will be able to sustain operations and enter the next stage of the life cycle. The competitive environment at this stage is often turbulent. Often customer needs for the new product are not that well understood and new firms enter with different product versions and new methods. During this early stage in an industry life cycle, some businesses must invest more into growing their businesses than they get back, which can create financial difficulties.

Exhibit 5.4   The Industry Life Cycle

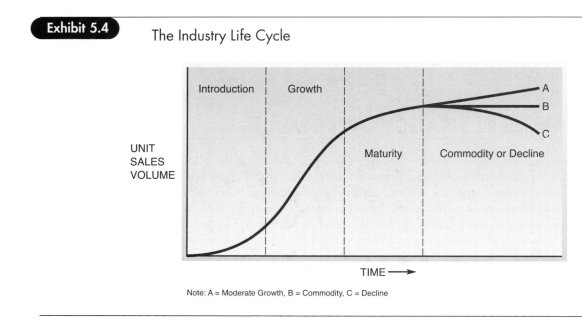

Note: A = Moderate Growth, B = Commodity, C = Decline

As Exhibit 5.4 illustrates, demand gradually builds during the introduction stage, as consumers come to understand the product and its uses. For example, in the earliest stage of the personal computer industry, most customers were hobbyists who built their own computers to practice programming. Over time, after a great deal of product and market development effort by the first personal computer companies, new customers were introduced to the new uses for the personal computer. During the introduction stage, most customers used computers at home—for programming, games (Atari and Commodore), and some small office word processing (Tandy).

In the introduction stage, firms also attempt to produce a product that is of sufficiently high quality that they will be able to establish a good reputation in the market. The emphasis is often on research and development and market education. Early producers sometimes enjoy a "first-mover advantage," because of the experience they are gaining, the reputation they build with customers, and the opportunity they may have to create barriers to entry such as patents or exclusive distribution channels.[53] In fact, products sometimes come to be associated with early innovators, as in the case of WeedEater, Scotch tape, Linoleum floor coverings and Xerox machines.

If the competitors are successful in meeting early customer needs, demand will begin to grow more aggressively—and the industry will enter the **growth stage**. In the personal computer industry, the growth stage was catalyzed by the introduction of the first spreadsheet program, called VisiCalc, and the entrance of IBM into the market. Both of these events signaled the legitimacy of the personal computer as a business office machine, which stimulated growth. During the growth phase, new competitors enter the market but, since demand is often growing so rapidly, there is enough market opportunity for practically everyone. Competitors can concentrate on designing products and services to meet customer needs and are able to avoid direct, head-on competition.

During the growth stage, as demand greatly expands and the number of competitors increases, existing competitors may attempt to erect entry barriers by building plants that are large enough to enjoy economies of scale, locking in contracts for supplies or distribution of products, or differentiating products through advertising and new features or service. As growth begins to level off toward the end of the growth stage and as some firms fail to develop product characteristics that customers value or try to grow faster than their resources allow, a **competitive shakeout** usually occurs.

In many industries, the efforts by competitors to develop new, innovative products may result in a **dominant design** that serves the needs of most of the market.[54] When it becomes apparent that customers are preferentially choosing one particular design configuration or bundle of services, many competitors will begin making the same product in order to access the large mainstream market segment. Those competitors who opt not to align with the dominant design will be forced to serve niche segments at either the very high end or very low end of the market. In the personal computer industry, the combination of an Intel microprocessor with Microsoft operating system, what was called a Wintel machine, became the dominant design. Most personal computer makers aligned with that dominant design, which has continued to this day. Apple Computer chose not to align with the dominant design and survived in a niche segment.[55]

Following the emergence of the dominant design, products are much more standardized and competition tends to focus on cost reductions, product quality and availability. If the rate of market growth is slowing, weaker competitors may discover that they can no longer generate enough sales or profits to sustain themselves. They sell off their assets, declare bankruptcy or are acquired by stronger competitors.

During the maturity stage, as demand growth continues to level off, efficient, high-volume production tends to dominate manufacturing strategy. Since the product has become standardized, in line with the dominant design, customers typically focus on price and dependability. When an organization discovers a successful innovation, it is quickly incorporated into other firm's products. Consequently, product differentiation becomes increasingly difficult. Marketing, distribution efficiency and low-cost operations gain increasing importance during this stage. Dell Computer, with its low-cost direct-to-consumer approach, was enormously successful during the maturity stage.

Finally, during the commodity or decline stage, tight cost controls leading to efficiency are essential to success. Since the product has become highly standardized at this point, price is still a very important basis for competition. Competition is intense, and firms may begin to drop out again, especially if demand takes the shape of curve C in Exhibit 5.4 and if exit barriers are low. Examples of exit barriers that might motivate organizations not to drop out include owning a lot of assets that can't be used for anything else, high costs of terminating contracts or tearing down buildings, or social costs such as laying off workers.[56] The personal computer arguably is in the commodity stage. Mergers and acquisitions have resulted in a few, very large manufacturers that compete largely on price. These manufacturers also produce a number of variations on the original personal computer concept, such as laptops and notebooks, which are increasingly popular as replacement products.

To avoid the full effects of decline, firms may focus on a particular niche in the market that is still growing. Or innovative firms may be able to introduce a product that totally replaces the old product and makes it obsolete. For example, personal computers and CDs have made typewriters and records obsolete. Finally, some organizations may just "hang on" until other firms have dropped out or are absorbed into larger firms through acquisition, at which time reduced competition can result in an improved financial situation.[57] This is happening right now in the tobacco industry. A recent example is Altria's acquisition of UST. Altria is the parent company of Phillip Morris, the largest manufacturer of cigarettes and UST was the largest U.S. producer of smokeless tobacco.

One of the lessons that we learn from the life cycle is that organizations must adapt as their products move through the stages of evolution. Whereas product innovation and attempts to differentiate products may have significant value in the early stages, once a dominant design emerges, the focus of strategy must shift toward low costs and service, even as efforts to develop new products continue.

In summary, identification of the stage of the industry life cycle can provide strategic direction as firms develop their business-level strategies. As organizations fine-tune their strategies, they need to specify the distinctive competencies they will try to develop in order to achieve a competitive advantage.

KEY POINTS SUMMARY

This chapter dealt with business-level strategy, which defines an organization's approach to competing in its chosen markets. The following are the important points from this chapter:

1. The responsibilities of business-level managers include establishing the overall direction of the business unit, ongoing analysis of the changing business situation, selecting generic business-level strategies and competitive tactics, and managing resources to create functional level strategies that support business-level strategies and develop strategic competencies.

2. The generic business-level strategies discussed in this chapter are cost leadership, differentiation, and best cost. Focus strategies apply one of the generic business-level strategies for a narrow target market.

3. Firms that are cost leaders actively pursue ways to produce products and services at the lowest possible cost. Low-cost leadership may be achieved through high capacity utilization, scale economies, technological advances and experience effects.

4. Organizations that pursue differentiation attempt to distinguish their products or services in such a way that they have greater value to their consumers. Differentiation is often pursued on the basis of satisfying customers through higher quality, state-of-the-art research and development, superior human resources, or establishing a strong reputation and/or brand through advertising.

5. Best-cost strategies combine elements from both differentiation and low-cost leadership.

6. Competitive tactics describe the actions firms take as they deal with the dynamics of a competitive environment. They include growth strategies, offensive tactics, defensive tactics, collaborative tactics, political tactics, avoidance tactics, and tactics that result in strategic flexibility.

7. International strategies provide opportunities for firms to achieve their growth and competitive strategies through a variety of international expansion options.

8. An understanding of the industry life cycle can assist in determining the distinct characteristics of a business-level strategy, and how changes in industry growth rate and competitiveness will influence strategy choices.

REFERENCES

1   S. Kapner, "Changing of the Guard at Wal-Mart," *Business Week* (March 2, 2009): 69–76; M. Rustillo, "New Chief at Wal-Mart Looks Abroad for Growth," *Wall Street Journal* (February 2, 2009): B1, B6.

2   H.J. Bryce, *Financial and Strategic Management for Nonprofit Organizations* (Englewood Cliffs, New Jersey: Prentice-Hall, 1987).

3   This whole discussion of generic strategies draws heavily from concepts found in M.E. Porter, *Competitive Strategy: Techniques for Analyzing Industries and Competitors* (New York: The Free Press, 1980): Chapter 2.

4   R. Jana, "Do Ideas Cost Too Much?" *Business Week* (April 20, 2009): 46–47.

5   E. Mansfield, "How Rapidly Does New Industrial Technology Leak Out?" *Journal of Industrial Economics* (December, 1985): 217.

6   P. Ghemawat, "Sustainable Advantage," *Harvard Business Review* (September/October, 1986): 53.

7   J. Weber, "Over a Buck for Dinner? Outrageous," *Business Week* (March 9, 2009): 57.

8   A. Zimmerman, "Retail Sales Show Signs of Life," *Wall Street Journal* (March 6, 2009): A1, A12.

9   This discussion of factors leading to cost savings is based, in part, on R. Stagner, "Corporate Decision Making: An Empirical Study," *Journal of Applied Psychology* 53 (1969): 1–3.

10 E. Bellman, "Tata Will Sell Inexpensive Car by Lottery," *The Wall Street Journal* (March 24, 2009): B2.

11 J. Uotila, M. Maula, T. Keil and S. Zahra, "Exploration, Exploitation and Financial Performance: Analysis of S&P 500 Corporations," *Strategic Management Journal* 30 (2009): 221–231.

12 W.J. Abernathy and K. Wayne, "Limits of the Learning Curve," *Harvard Business Review* (September/October, 1974): 109–119; W.B. Hirschman, "Profit from the Learning Curve," *Harvard Business Review* (January/February, 1964): 125–139.

13 Porter, *Competitive Strategy*.

14 M. Walton, *Deming Management at Work* (New York: G.P. Putnam's Sons, 1990).

15 A.A. Thompson, Jr., and A.J. Strickland, Jr., *Strategic Management: Concepts and Cases*, 11th ed. (Boston: Irwin/McGraw-Hill, 1999).

16 C.W.L. Hill, "Differentiation versus Low Cost or Differentiation and Low Cost: A Contingency Framework," *Academy of Management Review* 13 (1988): 403; A.I. Murray, "A Contingency View of Porter's 'Generic Strategies,'" *Academy of Management Review* 13 (1988): 390–400.

17 "A Conversation with Roberto Goizueta and Jack Welch," *Fortune* (December 11, 1995): 98–99.

18 N. Shirouzu and J. Murphy, "A Scion Drives Toyota Back to Basics," *Wall Street Journal* (February 24, 2009): A1, A4.

19 J. Schumpeter, *The Theory of Economic Development* (Cambridge, MA: Harvard University Press, 1934).

20 A. McConnon, "Making it Easier to Treat HIV/AIDS," *Business Week* (April 6, 2009): 46–47.

21 K.G. Smith, C. Grimm and M. Gannon, *Dynamics of Competitive Strategy* (London: Sage Publications, 1992).

22 G. Young, K.G. Smith and C. Grimm, "Austrian and Industrial Organization Perspectives on Firm-Level Competitive Activity and Performance," *Organization Science* 73 (1996): 243–254.

23 C.M. Grimm and K.G. Smith, *Strategy as Action: Industry Rivalry and Coordination* (St. Paul, MN: West Publishing, 1997).

24 W. Ferrier, K. Smith, and C. Grimm, "The Role of Competition in Market Share Erosion and Dethronement: A Study of Industry Leaders and Challengers," *Academy of Management Journal* 43 (1999): 372–388.

25 S. Ethiraj and D.H. Zhu, "Performance Effects of Imitative Entry," *Strategic Management Journal* 29 (2008): 797–817.

26 P. Ghemawat, *Strategy and the Business Landscape* (Upper Saddle River, NJ: Prentice Hall, 2001).

27 J. Gimeno and C. Woo, "Multimarket Contact, Economies of Scope, and Firm Performance," *Academy of Management Journal* 42 (1999): 323–341.

28   Grimm and Smith, *Strategy as Action*.

29   S.H. Ang, "Competitive Intensity and Collaboration: Impact on Firm Growth Across Technological Environments," *Strategic Management Journal* 29 (2008): 1057–1075.

30   B.R. Barringer and J.S. Harrison, "Walking a Tightrope: Creating Value Through Interorganizational Relationships," *Journal of Management*, 26 (2000): 367–404.

31   C. Dhanaraj and A. Parkhe, "Orchestrating Innovation Networks," *Academy of Management Review* 31 (2006): 659–669.

32   G.A. Fowler and J.E. Vascellaro, "Sony, Google Mount Challenge to Amazon Over Digital Books," *The Wall Street Journal* (March 19, 2009): B5.

33   R. Abramson, "Pegasus Gets a Lift From Online Hotel-Reservation Deal," *The Wall Street Journal* (February 12, 2002): B4; J.N. Ader and T. McCoy, "Web Storm Rising," *Lodging Industry* (August, 2002): 1.

34   J. Sapsford and P. Beckett, "Visa and MasterCard Must Allow Banks to Issue Rivals' Credit Cards, Judge Rules," *The Wall Street Journal* (October 10, 2001): A3.

35   Empirical support of this phenomenon is found in K.B. Grier, M.C. Munger and B.E. Roberts, "The Determinants of Industry Political Activity, 1978–1986," *American Political Science Review* 88 (1994): 911–925; a descriptive review of this problem is found in I. Maitland, "Self-defeating Lobbying: How More Is Buying Less in Washington," *Journal of Business Strategy* 7 (2) (1986): 67–78.

36   W.R. Scott, *Organizations: Rational, Natural, and Open Systems*, 3rd ed. (Englewood Cliffs, NJ: Prentice Hall, 1992).

37   W.C. Kim and R. Mauborgne, *Blue Ocean Strategy: How to Create Uncontested Market Space and Make the Competition Irrelevant* (Boston, Harvard University Business School Press, 2005).

38   "BOS Strategic Moves", http://www.blueoceanstrategy.com/about/lead/BandN.html (April 6, 2009).

39   K.R. Harrigan, "Strategic Flexibility in the Old and New Economies," in M.A. Hitt, R.E. Freeman and J.S. Harrison, eds. *Blackwell Handbook of Strategic Management* (Oxford, U.K.: Blackwell Publishers LTD, 2001): 98–123.

40   G.S. Yip, *Total Global Strategy II* (Upper Saddle River, New Jersey: Prentice Hall, 2003).

41   This discussion of tactics for global expansion was based, in part, on C.W.L. Hill, P. Hwang and W.C. Kim, "An Eclectic Theory of the Choice of International Entry Mode," *Strategic Management Journal* 11 (1990): 117–128; C.W.L. Hill and G.R. Jones, *Strategic Management: An Integrated Approach* (Boston: Houghton Mifflin, 1992): 254–259.

42   Some of the options contained in this list were based on information found in M.L. Fagan, "A Guide to Global Sourcing," *Journal of Business Strategy* (March/April, 1991): 21–25; J. Sheth and G. Eshghi, *Global Strategic Management Perspectives* (Cincinnati: South-Western Publishing Co., 1989) and M.J. Stahl and D.W. Grigsby, *Strategic Management for Decision Making* (Boston: PWS-Kent, 1992): 205–206.

43   K. Ohmae, "Managing in a Borderless World," *Harvard Business Review* (May/June, 1989): 152–61.

44   R. Jacob, "Trust the Locals, Win Worldwide," *Fortune* (May 4, 1992): 76.

45   P. Engardio and M. Arndt, "How Cummins Does It," *Business Week* (August 22, 2005): 82–84.

46   T. Levitt, "The Globalization of Markets," *Harvard Business Review* (May/June, 1983): 92.

47   S.P. Douglas and Y. Wind, "The Myth of Globalization," *Columbia Journal of World Business* (Winter, 1987): 19–29.

48   C.A. Bartlett and S. Ghoshal, "Managing Across Borders: New Organizational Responses," *Sloan Management Review* (Fall, 1987): 43–54.

49   "Glocalization," *Honda Motor Company, LTD Annual Report* (2002): 4.

50   P. Gumbel, "Nestle's Quick: Avid Mountaineer Peter Brabeck Wants His Firm to Move Faster, but Without Losing its Footing," *Time* (January 27, 2003): A6.

51   This discussion of strategy during the stages of product market evolution is based on C.R. Anderson and C.P. Zeithaml, "Stage of the Product Life Cycle, Business Strategy and Business Performance," *Academy of Management Journal* 27 (1984): 5–24; J.B. Barney and R.W. Griffin, *The Management of Organizations: Strategy, Structure, Behavior*

(Boston: Houghton Mifflin, 1992): 229–230; R.H. Hayes and W.C. Wheelwright, *Restoring Our Competitive Edge: Competing Through Manufacturing* (New York: John Wiley and Sons, 1984): Chapter 7; C.W. Hofer and D. Schendel, *Strategy Formulation: Analytical Concepts* (St. Paul: West Publishing, 1978): Chapter 5.

52   The term commodity to describe curves A and B was borrowed from Hayes and Wheelwright, *Restoring Our Competitive Edge*: 203.

53   M.B. Lieberman and D.B. Montgomery, "First-Mover Advantages," *Strategic Management Journal* 9 (1988): 41–58.

54   J.M. Utterback, *Mastering the Dynamics of Innovation* (Boston: Harvard Business School Press, 1994).

55   C.H. St. John, R.W. Pouder, A.R. Cannon, "Environmental Uncertainty and Product-Process Life Cycles: A Multi-Level Interpretation of Change Over Time," *Journal of Management Studies* (March, 2003): 513–543.

56   K.R. Harrigan and M.E. Porter, "End-Game Strategies for Declining Industries," *Harvard Business Review* (July-August, 1983): 111–120.

57   Harrigan and Porter, "End-Game Strategies for Declining Industries."

6

Corporate Strategies

STRATEGY IN FOCUS

Tata Group

Founded in 1868, Tata Group is an Indian conglomerate with significant operations in Europe, Asia Pacific, China, Africa, the United Kingdom, the Middle East and North and South America. Tata companies operate in seven business sectors: communications and information technology, engineering, materials, services, energy, consumer products and chemicals. The major Tata companies are Tata Steel, Tata Motors, Tata Consultancy Services (TCS), Tata Power, Tata Chemicals, Tata Tea, Indian Hotels and Tata Communications. Tata Steel is the sixth largest steel maker, Tata Tea is the second largest branded tea company, and Tata Motors is among the top five commercial vehicle manufacturers in the world. The company employs approximately 350,000 people globally, and over 60% of its revenues come from business outside of India.

Each of Tata's business enterprises operates independently, with its own board of directors and shareholders. In all, there are 27 publicly listed Tata enterprises with a combined market capitalization of around $60 billion and 3.2 million shareholders. In spite of their independent operations, Tata companies do share resources. For instance, its consultancy group, TCS, provides services to external companies such as British Airways and the Dutch bank ABN Amro, but it also helps Tata companies. TCS shares revenues from the new products and services it jointly creates with its sister companies.

Despite the diversity of its operations, the company is trying to instill an innovative spirit across the company. The 72-year-old chairman, Ratan Tata, recently told his employees, "Cut costs. Think out of the box. Even if the world around you is collapsing, be bold, be daring, think big." *Business Week* recently ranked Tata the thirteenth most innovative company in the world.

Throughout its history, the company created India's first steel mill, power plant, airline and domestically produced car. Tata Chemicals is working on an electricity-free, low-cost antimicrobial water system and Tata Power is about to unveil an advance in smart electricity grid technology. However, the innovation that has recently created the most stir is Tata Motor's $2000 car, the Nano. The car has numerous innovative features. Tata's premier automotive research center is not in India, but in the United Kingdom.

In addition to growth through internally produced innovations and market penetration, the company has pursued a vigorous acquisition strategy. The company bought the Pierre, which is a four-star New York hotel, and the Anglo-Dutch steel company, Corus. In more recent years, Tata acquired the luxury car maker Jaguar Land Rover as well as Eight O'Clock Coffee Company and General Chemical Industrial Products, both U.S. firms.[1]

Tata Group is pursuing a corporate-level strategy called unrelated diversification, which means that it is involved in a variety of businesses, some of which do not share common technologies or markets. In spite of the diversity of its operations, the company is trying to develop a distinctive competency in innovation, although one of Tata's executives admits that innovation, "has yet to be strongly embedded across the group."[2]

This chapter deals with the functions top executives perform as they formulate corporate-level strategy, some of the tools they use (such as mergers and acquisitions), and theory concerning how corporate-level actions enhance the value of organizations. We will discuss the way business units can be related to each other and provide a rationale for building distinctive competencies based on similarities among them. Then we will describe specific tactics firms use to diversify.

At the corporate level, primary strategy formulation responsibilities include setting the direction of the entire organization, formulation of a corporate strategy, selection of businesses in which to compete, selection of tactics for diversification and growth, and management of corporate resources and capabilities. These responsibilities and the key issues associated with each responsibility are listed in Exhibit 6.1.

DEVELOPMENT OF CORPORATE STRATEGY

The three broad approaches to corporate strategy are concentration, vertical integration and diversification.

Exhibit 6.1   Major Corporate-Level Strategic Management Responsibilities

Major Responsibilities	Key Issues
Direction setting	Establishment and communication of organizational mission, vision, enterprise strategy, and long-term goals
Development of corporate-level strategy	Selection of a broad approach to corporate-level strategy—concentration, vertical integration, diversification, and international expansion
	Selection of resources and capabilities in which to build corporate-wide distinctive competencies
Selection of business and portfolio management	Management of the corporate portfolio
	Emphasis given to each business unit—allocation of resources for capital equipment, R&D, etc.
Selection of tactics for diversification and growth	Choice among methods of diversification—internal venturing, acquisitions, and joint ventures
Management of resources	Acquisition of resources or development of competencies leading to a sustainable competitive advantage
	Coordination of business-level strategies and an appropriate management structure for the corporation
	Development of an appropriate corporate culture

Single Business/Concentration

Most organizations begin with a single or small group of products and services and a single market. This type of corporate-level strategy is called **concentration**. Federal Express, Domino's Pizza, Lands' End, and Delta Airlines are examples of firms that participate in just one business.

In the United States and other highly industrialized countries, concentration strategies have sometimes been found to be more profitable than other types of corporate, or multi-business, strategies.[3] Of course, the profitability of a concentration strategy is largely dependent on the industry and nation in which a firm is involved. When the industry and country conditions are attractive, the strengths of a concentration strategy are readily apparent. First, a single business approach allows an organization to master one business and industry environment. This specialization allows top executives to obtain in-depth knowledge of the business and industry, which should reduce strategic mistakes. Second, since all resources are directed at doing one thing well, the organization may be in a better position to develop the resources and capabilities necessary to establish a sustainable competitive advantage. By concentrating on a single business, firms are able to concentrate on a focused set of strategies to achieve growth and profitability, as was discussed in Chapter 5.

Third, a concentration strategy can prevent the proliferation of management levels and staff functions that are often associated with large multi-business firms, and that add overhead costs and limit flexibility of business units. Fourth, a concentration strategy allows a firm to invest profits back into the business, rather than competing with other corporate holdings for the investment funds.

On the other hand, concentration strategies entail several risks, especially when environments are unstable. Since the organization is dependent on one product or business area to sustain itself, change can dramatically reduce organizational performance. The airline industry is a good example of the effects of uncertainty on organizational performance. Prior to deregulation in the airline industry, most of the major carriers were profitable. They had protected routes and fixed prices. However, deregulation and the ensuing increase in competition hurt the profitability of all domestic carriers. Since most of the major carriers were pursuing concentration strategies, they did not have other business areas to offset their losses. Consequently, several airlines were acquired or went bankrupt. Deregulation and financial difficulties among the legacy carriers in the United States also opened up opportunities for regional carriers such as Southwest to expand into their core markets.

Product obsolescence and industry maturity create additional risks for organizations pursuing a concentration strategy. If the principal product of an organization becomes obsolete or matures, organizational performance can suffer until the organization develops another product that is appealing to the market. Some organizations are never able to duplicate earlier successes. Furthermore, since these organizations only have experience in one line of business, they have limited ability to switch to other areas when times get tough.

Concentration strategies can also lead to uneven cash flow and profitability. While the business is growing, the organization may find itself in a "cash poor" situation, since growth often entails additional investments in capital equipment and marketing. On the other hand, once growth levels off, the organization is likely to find itself in a "cash rich" situation, with limited opportunities for profitable investment in the business itself. In fact, this may be one of the most important reasons that organizations in mature markets begin to diversify.[4] Having

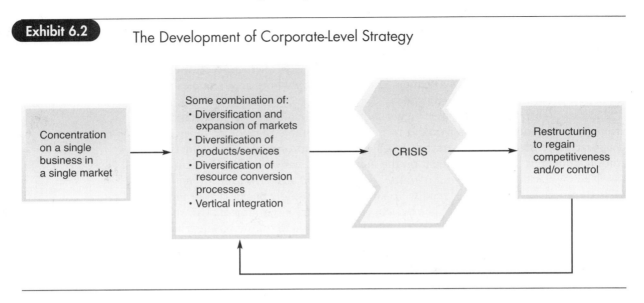

Exhibit 6.2   The Development of Corporate-Level Strategy

exhausted all reasonable opportunities to reinvest cash in innovation, renewal or revitalization, organizational managers may look to other areas for growth. Finally, a concentration strategy may not provide enough challenge or stimulation to managers. In other words, they may begin to get tired of doing the same things year after year. This is less true in organizations that are growing rapidly, since growth typically provides excitement and promotion opportunities.

Many successful organizations abandon their concentration strategies at some point due to market saturation, increased competition or some other reason. Corporate strategy typically evolves from concentration to some form of vertical integration or diversification of products, markets, or resource conversion processes (see Exhibit 6.2).[5] Firms may continue to diversify and/or vertically integrate for a considerable time until at some point they experience a significant drop in performance or some other sort of crisis. The final stage of Exhibit 6.2, restructuring, will be discussed in Chapter 8.

Vertical Integration

Vertical integration is the term used to describe the extent to which a firm is involved in several stages of the industry supply chain. A simplified industry supply chain, which is illustrated in Exhibit 6.3, begins with *extraction* of raw materials such as timber, ore, and crude oil. In *primary manufacturing*, these raw materials are converted into commodities such as wood pulp and iron. Primary manufacturing sometimes involves the creation of components that are used to assemble final products, such as the engine, transmission, and brake systems used in automobiles. *Final product manufacturing* involves the creation of a product that is in its final form prior to consumption, such as the final assembly of an automobile. At this point branding becomes very important, since consumers associate brand names of final products with particular levels of quality, service and reliability. Finally, *wholesaling* entails channeling final products to retail outlets, and *retailing* consists of selling these products to the ultimate consumer. Some products bypass the wholesaling and/or retailing stages due to direct sale by the manufacturer to customers.[6] Also, as firms increase their use of the Internet to coordinate their buying activities, some wholesale distribution channels are being largely eliminated in some industries.

Industry Supply Chain for Manufacturing Firms Exhibit 6.3

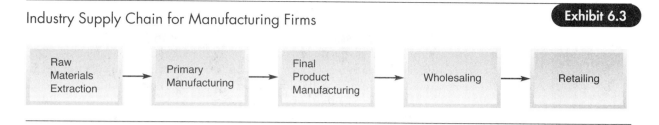

Some industries, such as steel and wood production, contain many firms that are predominantly vertically integrated. In other industries, such as apparel, vertical integration is limited and most organizations are only involved in one or two stages. Firms may pursue vertical integration for a variety of reasons, including increased efficiency, increased control over the quality of supplies or the way a product is marketed, better or more complete information about suppliers or markets, greater opportunity for product differentiation through coordinated effort, or simply because they believe they can enhance profits through assuming one of the functions that was previously performed by another company.[7] For example, Walt Disney Co. and other entertainment giants are involved in movie and television studios, movie distribution, broadcast and cable networks, theme parks, and retailing with the intention of controlling their product from concept to customers. **Transaction cost economics**, which is the study of economic exchanges and their costs, described in Exhibit 6.4, provides a cost perspective on vertical integration that helps explain when vertical integration may be appropriate.[8]

Research has not generally found vertical integration to be a highly profitable strategy relative to the other corporate-level strategies.[9] However, many of the firms that have been studied are old and large. They may have used vertical

Transaction Costs and Vertical Integration Exhibit 6.4

From a transaction cost perspective, firms can either negotiate on the open market for the products and services they need or they can produce these products and services themselves. If an organization can obtain required resources from a competitive open market without allocating an undue amount of time or other resources to the contracting process or contract enforcement, it is probably in its best interests to buy from the market instead of vertically integrating. However, when transaction costs are high enough to encourage an organization to produce a good or service in-house instead of buying it from the open market, a market failure is said to exist. The market is likely to "fail" under the following conditions:

- The future is highly uncertain. It may be too costly or impossible to identify all of the possible situations that may occur and to incorporate these possibilities into the contract.
- Only one or a small number of suppliers of a good or service exists, and these suppliers are likely to pursue their own self-interests.
- One party to a transaction has more knowledge about the transaction or a series of transactions than another.
- An organization invests in an asset that can only be used to produce a specific good or service, which makes use of the market difficult (asset specificity).

Sources: O.E. Williamson, *Markets and Hierarchies: Analysis and Antitrust Implications* (New York: The Free Press, 1975); O.E. Williamson, *The Economic Institutions of Capitalism* (New York: The Free Press, 1985).

integration with success as their industries were forming. As one vertical integration expert explained, vertical integration can "lock firms in" to unprofitable adjacent businesses.[10] However, this does not mean that all vertical integration is unprofitable. One study suggested that vertical integration may be associated with reduced administrative, selling, and R&D costs, but higher production costs. The researchers believe that the higher production costs may be a result of a lack of incentive on the part of internal suppliers to keep their costs down. Since the internal suppliers have a guaranteed customer, they do not have to be as competitive.[11]

An important point to remember with regard to all of the strategies is that some companies are pursuing them successfully. Furthermore, vertical integration often requires substantially different skills than those currently possessed by the firm. In this regard, vertical integration is similar to unrelated diversification, a topic that will be discussed later in this chapter.[12] A firm that can master one stage of the industry supply chain will not necessarily excel at other stages. For this reason, many firms avoid vertical integration and move directly into some form of diversification.

Diversification Strategies

A firm's diversification strategy describes the scope of the firm in terms of the industries and markets in which it competes. Diversification can be divided into two broad categories. **Related diversification** implies organizational involvement in activities that are somehow related to the dominant or "core" business of the organization, often through common markets or similar technologies. **Unrelated diversification** does not depend on any pattern of relatedness. Some of the most common reasons for diversification are listed in Exhibit 6.5.[13] They are divided into strategic reasons, which are frequently cited by executives in the popular business press, and personal motives that CEOs may have for pursuing diversification. As we discussed in Chapter 5, if CEOs pursue diversification for their own interests at the expense of the shareholders and other stakeholders then an agency problem exists.[14]

Unrelated Diversification. Large, unrelated diversified firms are often called **conglomerates**, since they are involved in a conglomeration of unrelated businesses. Tata Group, discussed in the introduction to this chapter, is a conglomerate. So also is Royal Philips:

> Royal Philips Electronics of the Netherlands has 161,500 employees in over 60 countries. The company has diversified into a wide variety of industries. Through its Semiconductors operations, it produces and markets semiconductors for the communications, consumer, automotive, and identification markets. Its Lighting division produces and markets lamps, luminaries, lighting electronics, automotive lighting, and special lighting. In Medical Systems, it operates in the areas of diagnostic imaging systems, customer services and clinical solutions. The Domestic Appliances and Personal Care division is involved in shaving, beauty, home environment care, foods, beverages, oral healthcare and consumer health and wellness. Finally, Philips' Consumer Electronics businesses are involved in connected displays, home entertainment networks and mobile "infotainment."[15]

Much of the research on U.S. firms has demonstrated that unrelated firms have lower profitability than firms pursuing other corporate-level strategies such

A Few Common Reasons for Diversification

Exhibit 6.5

Strategic Reasons

Risk reduction through investments in dissimilar businesses or less-dynamic environments

Stabilization or improvement in earnings

Improvement in growth

Cash generated in slower growing traditional areas exceeds that needed for profitable investment in those areas (organizational slack)

Application of resources, capabilities, and core competencies to related areas

Generation of synergy/economies of scope

Use of excess debt capacity (organizational slack)

Desire to learn new technologies

Increase in market power

Desire to turn around a failing business, leading to high returns

Motives of the CEO

Desire to increase power and status

Desire to increase compensation from running a larger enterprise

Desire to increase value of the firm

Craving for a more interesting and challenging management environment (boredom)

---

as concentration or related diversification.[16] There is also some evidence that unrelated diversification is associated with higher levels of risk than other corporate strategies.[17] Unrelated diversification places significant demands on corporate-level executives due to increased complexity and technological changes across industries. In fact, it is very difficult for a manager to understand each of the core technologies and appreciate the special requirements of each of the individual units in an unrelated diversified firm. Consequently, the effectiveness of management may be reduced.

Although unrelated diversification may be a poor performing strategy overall, some firms perform well. Royal Philips and Hitachi of Japan have enjoyed success with the strategy. General Electric, one of the biggest conglomerates in the world, also enjoyed many years of strong financial performance, although recently the company has been struggling.[18] In addition to these examples of conglomerates based in highly industrialized nations, there is also mounting evidence that high levels of diversification lead to higher financial performance in less-developed countries.[19] Large firms like Tata Group seem able to allocate resources to profitable business areas more effectively than the inefficient capital markets that often exist in those countries. Also, conglomerates, due to their vast resources, may be able to overcome some of the problems associated with a poorly developed infrastructure. For instance, a large, highly diversified firm may have skills and resources in business areas such as transportation, construction or power generation that can help its businesses overcome problems in these areas.

Related Diversification. When an organization chooses to diversify from its original core business into other businesses, it often decides to enter an industry segment that is similar or related to what it already knows. For instance, Procter & Gamble is using its considerable marketing muscle and experience with low-end cosmetics like CoverGirl and Max Factor to enter the luxury cosmetics industry.[20] Most of the research on diversification strategies indicates that some form of relatedness among diversified businesses, as opposed to no relatedness at all, leads to higher financial performance.[21]Also, related diversification appears to be associated with reduced financial risk, possibly because it allows a company to enjoy the financial advantages of reduced dependence on one business area without placing as many demands on managers.[22] Honda Motor Company pursues a related diversification strategy:

> Honda Motor Company, LTD. is a leading manufacturer of automobiles and the largest manufacturer of motorcycles in the world. Honda's diversification strategy focuses on developing and manufacturing products that make use of its highly efficient internal combustion engines. Honda offers a wide variety of automobiles in various styles suited to the countries in which they are sold. In North America, the Accord continues to be a top seller, but the company has also offered several very innovative vehicles including the Pilot large sport utility vehicle, the S2000 two-seat roadster, and the Element (nobody really knows what it is), not to mention its Acura luxury cars. In Japan, the Step Wagon and Stream minivans are popular. Honda's motorcycle business includes all terrain vehicles and personal watercraft. The company has enjoyed huge increases in unit sales in Asia due to new models like M-Living, a low-priced commuter motorcycle offered in China and a similar motorcycle called the Wave 125 in Thailand. In addition to its automobile and motorcycle businesses, Honda produces a line of power products such as snow blowers, tillers, lawn mowers and outboard boat engines.[23]

Related diversification is based on similarities that exist among the products, services, markets, or resource conversion processes of two businesses. In the case of Honda, the internal combustion engine is the common denominator of its operations. Similarities are supposed to lead to synergy, which means that the whole is greater than the sum of its parts. In other words, one organization should be able to produce two related products or services more efficiently than two organizations each producing one of the products or services on its own. The same reasoning applies to similar markets and similar resource conversion processes. For example, Johnson & Johnson is involved in a wide variety of diversified businesses; however, virtually all of them are related to converting chemical substances into drugs and toiletries.

Relatedness comes in two forms, tangible and intangible.[24] **Tangible relatedness** means that the organization has the opportunity to use the same physical resources for multiple purposes. Tangible relatedness can lead to synergy through resource sharing. For example, if two similar products are manufactured in the same plant, then they can benefit from operating synergy. Other examples of synergy resulting from tangible relatedness include (1) using the same marketing or distribution channels for multiple related products, (2) buying similar raw materials for related products through a centralized purchasing office to gain purchasing economies, (3) providing corporate training programs to employees from different divisions that are all engaged in the same type of work, and (4) advertising multiple products simultaneously. Maytag, for example, manufactures beverage vending machines using many of the same materials, equipment and facilities that it uses to produce household appliances, particularly refrigerators.

Intangible relatedness occurs any time capabilities developed in one area can be applied to another area. When executed properly, intangible relatedness can result in managerial synergy.[25] For example, Wal-Mart developed skill in retailing that was directly applicable to Sam's Club. Also, Campbell Soup has applied skills in manufacturing and packaging soup to a variety of other products. Synergy based on intangible resources such as brand name or management skills and knowledge may be more conducive to the creation of a sustainable competitive advantage, since intangible resources are hard to imitate and are never used up.[26]

Some types of relatedness are more imaginary than real. For example, the relatedness between oil and other forms of energy such as solar and coal has proved illusive to several of the large oil companies, who experienced performance problems in these "related business ventures." In addition, even if relatedness is evident, synergy *has to be created*, which means that the two related businesses must fit together *and* that organizational managers must work at creating efficiencies from the combination process.[27]

Two types of fit are required: strategic fit and organizational fit. **Strategic fit** refers to the effective matching of strategic organizational capabilities. For example, if two organizations in two related businesses combine their resources, but they are both strong in the same areas and weak in the same areas, then the potential for synergy is diminished. Once combined, they will continue to exhibit the same capabilities. However, if one of the organizations is strong in R&D, but lacks marketing power, while the other organization is weak in R&D, but strong in marketing, then there is real potential for both organizations to be better off—if managed properly. **Organizational fit** occurs when two organizations or business units have similar management processes, cultures, systems and structures.[28] Organizational fit makes organizations compatible, which facilitates resource sharing, communication, and transference of knowledge and skills. Strategic fit and organizational fit dramatically increase the likelihood that synergy will be created between two related businesses.

Assuming that an organization's leaders have decided to pursue diversification as a corporate strategy, they must still decide on the method that will be followed to carry it out. Methods for pursuing diversification will be discussed in the next section.

DIVERSIFICATION METHODS

Once an organization has decided to pursue a diversification strategy, it can pursue one of three basic approaches to carry it out: an internal venture to develop the new business on its own, an acquisition or a joint venture.

Internal Ventures

An **internal venture** depends on the research and development activities of the organization. Since only the core organization is involved, management has greater control over the progress of the venture. For instance, Tata Motors created its Nano by tapping its own research and development efforts. Furthermore, proprietary information need not be shared with other companies and all profits are retained within the organization. 3M Corporation has a long track record of developing successful new ventures internally. 3M has built on core capabilities in various chemistry disciplines to successfully launch new businesses that apply optical materials, abrasives, and adhesives to consumer, industrial, and medical markets. Virgin, a U.K.-based company, has used internal ventures to successfully enter a variety of businesses as diverse as airlines, music, mobile phones, vacations, wines and publishing. According to Virgin:

> We look for opportunities where we can offer something better, fresher and more valuable, and we seize them. We often move into areas where the customer has traditionally received a poor deal, and where competition is complacent . . . . When we start a venture, we base it on hard research and analysis.[29]

In spite of the benefits of internal ventures, the risks of failure are high and even successful ventures take many years to become profitable.[30] In fact, the slow speed of internal ventures often causes managers to think seriously about acquisitions when they want to diversify their firms. If a firm acquires an existing business, it gains immediate entrance into the new business area. Furthermore, if the acquired firm has been successful, the acquiring firm managers may feel that there is less risk of failure. Nevertheless, acquisitions come with their own risks and problems, as the next section will demonstrate.

Mergers and Acquisitions

As an alternative to corporate venturing, some organizations choose to buy diversification in the form of acquisitions. In fact, they are often considered a "substitute for innovation."[31] **Mergers** occur any time two organizations combine into one. **Acquisitions**, in which one organization buys a controlling interest in the stock of another organization or buys it outright from its owners, are the most common types of mergers.

Acquisitions are a relatively quick way to (1) enter new markets, (2) acquire new products or services, (3) learn new resource conversion processes, (4) acquire needed knowledge and skills, (5) vertically integrate, (6) broaden markets geographically or (7) fill needs in the corporate portfolio.[32] In the pharmaceutical industry, Pfizer bought rival Wyeth for $68 billion and Johnson & Johnson acquired breast implant maker Mentor for $1 billion.[33] In the computer industry, Oracle surprised a lot of industry observers with its $7.38 billion acquisition of Sun Microsystems, edging out IBM. Oracle spent $30 billion buying software companies prior to the Sun deal.[34] In the battered banking industry, Wells Fargo acquired Wachovia for $15 billion, dramatically increasing its market reach into the Eastern United States and making the company a truly national bank.[35]

Although merger and acquisition volume worldwide dropped from $42 trillion in 2007 to $29 trillion in 2008, low stock prices mean that companies look relatively inexpensive to potential buyers. Companies that have the financial resources can take advantage of the situation. Hewlett-Packard sold $2 billion worth of bonds, in part to pay for future acquisitions. Eli Lilly, in the wake of its ImClone Systems acquisition, is looking to spend another $15 billion on acquisitions.[36] Also, private equity firms, which helped fuel the last big merger wave, have an estimated $250 billion available to make acquisitions.[37]

Unfortunately, most of the research evidence seems to indicate that mergers and acquisitions are not, on average, financially beneficial to the shareholders of the acquiring firm.[38] In one study, researchers found that acquisitions were associated with declining profitability, reduced research and development expenditures, fewer patents produced, and increases in financial leverage.[39] Also, Michael Porter studied the diversification records of 33 large, prestigious U.S. companies over a period of nearly four decades and concluded that the corporate strategies of most companies reduced, rather than enhanced, shareholder value.[40] He discovered that most of these companies divested many more of their acquisitions than they kept.

A Few of Many Potential Problems with Mergers and Acquisitions   Exhibit 6.6

High Financial Costs

1. **High premiums typically paid by acquiring firms**. If a company was worth $50/share in a relatively efficient financial market prior to an acquisition, why should an acquiring firm pay $75 (a typical premium) or more to buy it?

2. **Increased interest costs**. Many acquisitions are financed by borrowing money at high interest rates. Leverage typically increased during an acquisition.

3. **High advisory fees and other transaction costs**. The fees charged by the brokers, lawyers, financiers, consultants, and advisors who orchestrate the deal often cost millions of dollars. In addition, filing fees, document preparation, and legal fees in the event of contestation can be very high.

4. **Poison pills**. These antitakeover devices make companies very unattractive to a potential buyer. Top managers of target companies have been very creative in designing a variety of poison pills. One example of a poison pill is the "golden parachute," in which target firm executives receive large amounts of severance pay (often millions of dollars) if they lose their jobs due to a hostile takeover.

Strategic Problems

1. **High turnover among the managers of the acquired firm**. The most valuable asset in most organizations is its people, their knowledge, and their skills. If most managers leave, what has the acquiring firm purchased?

2. **Short-term managerial distraction**. "Doing a deal" typically takes managers away from the critical tasks of the core businesses for long durations. During this time period, who is steering the ship?

3. **Long-term managerial distraction**. Sometimes organizations lose sight of the factors that lead to success in their core businesses because they are too distracted running diversified businesses.

4. **Less innovation**. Acquisitions have been shown to lead to reduced innovative activity, which can hurt long-term performance.

5. **No organizational fit**. If the cultures, dominant logics, systems, structures, and processes of the acquiring and target firms do not fit, synergy is unlikely.

6. **Increased risk**. Increased leverage often associated with mergers and acquisitions leads to greater financial risk. Acquiring firms also risk being unable to manage the newly acquired organization successfully.

Source: Information in this exhibit was compiled from M.A. Hitt, J.S. Harrison and R.D. Ireland. *Mergers and Acquisitions: A Guide to Creating Value for Stakeholders* (New York: Oxford University Press, 2001).

For example, CBS, in an effort to create an "entertainment company," bought organizations involved in toys, crafts, sports teams, and musical instruments. All of these businesses were sold due to lack of fit with the traditional broadcasting business of CBS. Exhibit 6.6 provides several explanations for why acquisitions, on average, tend to depress profitability (at least in the short term).

This does not mean that all mergers are doomed to failure. Fortunately, researchers have been able to identify factors that seem to be associated with successful and unsuccessful mergers. Unsuccessful mergers have been associated with a large amount of debt, overconfident or incompetent managers, poor ethics, changes in top management or the structure of the acquiring organization, inadequate analysis (due diligence) prior to the deal and diversification away from the core area in which the firm is strongest. The successful mergers were related to low-to-moderate amounts of debt, a high level of relatedness leading to synergy, friendly negotiations (no resistance), a continued focus on the core business, careful selection of and negotiations with the acquired firm, and a strong cash or debt position.[41]

Furthermore, researchers have discovered that the largest shareholder gains from mergers occurred when the cultures and the top management styles of the two companies were similar (organizational fit).[42] In addition, sharing resources and activities was found to be important to post-merger success.[43] However, it is fair to say that "there are no rules that will invariably lead to a successful acquisition."[44]

Many of the diversification objectives sought by organizations through acquisitions are also available through strategic alliances and joint ventures, which are the topic of the next section.

Strategic Alliances and Joint Ventures

A **strategic alliance** is formed when two or more organizations join in a common purpose. Alliances may be formed to develop new products or services, enter new markets, influence government bodies, conduct research, improve technology, or a host of other reasons.[45] Strategic alliances of all types are very popular.[46] When the arrangement is contractual and the alliance operates independently of the organizations that form them, then the alliance typically is called a **joint venture**. Many of the partnerships with external stakeholders discussed in Chapter 2 are examples of strategic alliances and joint ventures.

Strategic alliances and joint ventures can help organizations achieve many of the same objectives that are sought through mergers and acquisitions. They can lead to improved sales growth, increased earnings, or provide balance to a portfolio of businesses, which are some of the most commonly cited reasons for acquisitions.[47] For example, Yahoo and eBay created a broad partnership in which Yahoo is promoting eBay's PayPal payment services as a way to pay for Yahoo services and eBay is displaying advertisements that are brokered by Yahoo on its online auction site. In another tech alliance, Dell agreed to install Google software on its personal computers before it ships them.[48] Cisco Systems has reported that more than 10% of its revenues come from its strategic alliance relationships. One of its recent alliances teams Cisco with Intel and Oracle to increase sharing and exchange of medical information.[49]

The strongest rationale for forming a joint venture is resource sharing. Since joint ventures involve more than one company, they can draw on a much larger resource base. The resources that are most likely to be transferable through a joint venture are:

1. *Marketing.* Companies can gain marketing information and resources not easily identified by outsiders, such as knowledge of competition, customer behavior, industry condition, and distribution channels.
2. *Technology.* Those participating in a joint venture can use technological skills and specific knowledge that is not generally available.
3. *Raw Materials and Components.* Some joint ventures are formed to have access to different elements of the manufacturing process.
4. *Financial.* Companies can obtain external capital, usually in conjunction with other resources.
5. *Managerial.* Joint venture participants can use specific managerial and entrepreneurial capabilities and skills, usually in conjunction with other resources.

6. *Political.* Some joint ventures are obligatory to enter developing countries because of either formal or informal political requirements; others are formed to gain political commitments.[50]

In addition to the advantages associated with resource sharing, joint ventures can enhance speed of entry into a new field or market because of the expanded base of resources from which ventures can draw. For instance, Procter & Gamble's venture into luxury cosmetics is being pursued through a partnership with Dolce & Gabbana, the luxury fashion retailer.[51] A firm that wants to enter a foreign market can save a great deal of time if a partner is sought that already has significant resources in the target market. For example, CEMEX joined forces with firms in four countries to provide information technology consulting services and then formed a joint venture with ReadyMix USA to provide construction services and products to the southeastern United States.[52] Joint ventures also spread the risk of failure among all of the participants. That is, a failure will result in a smaller loss to each partner than it would to an organization that pursues the venture on its own. Consequently, compared to mergers or internal venturing, joint ventures are sometimes considered a less risky diversification option.

Joint ventures can also increase strategic flexibility by allowing a firm to more easily leave a business and invest resources elsewhere.[53] Recently, a great deal of emphasis has been placed on learning from joint ventures and other forms of partnerships. As mentioned in Chapter 3, organizational knowledge is a particularly important resource because it has an impact on virtually all parts of the organization.[54]

In spite of their strategic strengths, joint ventures are limiting, in that each organization only has partial control over the venture and enjoys only a percentage of the growth and profitability it creates. They can also create high administrative costs associated with developing the multiparty equity arrangement and managing the venture once it is undertaken.[55] As in mergers and acquisitions, lack of organizational fit has the potential to reduce cooperation and lead to venture failure. Also, if one party to a multi-firm venture decides to withdraw, the success of the venture may be put in jeopardy.[56]

Joint ventures also entail a risk of opportunism by venture partners. For instance, a company may gain knowledge or contacts from its venture partner which it can then use in future competition with that same partner after severing the relationship. Good written contracts can help to alleviate but cannot eliminate this risk. Joint ventures with firms in other countries add even more risks due to potential problems such as miscommunications (especially where languages are different), differences in management systems and styles between the firms, and lack of understanding of the political, economic and legal environments of the partner firms.

Successful joint ventures and other types of alliances require careful planning and execution. Managers should communicate the expected benefits of the venture to the important external and internal stakeholders so they will understand the role the alliance will play in the organization.[57] They should also develop a strategic plan for the venture which consolidates the views of the partners about market potential, competitive trends, and potential threats. There are several additional steps which may be used to improve the likelihood of success:

1. Through careful systematic study, identify an alliance partner that can provide the capabilities that are needed. Avoid the tendency to align with another firm just because alliance-forming is a trend in the industry.

2. Clearly define the roles of each partner and ensure that every joint project is of value to both.
3. Develop a strategic plan for the venture that outlines specific objectives for each partner.
4. Keep top managers involved so that middle managers will stay committed.
5. Meet often, informally, at all managerial levels.
6. Appoint someone to monitor all aspects of the alliance and use an outside mediator when disputes arise.
7. Maintain enough independence to develop own area of expertise. Avoid becoming a complete "captive" of the alliance partner.
8. Anticipate and plan for cultural differences.[58]

For all of the corporate-level strategies, skill in execution is of critical importance. Even a strategy that is considered less attractive can be successful if it is executed well. The next section describes a tool used by diversified companies to manage their portfolios of businesses.

PORTFOLIO MANAGEMENT

Portfolio management refers to managing the mix of businesses in the corporate portfolio. CEOs of large diversified organizations like General Electric continually face decisions concerning how to divide organizational resources among diversified units and where to invest new capital. Portfolio models are designed to help managers make these types of decisions.

In spite of their adoption in many organizations, portfolio management techniques have been the subject of a considerable amount of criticism.[59] However, since they are still in wide use, it is important for students to understand what they can and cannot do. We will begin by describing the simplest and first widely-used portfolio model, the Boston Consulting Group Matrix. The model has many shortcomings, stemming mostly from its simplicity and the tendency of those who apply the model to do so without understanding the assumptions that underlie it. However, most of the other portfolio techniques are adaptations of it, and its simplicity makes it a good starting point. Following this discussion, we will then describe a more complete model.

Boston Consulting Group Matrix

The Boston Consulting Group (BCG) Matrix, which is displayed in Exhibit 6.7, is based on two factors, industry growth rate and relative market share. Industry growth rate is the growth rate of the industry in which a particular business unit is involved. Relative market share is calculated as the ratio of the business unit's size to the size of its largest competitor. The two factors are used to plot all of the businesses in which the organization is involved, represented as Stars, Question Marks (also called Problem Children), Cash Cows and Dogs. The size of the circles in Exhibit 6.7 represents the size of the various businesses of an organization. Remember that only one organization, comprised of many different business units, is plotted on each matrix.

The BCG Matrix is sometimes used in planning cash flows. In simple terms, Cash Cows should generate more cash than they can effectively reinvest, whereas Question Marks require additional cash to sustain rapid growth and Stars

The Boston Consulting Group Matrix

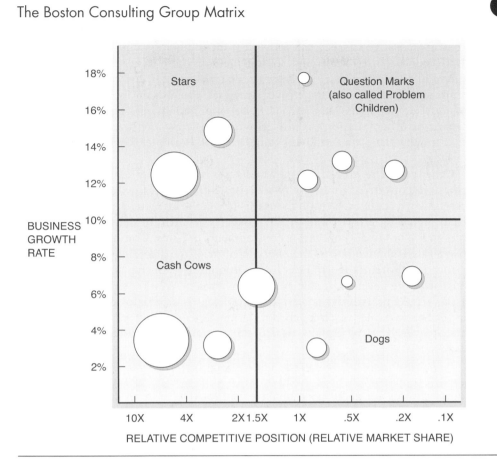

Source: Reprinted with permission from *Long Range Planning*, Vol. 10 (February), by B. Hedley, "Strategy and the Business Portfolio," p. 12. Copyright © 1977, with permission from Elsevier.

generate about as much cash as they use, on average.[60] In the original development of the model, the Boston Consulting Group used market share as a surrogate measure for the length of time an organization had participated in an industry, concluding that firms with more experience in an industry are more likely to have achieved economies of scale, as well as cost reductions from learning and experience effects. Therefore, Stars and Cash Cows, with their superior market share positions, tend to be the most profitable businesses.[61]

Consequently, the optimal BCG portfolio contains a balance of Stars, Cash Cows, and Question Marks. Stars have the greatest potential for growth and tend to be highly profitable. However, as the industries in which Stars are involved mature and their growth slows, they should naturally become Cash Cows. Question Marks are important because of their potential role as future Stars in the organization. Dogs are the least attractive types of business. The original prescription was to divest them.[62] However, even Dogs can be maintained in the portfolio as long as they do not become a drain on corporate resources. Also, some organizations are successful at positioning their Dogs in an attractive niche in their industries.

One of the shortcomings of the BCG Matrix is that it does not allow for changes in strategy due to differing environments. The standard BCG prescription is this: achieve high market share leadership and become a Star or a Cash Cow. The problem with this prescription is that it may only be valid for firms pursuing a low-cost leadership strategy. The use of market share as a measure of competitive strategy carries with it the implicit assumption that size has led to economies of scale and learning effects, and that these effects have resulted in competitive success through the creation of a low-cost position. Differentiation and focus competitive strategies are not incorporated into the model. Also, companies that are successful in pursuing focus strategies (through low cost or differentiation) in low-growth industries may be classified as Dogs even though they are attractive businesses. For example, Rolex would qualify as a Dog.

Other problems with the BCG Matrix are related to its simplicity. Only two factors are considered and only two divisions, high and low, are used for each factor. Also, as conveyed throughout this book, the attractiveness of an industry is determined by growth and profit prospects, which are determined by many forces in the broad and operating environments of firms. Consequently, a simple growth rate is inadequate as the only indicator of the attractiveness of an industry and, therefore, its worthiness for additional investment. Some fast-growing industries have never been particularly profitable.[63] Market share, for all of the reasons stated previously, is also an insufficient indicator of competitive position. Other variables, such as corporate image, cost position, or R&D advantages, are likely to be equally or more important to the competitiveness of a business.

A common criticism that applies to many portfolio models, and especially the BGG Matrix, is that they are based on the past instead of the future.[64] Given that strategy choices are about positioning a firm for the future in an environment of change, this criticism is valid. Also, historical industry growth rate and business market share are widely known information in industries comprised of mostly public companies. Therefore, the logic of strategy choices made by firms that follow a rigid interpretation of the BCG model (invest, divest) would be widely known to competitors—which can undermine competitive positioning over time.

In conclusion, the BCG Matrix is most applicable to firms in particular operating environments that are pursuing low-cost leadership strategies based on the experience curve. Nevertheless, the Matrix may help firms anticipate cash needs and flows. Numerous organizational managers and business writers have developed portfolio matrices that overcome some of the limitations of the BCG Matrix. One of these approaches will now be described.

The General Electric Business Screen

Virtually any variables or combination of variables of strategic importance can be plotted along the axes of a portfolio matrix. The selection of variables depends on what the organization considers important. Many matrices contain factors that are composites of several variables. One of the most famous of these, developed at General Electric, is illustrated in Exhibit 6.8. The G.E. model is referred to as the G.E. Portfolio Matrix, the Nine-Cell Grid, or the G.E. Business Screen.

In the G.E. Business Screen, the area in the circles represents the size of the industries in which each business competes. The slice out of the circle is the market share of the business unit in each of these industries. The variables that are used to assess industry attractiveness are typically derived from the objectives and characteristics of the organization (i.e., attitude toward growth, profitability, or social responsibility) and the industries themselves. Assessment of competitive

The General Electric Business Screen

Exhibit 6.8

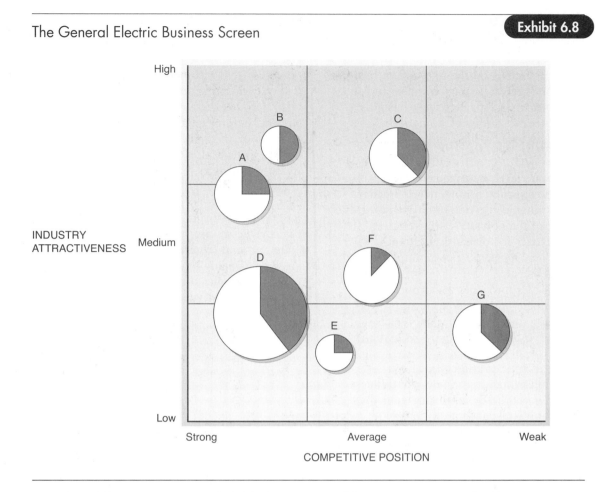

position is based on a firm's position with respect to the key success factors in an industry.[65] An organization aspires to have all of its businesses in the top left cell. These businesses are called Winners. However, some of these Winners should be established businesses that are not growing rapidly so that a portion of their cash flow can be used to support developing winners.

The way an organization allocates its internal resources reconfirms its selection of businesses. For example, business units that are considered critical to the future success of an organization should receive high priority in resource allocation decisions, whereas unimportant businesses may receive only maintenance levels of support. From a portfolio management perspective, businesses that are in a strong competitive position in attractive industries should be given the highest priority.

In conclusion, while all portfolio management models have weaknesses and limitations, they provide an additional tool to assist managers in anticipating cash flows and making resource allocation decisions. The G.E. Business Screen, in particular, is flexible enough to accommodate a wide variety of indicators of industry attractiveness and competitive strength and may be used to employ many of the concepts reviewed in earlier chapters of this book.

KEY POINTS SUMMARY

Corporate strategy focuses on the selection of businesses in which the organization will compete and on the tactics used to enter and manage those businesses and other corporate-level resources. Some of the most important points discussed in this chapter include the following:

1. At the corporate level, management responsibilities include direction setting, development of a corporate strategy, selection of businesses and management of the portfolio of businesses, selection of tactics for diversification and growth, and management of corporate-level resources.

2. The three broad approaches to corporate strategy are single business/concentration, vertical integration and diversification, which is divided into two broad categories, related and unrelated.

3. Single business/concentration strategies allow an organization to focus on doing one business very well; however, a key disadvantage is that the organization is dependent on that one business for survival.

4. Vertical integration allows an organization to become its own supplier or customer. However, according to the theory of transaction cost economics, if required resources can be obtained from a competitive open market without allocating an undue amount of time or other resources to the contracting process or contract enforcement, it is probably in the best interests of an organization to buy from the market instead of vertically integrating.

5. Research indicates that unrelated diversification is not a particularly successful strategy; however, some firms perform well with it.

6. Related diversification is a very popular strategy. Businesses are related if they share a common market, technology, raw material, or any one of many other factors. However, for a related diversification strategy to have its full positive impact, strategic and organizational fit is required.

7. Diversification can be accomplished through internal venturing, acquisition of existing businesses, or strategic alliances/joint ventures. Each of these tactics has advantages and disadvantages.

8. Portfolio models help organizations manage their portfolio of diversified businesses. Two examples are the Boston Consulting Group Matrix and the G.E. Business Screen.

REFERENCES

1   M. Kripalani, "Tata Taps a Vast R&D Shop—Its Own" *Business Week* (April 20, 2009): 50; "Leadership with Trust," http://www.tata.com/aboutus/sub_index.aspx?sectid=8hOk5Qq3EfQ= (April 27, 2009).

2   Kripalani, "Tata Taps a Vast R&D Shop—Its Own."

3   Three classic studies for U.S. firms are found in R.P. Rumelt, *Strategy, Structure and Economic Performance* (Boston: Harvard Business School, 1974); R.P. Rumelt, "Diversification Strategy and Profitability," *Strategic Management Journal* 3 (1982): 359–369; and L.H.P. Lang and R.M. Stulz, "Tobin's q, Corporate Diversification and Firm Performance," *Journal of Political Economy* 102 (1994): 1248–80. The general proposition that low levels of diversification (especially unrelated) in highly industrialized countries is associated with higher performance has been confirmed several times, most recently in W.P. Wan and R.E. Hoskisson, "Home Country Environments, Corporate Diversification Strategies, and Firm Performance," *Academy of Management Journal* 46 (2003): 27–45.

4   H.I. Ansoff, *Corporate Strategy: An Analytical Approach to Business Policy for Growth and Expansion* (New York: McGraw-Hill, 1965): 129–130.

5   A.D. Chandler, Jr., *Strategy and Structure: Chapters in the History of the Industrial Enterprise* (Cambridge, Massachusetts: MIT Press, 1962).

6   J.R. Galbraith and R.K. Kazanjian, *Strategy Implementation: Structure, Systems and Process*, 2nd ed. (St. Paul: West Publishing, 1986), Chapter 4.

7   L.F. Mesquita, J. Anand and T.H. Brush, "Comparing the Resource-Based and Relational Views:

Knowledge Transfer and Spillover in Vertical Alliances," *Strategic Management Journal* 29 (2008): 913–941; K.R. Harrigan, "Formulating Vertical Integration Strategies," *Academy of Management Review* 9 (1984): 639.

8   O.E. Williamson, *Markets and Hierarchies: Analysis and Antitrust Implications* (New York: The Free Press, 1975) and *The Economic Institutions of Capitalism* (New York: The Free Press, 1985).

9   Rumelt, *Strategy, Structure and Economic Performance*; Rumelt, "Diversification Strategy and Profitability."

10 Harrigan, "Formulating Vertical Integration Strategies."

11 R.A. D'Aveni and D.J. Ravenscraft, "Economies of Integration Versus Bureaucracy Costs: Does Vertical Integration Improve Performance?" *Academy of Management Journal* 37 (1994): 1167–1206.

12 R.E. Hoskisson, J.S. Harrison and D.A. Dubofsky, "Capital Market Implementation of M-Form Implementation and Diversification Strategy," *Strategic Management Journal* 12 (1991): 271–279.

13 H.I. Ansoff, *Corporate Strategy: An Analytical Approach to Business Policy for Growth and Expansion* (New York: Mc Graw-Hill, 1965): 130–132; J.S. Harrison, "Alternatives to Merger–Joint Ventures and Other Strategies," *Long Range Planning* (December, 1987): 78–83; C.W.L. Hill and G.S. Hansen, "A Longitudinal Study of the Cause and Consequence of Changes in Diversification in the U.S. Pharmaceutical Industry," *Strategic Management Journal* 12 (1991): 187–199; W.G. Lewellen, "A Pure Financial Rationale for the Conglomerate Merger," *Journal of Finance* 26 (1971): 521–537; F.M. McDougall and D.K. Round, "A Comparison of Diversifying and Nondiversifying Australian Industrial Firms," *Academy of Management Journal* 27 (1984): 384–398; R. Reed and G.A. Luffman, "Diversification: The Growing Confusion," *Strategic Management Journal* 7 (1986).

14 S. Chatterjee, J.S. Harrison and D. Bergh, "Failed Takeover Attempts, Organizational Governance and Refocusing," *Strategic Management Journal* 24 (2003): 87–96.

15 "Businesses," http://www.philips.com/About/company/businesses/Index.html (April 27, 2009).

16 A few examples of the many studies that demonstrate low performance associated with unrelated diversification are R. Amit and J. Livnat, "Diversification Strategies, Business Cycles, and Economic Performance," *Strategic Management Journal* 9 (1988): 99–110; R.A. Bettis and V. Mahajan, "Risk/Return Performance of Diversified Firms," *Management Science* 31 (1985): 785–799; D. Ravenscraft and F.M. Scherer, *Mergers, Selloffs, and Economic Efficiency* (Washington, D.C.: Brookings Institution, 1987); P.G. Simmonds, "The Combined Diversification Breadth and Mode Dimensions and the Performance of Large Diversified Firms," *Strategic Management Journal* 11 (1990): 399–410; P. Varadarajan and V. Ramanujam, "Diversification and Performance: A Reexamination Using a New Two-Dimensional Conceptualization of Diversity in Firms," *Academy of Management Journal* 30 (1982): 380–393. On the other hand, the following studies are among those that support the superiority of unrelated diversification: R.M. Grant and A.P. Jammine, "Performance Differences Between the Wrigley/Rumelt Strategic Categories," *Strategic Management Journal* 9 (1988): 333–346; A. Michel and I. Shaked, "Does Business Diversification Affect Performance?" *Financial Management* (Winter, 1984): 18–25.

17 M.C. Lauenstein, "Diversification–The Hidden Explanation of Success," *Sloan Management Review* (Fall, 1985): 49–55; M. Lubatkin and R.C. Rogers, "Diversification, Systematic Risk and Shareholder Return: A Capital Market Extension of Rumelt's 1974 Study," *Academy of Management Journal* 32 (1989): 454–465.; M. Lubatkin and H.G. O'Neill, "Merger Strategies and Capital Market Risk," *Academy of Management Journal* 30 (1987): 665–684; M. Lubatkin, "Value Creating Mergers: Fact or Folklore," *Academy of Management Executive* (November, 1988): 295–302; C.A. Montgomery and H. Singh, "Diversification Strategy and Systematic Risk," *Strategic Management Journal* 5 (1984): 181–191.

18 J. McGregor, "From Great to Good," *Business Week* (April 13, 2009): 32–35.

19 W.P. Wan and R.E. Hoskisson, "Home Country Environments, Corporate Diversification Strategies, and Firm Performance," *Academy of Management Journal* 46 (2003): 27–45; R.E. Hoskisson, R.A. Johnson, D. Yiu and W.P. Wan, "Restructuring Strategies of Diversified Business Groups: Difference Associated with Country Institutional Environments," in M.A. Hitt, R.E. Freeman and J.S. Harrison, eds. *The Blackwell Handbook of Strategic Management* (Oxford: Blackwell Publishers LTD, 2001): 444; M.R. Aleson and M.E. Escuer, "The Impact of Product Diversification on the Corporate Performance of Large Spanish Firms," *Spanish Economic Review* 4(2): 119–129.

20 R. Dodes and E. Byron, "P&G Flirts with Luxury Cosmetics," *Wall Street Journal* (March 9, 2009): B1.

21 A detailed review of this literature is found in R.E. Hoskisson and M.A. Hitt, "Antecedents and Performance Outcomes of Diversification: A Review and Critique of Theoretical Perspectives," *Journal of Management* 16 (1990): 468. More recent evidence is found in P.S. Davis, R.B. Robinson, Jr., J.A. Pearce and S.H. Park, "Business Unit Relatedness and Performance: A Look at the Pulp and Paper Industry," *Strategic Management Journal* 13 (1992): 349–361 and in J.S. Harrison, E.H. Hall, Jr., and R. Nargundkar, "Resource Allocation as an Outcropping of Strategic Consistency: Performance Implications," *Academy of Management Journal* 36 (1993): 1026–1051.

22 M. Lubatkin and S. Chatterjee, "Extending Modern Portfolio Theory into the Domain of Corporate Diversification: Does It Apply?" *Academy of Management Journal* 37 (1994): 109–136.

23 "Corporate Profile," http://world.honda.com/profile (April 27, 2009).

24 M.E. Porter, *Competitive Advantage: Creating and Sustaining Superior Performance* (New York: The Free Press, 1985): 317–363.

25 H.I. Ansoff, *Corporate Strategy* (New York: Mc Graw-Hill, 1965).

26 H. Itami, *Mobilizing Invisible Assets* (Cambridge, Massachusetts: Harvard University Press, 1987).

27 P.R. Nayyar, "On the Measurement of Corporate Diversification Strategy: Evidence From Large U.S. Service Firms," *Strategic Management Journal* 13 (1992): 219–235; R. Reed and G.A. Luffman, "Diversification: The Growing Confusion," *Strategic Management Journal* 7 (1986): 29–36.

28 M.A. Hitt, J.S. Harrison and R.D. Ireland, *Mergers and Acquisitions: A Guide to Creating Value for Stakeholders* (Oxford: Oxford University Press, 2001); D.B. Jemison and S.B. Sitkin, "Corporate Acquisitions: A Process Perspective," *Academy of Management Review* 11 (1986): 145–163.

29 "The Virgin Story," http://www.virgin.com/aboutus/story.shtml (April 16, 2003).

30 E.R. Biggadike, "The Risky Business of Diversification," *Harvard Business Review* (May/June, 1979): 103–111.

31 M.A. Hitt, R.E. Hoskisson, R.D. Ireland and J.S. Harrison, "Effects of Acquisitions on R&D Inputs and Outputs". *Academy of Management Journal* 34 (1991): 693–706.

32 M. Lubatkin, "Value Creating Mergers: Fact or Folklore?" *Academy of Management Executive* (May, 1988): 295–302; J. Pfeffer, "Merger as a Response to Organizational Interdependence," *Administrative Science Quarterly* 17 (1972): 382–394.; J.H. Song, "Diversifying Acquisitions and Financial Relationships: Testing 1974-1976 Behaviour," *Strategic Management Journal* 4 (1983): 97–108; F. Trautwein, "Merger Motives and Merger Prescriptions," *Strategic Management Journal* 11 (1990): 283–295.

33 J. Silver-Greenberg, "Dealmakers Test the Waters," *Business Week* (March 2, 2009): 18–20.

34 D. Clark and B. Worthen, "Oracle Snatches Sun, Foiling IBM," *Wall Street Journal* (April 21, 2009): A1.

35 M.D. Hovanesian, "Why Well Fargo is So Wary," *Business Week* (April 6, 2009): 28.

36 J.D. Rockoff, "Eli Lilly is on Hunt for Acquisitions," *Wall Street Journal* (March 31, 2009): B1.

37 Silver-Greenberg, "Dealmakers Test the Waters."

38 One of the most active proponents of the view that mergers and acquisitions create value for acquiring-firm shareholders is Michael Lubatkin: see M. Lubatkin, "Value-Creating Mergers: Fact or Folklore?" *Academy of Management Executive* (November, 1988): 295–302. However, he reported strong evidence that contradicts his earlier conclusions in S. Chatterjee, M.H. Lubatkin, D.M. Schweiger, and Y. Weber, "Cultural Differences and Shareholder Value in Related Mergers: Linking Equity and Human Capital," *Strategic Management Journal* 13 (1992): 319–334. Other strong summary evidence that mergers and acquisitions do not create value is found in W.B. Carper, "Corporate Acquisitions and Shareholder Wealth," *Journal of Management* 16 (1990): 807–823; D.K. Datta, G.E. Pinches and V.K. Narayanan, "Factors Influencing Wealth Creation from Mergers and Acquisitions: A Meta-Analysis," *Strategic Management Journal* 13 (1992): 67–84.

39 M.A. Hitt, R.E. Hoskisson, R.D. Ireland and J.S. Harrison, "Are Acquisitions a Poison Pill for Innovation?" *Academy of Management Executive* (November, 1991): 20–35.

40 M.E. Porter, "From Competitive Advantage to Corporate Strategy": 59.

41 Hitt, Harrison and Ireland, *Mergers and Acquisitions*; M. Hitt, J. Harrison, R.D. Ireland and A. Best, "Attributes of Successful and Unsuccessful Acquisitions of U.S. Firms," *British Journal of Management* 9 (1998): 91–114; J.B. Kusewitt, Jr., "An Exploratory Study of Strategic Acquisition Factors Relating to Success," *Strategic Management Journal* 6 (1985): 151–169; L.M. Shelton, "Strategic Business Fits and Corporate Acquisition: Empirical Evidence," *Strategic Management Journal* 9 (1988): 279–287.

42 S. Chatterjee, M.H. Lubatkin, D.M. Schweiger and Y. Weber, "Cultural Differences and Shareholder Value in Related Mergers: Linking Equity and Human Capital," *Strategic Management Journal* 13 (1992): 319–334; D.K. Datta, "Organizational Fit and Acquisition Performance: Effects of Post-Acquisition Integration," *Strategic Management Journal* 12 (1991): 281–297; D.B. Jemison and S.B. Sitkin, "Corporate Acquisitions: A Process Perspective," *Academy of Management Review* 11 (1986): 145–163.

43 T.H. Brush, "Predicted Change in Operational Synergy and Post-Acquisition Performance of Acquired Businesses," *Strategic Management Journal* 17 (1996): 1–24.

44 F.T. Paine and D.J. Power, "Merger Strategy: An Examination of Drucker's Five Rules for Successful Acquisition," *Strategic Management Journal* 5 (1984): 99–110.

45 B. Boyrs and D.B. Jemison, "Hybrid Arrangements as Strategic Alliances: Theoretical Issues in Organizational Combinations," *Academy of Management Review* 14 (1989): 234–249; K.R. Harrigan, "Joint Ventures and Competitive Strategy," *Strategic Management Journal* 9 (1988): 141–158.

46 F.T. Rothaermel and W. Boeker, "Old Technology Meets New Technology," *Strategic Management Journal* 29 (2008): 47–77; B.R. Barringer and J.S. Harrison, "Walking a Tightrope: Creating Value Through Interorganizational Relationships," *Journal of Management* 26 (2000): 367–403.

47 J.S. Harrison, "Alternatives to Merger–Joint Ventures and Other Strategies," *Long Range Planning* (December, 1987): 78–83.

48 K.J. Delaney, M. Mangalindan and R.A. Guth, "New Tech Alliances Signal More Scrambling Ahead," *Wall Street Journal* (May 26, 2006): B1.

49 J. Carless, "A Roadmap for Driving Strategic Alliances to Success," http://newsroom.cisco.com/ddls/hd_052903.html (February 22, 2006).

50 A.C. Inkpen, "Knowledge Transfer and International Joint Ventures: The Case of NUMMI and General Motors," *Strategic Management Journal* 29 (2008): 447–453; C.E. Schillaci, "Designing Successful Joint Ventures," *Journal of Business Strategies* (Fall, 1987): 60; J. Hennart, "A Transactions Costs Theory of Equity Joint Ventures," *Strategic Management Journal* 9 (1988): 361–374.

51 Dodes and Byron, "P&G Flirts with Luxury Cosmetics."

52 *CEMEX 2005 Annual Report*, http://www.cemex.com (August 1, 2006).

53 Barringer and Harrison, "Walking a Tightrope: Creating Value through Interorganizational Relationships."

54 M. Kotabe, X. Martin and H. Domoto, "Gaining from Vertical Partnerships: Knowledge Transfer, Relationship Duration, and Supplier Performance Improvement in the U.S. and Japanese Automotive Industries," *Strategic Management Journal* 24 (2003), 293–316.

55 Harrigan, "Joint Ventures and Competitive Strategy"; R.N. Osborn and C.C. Baughn, "Forms of Interorganizational Governance for Multinational Alliances," *Academy of Management Journal* 33 (1990): 503–519.

56 Y. Luo, "Structuring Interorganizational Cooperation: The Role of Economic Integration in Strategic Alliances," *Strategic Management Journal* 29 (2008): 617–637.

57 P. Lorange and J. Roos, "Why Some Strategic Alliances Succeed and Others Fail," *The Journal of Business Strategy* (January/February, 1991): 25–30.

58 G. Develin and M. Bleackley, "Strategic Alliances—Guidelines for Success," *Long Range Planning* 21(5) (1988): 18–23; Lorange and Roos, "Why Some Strategic Alliances Succeed and Others Fail."

59 R.A. Kerin, V. Mahajan and P.R. Varadarajan, *Strategic Market Planning* (Needham Heights, Massachusetts: Allyn & Bacon, 1990): 94; J.A. Seeger, "Reversing the Images of BCG's Growth Share Matrix," *Strategic Management Journal* 5 (1984): 93–97; S.F. Slater and T.J. Zwirlein, "Shareholder Value and Investment Strategy Using the General Portfolio Model," *Journal of Management* 18 (1992): 717–732; R. Wensley, "PIMS and BCG: New Horizons or False Dawn," *Strategic Management Journal* 3 (1982): 147–158.

60 D.C. Hambrick, I.C. MacMillan and D.L. Day, "Strategic Attributes and Performance in the BCG Matrix—A PIMS-Based Analysis of Industrial Product Businesses," *Academy of Management Journal* 25 (1982): 518.

61 Hambrick, MacMillan and Day, "Strategic Attributes and Performance in the BCG Matrix."

62 B.D. Henderson, *Henderson on Corporate Strategy* (Cambridge, Massachusetts: Abt Books, 1979): 164.

63 C.W. Hofer and D. Schendel, *Strategy Formulation: Analytical Concepts* (St. Paul: West Publishing Company, 1978): 31.

64 Slater and Zwirlein, "Shareholder Value"; Seeger, "Reversing the Images."

65 Hofer and Schendel, *Strategy Formulation*: 73–76.

7

Strategy Implementation

Hewlett-Packard

Hewlett-Packard Company (HP) is one of the leading providers of personal computing devices, imaging and printing-related products, enterprise information technology, and technology services, consulting, and outsourcing. The company has made several large acquisitions in recent years, including computer industry rivals Compaq and Electronic Data Systems. HP is now the market share leader in desktop personal computers, portable personal computers, inkjet printers and laser printers. While acquisitions have contributed to substantial growth in company revenues, HP's increasing profit margins are more a function of cost cutting and internal efficiency measures.

One of HP's most successful efficiency programs is what the company calls its "information technology transformation." The company completely rebuilt its information technology (IT) infrastructure and processes to reduce costs, provide more reliable information, improve business continuity, create a more simplified system, and support company growth. For instance, 85 internal data centers were consolidated into six next-generation centers, 6,000 standard applications were consolidated to 1,500 applications, annual energy consumption was reduced by 60% and processing power was increased by 250%. The company expects to flip its ratio of IT spending from 75% on maintenance and 25% on innovation to 25% on maintenance and 75% on innovation. HP's goal is "to have the best operations of any company in the world." Operating margins increased from 4% to 8.8% in just three years.

Mark Hurd, CEO, is leading HP's quest for internal efficiency. He is a numbers-oriented manager who uses a personal spreadsheet program to track and analyze his own daily schedule. He not only preaches internal efficiency to internal managers and employees, but is known to share HP's philosophy with other stakeholders as well. For instance, Hurd was telling some of HP's customers about its IT consolidation efforts when someone asked what would happen if a senior-level employee wanted to purchase his own customer relationship management (CRM) software package. Hurd explained that HP painstakingly chose just one CRM package for the entire company and that extraordinary requests are not tolerated. In fact, he explained that if the manager purchased his own CRM system he would not be working for HP anymore.

Looking forward, Hurd believes that HP's significant competitive advantages include "a strong balance sheet, diversified revenues with one-third of our revenue and well over half of our profits from recurring sources such as services and supplies, a lean, variable cost structure and commitment to continue to eliminate all costs that are not core to the company's success, and proven financial and operational discipline."[1]

Some of the most successful companies of our time—Wal-Mart, Hewlett-Packard, Toyota—are operating in intensely competitive industries. One of the reasons for their extraordinary success is their attention to the details associated with strategy execution. The HP example illustrates the importance of functional-level strategies in implementing a cost leadership strategy. Until strategies are implemented, they are only ideas and intentions, with no real effect on the organization's direction. Hewlett-Packard has achieved extraordinary performance through attention to its own information technology infrastructure and processes. Mark Hurd has also influenced HP's culture to get employees to support the company's cost cutting measures.

Strategy execution typically goes hand-in-hand with strategy formulation, and we have made no attempt to create an artificial barrier between the two activities. For instance, the chapter on business-level strategies included fairly substantial detail regarding how particular strategies might be implemented, and the chapter on corporate-level strategies included a whole section on tactics for achieving diversification. However, several additional topics are essential to understanding how strategies are implemented successfully. These topics, the subjects of this chapter, include functional-level strategy development, design of organizational structure, and organizational culture. Because innovation and entrepreneurship is so essential to success in today's competitive environment, we have devoted a separate section to the topic.

FUNCTIONAL STRATEGIES

Business-level strategies are implemented through day-to-day decisions made at the operating level of the firm.[2] The competitive advantages and distinctive competences that are sought by firms are often embedded in the skills, resources, and capabilities at the functional level. Functional strategies are the plans for matching those skills, resources, and capabilities to the business and corporate strategies of the organization. For example, luxury car maker BMW, which actually increased its market share in the economic downturn, has a dealer compensation system that is tied directly to customer satisfaction scores and how well dissatisfied customers are dealt with.[3] JetBlue's success in the airline industry is also attributable to paying attention to details. After a survey of airline customers that found JetBlue far ahead of other discount carriers, J.D. Power and Associates, who conducted the survey, concluded: "The study finds that 'process' factors, such as check-in, how passengers board the plane and how baggage is delivered at the destination; and 'people' factors, such as hiring the right people and training and enabling them to be successful, are what differentiate carriers in the eyes of passengers."[4]

The collective pattern of day-to-day decisions made and actions taken by employees responsible for value activities create **functional strategies**, detailed action plans for implementing the growth and competitive strategies of the company. A helpful tool for developing functional strategies is found in Exhibit 7.1.

In the following sections, we will discuss the responsibilities and patterns of decisions made by marketing, operations, R&D, human resources, finance, and information systems. Along with a brief description of the responsibilities of each area, the discussion will emphasize that each functional area is a piece of a larger system and coordination among the pieces is essential to successful strategy execution. Furthermore, each functional area should support the various business- and corporate-level strategies of the firm. Therefore, well-developed functional strategies should have the following characteristics:

1. *Decisions made within each function should be consistent with each other.* For example, if marketing chooses to spend a great deal of effort and money creating a premium brand name for a new product, it should take advantage of distribution channels that allow the product to reach customers who will pay a premium price. If the wrong distribution channels are chosen, then the efforts spent on brand management including advertising, promotion, and product placement will be lost. Several years ago, one of the synthetic fiber producers allowed one of its best branded products to become associated with discount retail outlets and its investment in the brand was lost almost instantly.

2. *Decisions made within one function should be consistent with those made in other functions.* Unfortunately, it is common for the decisions made by one department to be inconsistent with those of another department. Marketing and operations frequently advocate very different approaches to the many interdependent decisions that exist between them. Left to their own devices, with no guidance from executive leadership, it is likely that marketing, over time, will make decisions that implement a differentiation strategy in an effort to better serve the customers that they represent. Meanwhile operations managers are likely to implement a low-cost strategy over time as they respond to pressure to improve productivity and reduce costs. These tendencies are completely logical in the absence of leadership about the priority of trade-offs.

3. *Decisions made within functions should be consistent with the strategies of the business.* For example, in a healthy business environment, marketing may pursue market share increases and revenue growth as its top priority. If the business environment changes—demand slows down and profits are squeezed—then the focus of marketing may have to change to stability and profit improvement over sales volume increases. Unless prodded by the organization, marketing may be very reluctant to change from its traditional way of doing business.[5]

Marketing Strategy

One of the most critical responsibilities of marketing employees is to span the boundary of the organization and interact with current and potential customers. Marketing is responsible for bringing essential information about new customer needs, projected future demand, competitor actions, and new business opportunities into the organization. These pieces of information influence plans for continuous improvements, capacity and workforce expansions, new technologies, and new products and services.

Marketing strategy is the plan for investing marketing efforts and resources (advertising, branding, distribution, etc.) to achieve business goals. To support growth strategies, marketing identifies new customer opportunities, suggests product opportunities, creates advertising and promotional programs, arranges distribution channels, and creates pricing and customer service policies which help position the company's products for the proper customer groups.

Marketing strategy is also used to implement a firm's generic business-level strategy. Low-cost leadership strategies require low-cost channels of distribution and low-risk product and market development activities. If demand can be

Exhibit 7.1	Conducting a Functional Strategy Audit

The functional strategy audit is a procedure for systematically reviewing the decisions in each of the functional areas to determine which ones should be changed to support the new strategy and needs of stakeholders. The format for the audit is shown.

	Needed	Current	Change

Marketing Strategy Decision Areas
Target customers
   (few versus many, what groups, what regions)
Product positioning
   (premium, commodity, multiuse, specialty use)
Product line mix
   (a mix of complementary products)
Product line breadth
   (a full line offering of products)
Pricing strategies
   (discount, moderate, premium prices)
Promotion practices
   (direct sales, advertising, direct mail)
Distribution channels
   (few or many, sole contract relationships)
Customer service policies
   (flexibility, responsiveness, quality)
Product/service policies
   (premium quality, good price, reliable)
Market research
   (accuracy and frequency of information on customers and competitors)

Operations Strategy Decision Areas
Capacity planning
   (lead demand to ensure availability or lag demand to achieve capacity utilization)
Facility location
   (locate near suppliers, customers, labor, natural resources, transportation)
Facility layout
   (continuous or intermittent flow)
Technology and equipment choices
   (degree of automation, computerization)
Sourcing arrangements
   (cooperative relationships with a few versus competitive bid)
Planning and scheduling
   (make to stock, make to order, flexibility to customer requests)
Quality assurance
   (acceptance sampling, process control, standards)
Workforce policies
   (training levels, cross-training, reward systems)

R&D/Technology Strategy Decision Areas
Research focus
   (product, process, applications)
Orientation
   (leader versus follower)

Continued

Exhibit 7.1

	Needed	Current	Change

Project priorities
    (budget, quality, creativity, time)
Linkages with external research organizations

Human Resources Strategy Decision Areas
Recruitment
    (entry-level versus experienced employees)
Selection
    (selection criteria and methods)
Performance appraisal
    (appraisal methods, frequency)
Salary and wages
    (relationship to performance, competitiveness)
Benefits
    (bonuses, stock-ownership programs, other benefits)
Personnel actions
    (disciplinary plans, outplacement, early retirements)
Training
    (types of training, availability to all employees)

Financial Strategy Decision Areas
Capital
    (debt versus equity versus internal financing)
Financial reporting to stockholders
Minimum return on investment levels
    (relationship to cost of capital)
Basis for allocating overhead costs
    (direct labor, machine use, sales volume, activity)

Information Systems Strategy Decision Areas
Hardware capability and integration across the organization
    (mainframe, network, hardwire linkages, dial-up)
Software capability and integration across the organization
    (user support, compatibility, security, standardization)
Linkages with customers and suppliers
    (direct links, shared systems)
Investments in new technologies
    (Internet, bar-code scanners, satellite technology)
Strategic use of internal and external information
    (decision support, operations support, marketing support, forecasting)
Possible development of an Enterprise Resource Planning (ERP) system
    (multiple functional areas sharing a common database)

influenced by advertising or price discounts, then marketing may pursue aggressive advertising and promotion programs or deep price discounts to get demand to a level that will support full capacity utilization and economies of scale within operations, as when the soft drink companies advertise and discount their products. Differentiation strategies require that marketing identify the attributes of products and services that customers will value, price and distribute the product or service in ways that capitalize on the differentiation, and advertise and promote the image of difference.

Marketing strategies become even more complicated as a firm increases the scope of its operations through diversification. Related diversification strategies suggest that firms may be able to take advantage of common markets through joint advertising and promotional strategies. For instance, Hewlett-Packard sometimes offers special deals on its printers to consumers who buy their personal computers. Firms may also pursue a variety of co-branding arrangements with other companies.[6] The term "co-branding" has taken on a number of different meanings in recent years; however, the general idea is that a single product or service is promoted through more than one brand name. Combining multiple brands into the same product or service is intended to increase the premium consumers are willing to pay for it. An obvious example is a clothing item that contains the logo of a famous brand. Sponsorships are another example of co-branding, as when Coca-cola sponsors a major event such as a concert. Another interesting example is when a restaurant company locates two different restaurants, such as a Kentucky Fried Chicken and a Pizza Hut, in the same location. In this case, both restaurants are subsidiaries of Yum! Brands.

Operations Strategy

Operations strategy is the plan for aligning the production and/or service operations of the firm with the intended business strategies. The task of operations managers is to design and manage an operations organization that can create the products and services the firm must have to compete in the marketplace. An effective operations unit "is not necessarily one that promises maximum efficiency or engineering perfection, but rather one that fits the needs of the business—that strives for consistency between its capabilities and policies and the competitive advantage being sought."[7]

Operations managers, like marketing managers, must manage multiple stakeholder interests in their daily decision-making. **Supply chain management**, one of the most important areas in operations management, involves, at a minimum, the integration of the interests of the focal company, the company's customers, and the company's suppliers. The management of these key relationships can often be quite complex. For example, in the organic foods business, the efforts of retailers to boost revenue have resulted in serious supply shortages. According to Marty Mesh, executive director of Florida Organic Growers, "Pick any organic product, industry-wide, whether its milk, meats, or grains, and you'll see that either we're already in a supply shortage or we could fast find ourselves in a shortage."[8] Successful supply chain management requires excellent communications. As we have elaborated on previously, open and productive communications are facilitated by trust based on fair distributions of value among stakeholders in the supply chain, decision-making processes that account for their needs, and excellent treatment of them as transactions occur.

Operations managers face many challenges in aligning operations to the priorities of a particular strategy. Growth strategies may require capacity expansions, hiring of new employees, and new sourcing agreements, which can in turn put pressure on the systems and procedures used to schedule customer orders, plan employee work arrangements, and manage supply chain relationships. Differentiation strategies based on flexibility and high-quality service may require a flexible or temporary workforce, special arrangements with suppliers, and very high levels of training for employees. Automation needed to increase productivity and ensure standardization may result in lay-offs which work against human resource policies and hurt morale. How operations managers handle these types of trade-off decisions can have a substantial influence on the performance of the firm. For example, in attempting a turn-around at Xerox, Ursula Burns, former head of manufacturing, focused "…on the guts of the company. How do we buy parts? How do we assemble things? How do we whack $1 billion out of production costs but still increase productivity?"[9]

Research and Development Strategy

In many organizations, R&D efforts are essential for effective strategy implementation. A firm's **research and development strategy** should define the priorities for new product and service development, long-range innovation efforts, the role of intellectual property protection, and any alliances or partnerships needed to advance innovation goals. For example, a firm that is pursuing a market development growth strategy will invest in applications development so that its products can be tested and qualified for more uses. Fabric manufacturers, for example, put their industrial fabrics through extensive wear-testing to qualify them for everything from conveyor belts to tents to bandages.

If the firm is seeking growth through product line development, the engineers and scientists within R&D will modify the product to improve its performance or extend its application to different markets. For example, Bose has a very strong brand name in sound equipment such as speakers. Underlying their exceptional reputation is a strong R&D program pursuing research into how the ear responds to sound. Also, Bose engineers design automated tone controls on their products that assess room acoustics and then make automatic adjustments.[10] More will be said about fostering innovation later in this chapter.

Human Resources Strategy

An organization's **human resources strategy** defines its approach to recruitment, selection, training, performance evaluation, performance rewards, and other key human resource management practices. Nucor Corporation is the largest steel producer and the largest recycler in the United States, with revenues in 2008 of $23.6 billion and net income of $1.8 billion.[11] One of Nucor's strengths is its employee incentive system. Although base salaries are below industry averages, Nucor has a pay-for-performance system based on defect-free production and profit sharing that mean its workers are among the highest paid in the industry. It is a win-win situation because both the company and its employees benefit from high performance.[12]

Managers within the human resources department serve a coordinating role between the organization's management and employees, and between the organization and external stakeholder groups including labor unions and government regulators of labor and safety practices (i.e., the Equal Employment Opportunity Commission and the Occupational Safety and Health Administration in the United States). Although the human resources staff serves as a resource, most of the actual human resources decisions are made by line managers. All managers, whether they are involved in marketing, operations, R&D, or information systems, play the key roles in deciding employee performance levels, training needs, selection criteria, and salary levels.

Different industry environments and organizational strategies tend to reinforce different human resources practices. In high technology and growth organizations, employees are usually hired from outside the organization to fill positions at all levels, entry positions through top-level management. Compensation systems emphasize long-range performance goals, with frequent use of bonus and profit-sharing plans.[13] Therefore, in organizations pursuing growth strategies, like Microsoft in software and Merck in pharmaceuticals, the human resources strategy focuses on hiring, training, and placing employees at all levels in the organization, and on developing performance-based compensation strategies. On the other hand, mature or cost-oriented businesses usually hire employees at the entry level and promote from within to fill higher level positions. They are more likely to focus rewards on short-range performance goals and to include seniority issues in compensation systems.[14]

As companies become more global, the challenges of managing human resources are becoming more complex. The human resources staff must determine what skills are needed to manage people of different cultures, recruit top candidates world-wide, create training programs and experiences which help employees appreciate other cultures, and conduct relocations world-wide. Furthermore, they may need to create compensation strategies for employees who, because of their national culture, value different reward and benefit packages. For example, in cultures that value personal accomplishment, control of one's destiny and independence, such as the United States and Britain, compensation strategies may focus on individual performance. In cultures that value team accomplishment, sacrifice for others, and external control or fate, as in the case in many Asian countries, the rewards may focus on group measures and seniority.[15]

Financial Strategy

The finance and accounting functions play a strategic role within organizations because they control the funds that are needed to acquire, develop, and utilize strategic resources. All of these activities are essential to successful strategy implementation. In implementing strategy, two sources of funds are needed: (1) large amounts of capital required for growth strategies and to maintain sufficient resources to maintain competitive position and (2) expense budgets to support the on-going, daily activities of the business. The primary purpose of a **financial strategy** is to provide the organization with the capital structure and operating funds that are appropriate for implementing growth and competitive strategies.

The finance/accounting group, often led by an individual called the Chief Financial Officer, decides the appropriate levels of debt, equity, and internal financing needed to support strategies by weighing the costs of each alternative, the plans for the funds, and the financial interests of various internal and external stakeholder groups. Finance also determines dividend policies and, through preparation of financial reports, influences how financial performance will be interpreted and presented to stockholders. In fact, financial reports may be the only contact some members of the investment community and most stockholders have with the organization.

Capital and expense budgets are an extremely important means for allocating funds to those departments, projects, and activities that need them to support strategies. All expenditures in capital and expense budgets should be linked back to the strategies of the firm. "The structure that a mature enterprise takes on at any point in time essentially represents the accumulation of a long series of prior resource allocation decisions. If a company wants to develop in a specific direction, it must make these resource allocation decisions in an organized fashion."[16]

The trade-offs that are embedded in financial decisions carry significant implications for strategy implementation. Should the firm pay earnings out in dividends to satisfy stockholders who want a fast return on their investment, or invest them back into the company to benefit employees, communities, and stockholders who want a longer-term increase in share price? In assessing expenses, investments, and earnings, should long-run or short-run performance be given more emphasis and how should that information be presented to stockholders and the investment community? Which internal stakeholder groups—marketing, operations, R&D, employees—should be most influential in capital allocation decisions? All of these decisions have a bearing on how a firm's stakeholders view the firm; specifically, whether they perceive that the firm is considering their interests in the decisions that are made and is fair in the way value is shared among the stakeholders that helped to create it.[17]

Another important role for the finance and accounting functions is to ensure compliance with both the letter and the spirit of all ethical and regulatory guidelines in the management of the financial resources of the firm. Following a series of corporate scandals involving inappropriate accounting practices and a failure by audit firms to exercise proper oversight, the Sarbanes-Oxley Act was passed to protect investors by improving the accuracy and reliability of information reported by publicly traded companies.[18] Although there continue to be differences of opinion as to whether the new regulations have accomplished their intended purpose, compliance is an important part of the duties of finance and accounting professionals within corporations.

Information Systems Strategy

The purpose of an **information systems strategy** is to provide the organization with the technology and systems which, at a minimum, are necessary for operating, planning, and controlling the business. They are central to knowledge creation, storage and distribution. In many organizations, computer information systems affect every aspect of business operations and serve a major role in linking stakeholders. In some instances, well-designed integrated information systems serve as the foundation for a competitive advantage by allowing more aggressive cost management than competitors, by providing more effective use of timely market information, or by allowing integrated transactions within the supply chain of customers and suppliers. For example, at United Parcel Service, a parcel shipping company, the senior vice-president and chief information officer manages an annual budget of over $1 billion, a division with almost 5,000 employees who are responsible for maintaining over 8,500 servers, 15 mainframes, and a website with over 18 million visitors a day.[19]

Information systems and technologies span across all functions of a business organization and must be effectively coordinated between functions and with the overall strategy of the firm. With spreadsheet packages, expert systems, and other decision-support software, employees at the lowest levels of the organization have the information and the tools to make decisions that were once reserved to middle managers. Computer-aided design (CAD) systems help marketing, manufacturing and R&D employees develop designs faster and with fewer errors. In computer-integrated manufacturing (CIM) environments, product designs and production schedules are linked directly to manufacturing equipment, which increases accuracy, flexibility and speed in meeting customer orders. Direct linkages with suppliers help in managing just-in-time delivery arrangements. Real-time inventory systems linked to order-taking systems provide valuable information which improves customer service. Direct computer linkages with customers provide real-time sales data that the organization may use to plan for the future.[20]

Many organizations are creating **enterprise resource planning** (ERP) systems to manage the flow of information throughout the entire organization.[21] An ERP system supports a wide variety of functions, such as operations and supply chain management, finance and accounting, human resources, distribution and customer relationship management from a shared data source. Each functional area may have its own software and applications that contribute to draw what is needed from a common database. The information contained in the database should be current, reliable and easily accessible.

ERP systems are found in most of the successful large retailers in the United States Scanners are used to record sales data by product and by store. Store managers use the data to update inventory records and reorder products so that their in-stock position will be assured. The sales data from hundreds of stores is transmitted daily to the corporate office where it is studied by product and by store to determine patterns and trends in customer buying behavior. The data are also fed into the distribution system. Expense data obtained from other sources, such as human resources and marketing, is combined with the sales data to create periodic financial reports. These examples barely scratch the surface of the potential uses and sources of information contained in a typical ERP system. As the cost of information management and storage continues to drop, these types of systems will continue to increase in popularity across many industries.

ERP systems are useful in achieving the goal of integration across functional strategies. The effectiveness of strategy implementation efforts is increased in firms where employees work as a coordinated system with all of their separate but interdependent efforts directed toward the goals of the firm.[22] Value chain analysis, which was introduced earlier in this book, is also useful in planning the coordination of functional activities during strategy implementation. For managers, the key task of strategy implementation is to align or fit the activities and capabilities of the firm with its chosen strategy. An understanding of the linkages and interdependencies among the value-adding activities becomes critical.

Organizations are linked together by their information systems. However, they are also tied together through a system that defines who reports to whom and how work is divided. These are elements of an organization's structure.

ORGANIZATIONAL STRUCTURE

The **formal organizational structure** specifies the number and types of departments or groups and provides the formal reporting relationships and lines of communication among internal stakeholders. An organization's structure should be designed to support the strategies of the firm.[23] The underlying assumption is that a strategy-structure fit will lead to superior organization performance. When making decisions about how to structure an organization, it is important to remember the following:

1. Structure is not an end, but a means to an end. The "end" is successful organizational performance.
2. There is no one best structure. A change in organization strategy may require a corresponding change in structure to avoid administrative inefficiencies, but the organization's size, strategies, external environment, stakeholder relationships, and management style all influence the appropriateness of a given structure. All structures embody trade-offs.[24]
3. Once in place, the new structure becomes a characteristic of the organization that will serve as a constraint on future strategic choices.
4. Administrative inefficiencies, poor service to customers, communication problems, or employee frustrations may indicate a strategy-structure mismatch.

When managers organize the activities of a business, they usually seek a structure that will support their growth and competitive strategies. Some of the standard, or traditional, structures are described below.

Standard Structural Forms

Because structures are designed to fit the specific strategies, tasks and human resources of the firm, practically every organization structure is unique. The simple structures illustrated in Exhibit 7.2 are important not because an organization will make use of one precisely as it is illustrated, but because they provide visual examples of some of the underlying principles upon which structures are developed. One of these principles is whether people are grouped on the basis of the inputs they provide or the outputs they create. For instance, a **functional structure** (Exhibit 7.2a) is organized around the inputs or activities that are required to produce products and services, such as marketing, operations, finance, and R&D.[25] This sort of structure causes people to become very focused on a particular function in the firm. They become experts, which can enhance the quality and efficiency of what they do. In contrast, a **divisional structure** is organized around the outputs of

---

Standard Structural Forms   Exhibit 7.2

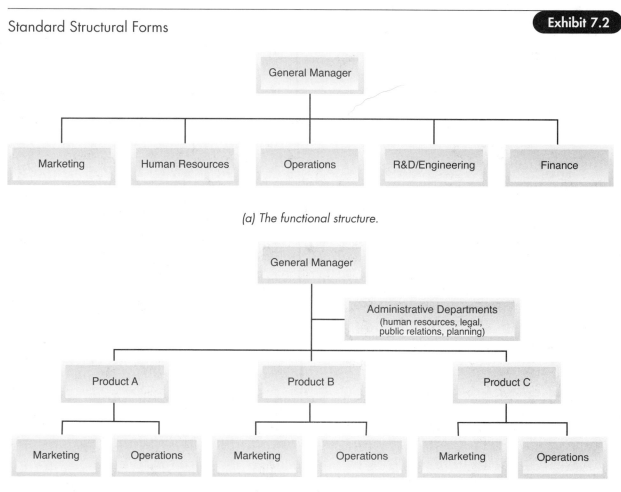

(a) The functional structure.

(b) Divisional structure.

(Continued)

Exhibit 7.2   Continued

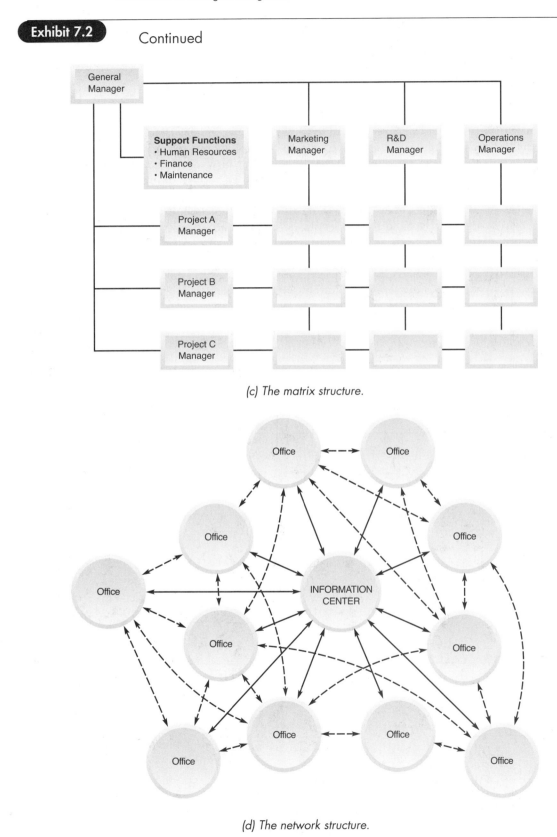

(c) The matrix structure.

(d) The network structure.

the organization, such as products, customers, or geographical regions.[26] People may still work in a functional department such as marketing or operations, but reporting is through a division manager. Divisional structures frequently are referred to as multidivisional, although some might argue that the term multidivisional is better suited to the largest and most highly diversified firms.[27]

Divisional structures come in a wide variety of forms. The example found in Exhibit 7.2b might also be called a product structure because it is organized around the products of the firm. For instance, an electronics firm might be divided into hand-held electronics, military guidance systems, and home alarm systems. Divisions might also represent customer groups, such as consumer or military, or markets, such as the Southern division, Northern division, Midwestern division and Western division. At an international level, divisions like North America, Pacific Rim, Western Europe, Eastern Europe, and China might make sense. The point is that people tend to relate closely to their divisions, which allows them to focus more on satisfying the needs of their consumers. A disadvantage is that the same functions are performed by more than one person or group in a divisional structure. For instance, there is potential for overlap of functions in areas like marketing, R&D, and purchasing. Typically firms try to overcome some of the redundancies by centralizing some functions, such as human resources, legal, public relations and planning.

The notion of centralization brings us to another important principle to consider when developing a structure. Structures should be created based on where critical decisions should be made—the degree of centralization. In the functional structure example found in Exhibit 7.2, the general manager will tend to make all of the key strategic decisions for the firm. In the divisional structure, strategic decisions are shared between the general manager and the product managers. The guiding principle is that the product manager is best suited to make most of the strategic decisions regarding his/her own product area, while the general manager is the best person to make decisions that affect the entire organization.

The **matrix structure** combines elements of the functional and divisional structures. Decision-making is both decentralized and divided. For instance, in the example found in Exhibit 7.2c, a marketing manager will make decisions regarding the marketing of products across all of the project groups, but must do so in cooperation with each of the project group managers. While this example is based on division into project groups, the left diagonal of a matrix could be based just as easily on product groups, geographic markets, or type of customer. Some observers view the matrix structure as a transition stage between a functional form and a product/market group structure, whereas others see the structure as a complex form necessary for complex environments.[28]

Matrix structures are most common in organizations that experience their workload in the form of projects (i.e., construction firms, consulting firms, architectural firms, movie and television production, and engineering firms). At any given point in time, experts drawn from the functional areas are assigned to various project duties—sometimes spanning across several projects. This provides a lot of flexibility with regard to how human resources are allocated to the productive activities of the firm. Fluor Corporation, one of the world's largest engineering design and construction companies, employs a matrix structure:

> At Fluor Corporation, it is very common for design engineers to report to two or more managers: the project manager on a particular contract and the functional manager of their particular design area, such as electrical or mechanical systems. The dual-reporting relationships of the matrix structure

emphasize the equal importance of functional design performance and service on the particular project. The functional dimension encourages employees to share technical information from one project to the next (learning) and helps avoid unnecessary duplication of skills. The project dimension allows the organization to focus on serving the needs of the customer while simultaneously encouraging cooperation and coordination among the different interdependent functions.

Unfortunately, matrix structures can be disconcerting for employees because of the "too many bosses" problem. Not only is it difficult to balance the needs of the different lines of authority and coordinate among the many people and schedules, but the sheer number of people that must be involved in decision-making can slow decision processes and add administrative costs.[29] The overall complexity of the structure can create ambiguity and conflict between functional and product managers and between individuals, but it is increasingly common to see a form of this structure in business environments where the expertise of individuals must be used across a variety of different projects or markets.

Some organizations, particularly large integrated service organizations, use the network, or "spider's web" structure.[30] A **network structure** is very decentralized and organized around customer groups or geographical regions. As shown in Exhibit 7.4d, a network structure represents a web of independent units, with little or no formal hierarchy to organize and control their relationship. The independent units are loosely organized to capture and share useful information. Other than information sharing, however, there is little formal contact among operating units. When formal contact is needed, committees and task forces are created on an ad hoc basis. The network structure is particularly appropriate in knowledge-intensive industries where decentralization and duplication of resources are required to service a broad geographical market, yet there are no manufacturing or technology economies of scale to drive centralization, as in large medical and legal practices, investment banking firms, and charitable institutions like United Way and Girl Scouts of America. In a network structure, most communication and knowledge sharing take place via technology rather than face-to-face.

A network structure may not be appropriate when high levels of coordination and resource sharing are required since it represents an extreme form of decentralization, with executive-level management serving primarily an advisory function and lower-level managers controlling most decisions. The weaknesses of the network structure include the potential for lost control of the autonomous units and high costs from the extensive duplication of resources.

More Complex Structures

A simple functional structure may work well in young firms or firms that are not very diversified. However, as organizations grow and pursue different business opportunities, administrative problems and complexity create pressures to break the organization into more manageable units. When an organization is broadly diversified with several businesses in its portfolio, management may choose to form **strategic business unit** (SBU), with each unit incorporating a few businesses that have something in common. Commonality can result from a number of factors, including similarities in technology, products customers, raw materials, or locations. The related businesses are grouped into SBUs in order to facilitate information sharing and coordination of related activities. Managers of the related businesses report to a SBU manager, who reports to corporate headquarters.

Johnson & Johnson has over 115,600 employees in more than 250 operating companies in 57 countries around the world.[31] All of the operating companies fit within three principal strategic business units or groups: Pharmaceuticals, Consumer, and Medical Devices and Diagnostics. The management team describes the logic of their structure:

> The Company's structure is based upon the principle of decentralized management. The Executive Committee of Johnson & Johnson is the principal management group responsible for the operations and allocation of the resources of the Company. This Committee oversees and coordinates the activities of the Consumer, Pharmaceutical and Medical Devices and Diagnostics business segments. Each subsidiary within the business segments is, with some exceptions, managed by citizens of the country where it is located.[32]

The Johnson & Johnson structure and philosophy has some of the characteristics of the network structure described earlier, but with some additional formal structuring to accommodate the size of the organization.

The increasing need for strategic flexibility in an increasingly competitive global marketplace has led to the adoption of alternative, less-structured corporate forms of organization. Sometimes called "modular," "virtual" or "network," these are loosely interconnected organizational components with boundaries that are not well defined, which are analogous to the network structure described earlier.[33] They differ in that they involve an extended network of relationships with external firms, including suppliers, sub-contractors, distributors, technology partners, and other groups as appropriate. In these types of firms, production can involve many firms simultaneously through a variety of cooperative relationships and joint ventures. They are joined through common goals and allow components to be recombined into a variety of configurations. Companies like Dell, Microsoft and Reebok have participated with success in such arrangements through alliances and outsourcing. Often these types of structures are supplemental to an existing hierarchical structure within the firm (such as those described in this chapter).

Foreign Subsidiaries

In some multinational organizations, foreign subsidiaries are treated as branch locations, but in others, subsidiaries are much more autonomous.[34] In general, foreign subsidiaries play one of three roles:

1. *Local Implementation*—These subsidiaries focus on one country, make minor adjustments to business strategy in order to meet local market needs, execute a strategy planned by the corporate management, and have little independence.
2. *Specialized Contribution*—These subsidiaries play a unique role as a member of an interdependent network of subsidiaries, often as a production arm of the network or as a distributor into a particular region.
3. *Global Mandate*—These subsidiaries are responsible for an entire global business. They are more autonomous and have the responsibility for crafting and executing strategies.[35]

The corporate office is responsible for determining the role each subsidiary will play based on the degree of autonomy required, the need for coordination with other divisions or subsidiaries, and the degree of fit with the overall corporate strategy and approach.

ORGANIZATIONAL CULTURE AND ENERGY

An **organization's culture**, the system of shared values that guides employees, is another important factor that influences the success of strategy implementation. Organizational culture often reflects the values and leadership styles of executives and managers that guide the firm. An organization's culture is also reflected in what might be called the **organization's energy**–how enthusiastic and focused it is in moving toward its goals.

Researchers have explored the idea of organizational energy from several points of view.[36] Heike Bruch and Sumantra Ghoshal proposed a framework for describing organization energy, as shown in Exhibit 7.3. Organization energy can be described in terms of its intensity and its quality.[37] For example, an organization with intense, high-quality energy exhibits "Passion." HP, described in the introduction to this chapter, is a company with a lot of passion. However, when intense energy is of negative quality, the outcome can be "Aggression." An aggressive company will exhibit a highly competitive win-at-all-costs posture, exemplified by MCI in the 1990s.

Companies with low intensity, positive energy are generally satisfied and "Comfortable." Although this type of energy can be effective in some cases, it can also lead to complacency and unwillingness to recognize the need for change. U.S. automobile companies for many years were comfortable in spite of looming changes in their industry. Finally, firms with a low energy intensity coupled with negative quality of energy are generally in a stage of "Resignation." U.S. automobile companies entered a stage of resignation as the reality of their competitive situations began to sink in. Much of the challenge of turning those companies around depends on whether their organizational energy improves. Companies cannot function effectively over the long term with low intensity, negative energy.

An organization's energy and culture can be its greatest strengths or its greatest weaknesses. In some organizations, poor morale and a cynical attitude toward customers often undermine organizational performance. Other organizations have succeeded in creating cultures that are completely consistent with what the organization is trying to accomplish—high-performance cultures. At Nucor, the largest steel producer in the United States, the company's stated commitment to a low-cost strategy is supported by a culture that expects efficiency and tight fiscal policy. When these values are coupled with intense, high-quality

Exhibit 7.3	Organizational Energy		
		High Energy–excitement, alertness	Low Energy–inertia, tiredness
Positive Energy—enthusiasm, satisfaction		Passion	Comfort or Complacency
Negative Energy—fear, frustration		Aggression	Resignation

energy—the outcome is a powerful commitment to excellence and a high level of organizational camaraderie. As noted by *Business Week*, "At times, workers and managers exhibit a level of passion for the company that can border on the bizarre. Executive Vice-President Joseph A. Rutkowski, an engineer who came up through the mills, speaks of Nucor as a 'magic' place, representing the best of American rebelliousness." He says, "We epitomize how people should think, should be."[38]

The role of executive leadership with regard to culture is to define and then live by the values that are sought, and to harness or redirect the organization's energy toward the important strategic priorities of the company. Also, human resource management practices, such as recruitment, training, and performance evaluation, tend to reinforce certain types of behavior. Often the most successful companies have managers and human resource practices that encourage innovation and entrepreneurship.

FOSTERING INNOVATION AND ENTREPRENEURSHIP

The long-term success of established firms is at least partially a function of the ability to meld entrepreneurship with strategic management.[39] Entrepreneurship creates new firm value from innovative ideas. Innovation and entrepreneurship are essential for a firm to differentiate its goods or services from competitors and create additional or new value for customers, both of which are critical to achieving competitive advantage.[40]

Innovation and entrepreneurship have been common topics in this book. Chapter 1 defined entrepreneurship as the process through which individuals, groups or firms pursue opportunities to create new value.[41] It also described the elements of strategic thinking that encourage innovation and entrepreneurship in firms. Chapter 2 defined an innovation as an invention that can be replicated reliably and on a meaningful scale. The chapter also demonstrated how firms can use analysis of their broad and industry environments as springboards to higher levels of innovation. Chapter 3 argued that a firm's learning and knowledge resources are central to developing and maintaining competitive advantage. The strategic direction and strategy formulation chapters likewise contained many principles and ideas associated with innovation and entrepreneurship. Exhibit 7.4 contains a summary of some of the most important ideas associated with innovation and entrepreneurship that have been found throughout the book, as well as some new ones that relate specifically to strategy implementation.

As Exhibit 7.4 points out, firms with lots of innovation and entrepreneurship have a strategic direction, culture and leaders that encourage creativity, learning and risk taking. Information flows easily throughout these organizations, both in face-to-face interactions and through the firm's information system.[42] It is also helpful if the firm has slack financial resources, which are financial resources that are not completely committed to paying existing obligations. High liquidity reflected in higher-than-necessary cash balances and low debt levels allow a firm the flexibility it may need to pursue promising new ventures.[43] Furthermore, human resources systems reward behavior that leads to innovation and entrepreneurship. Also, systems are in place to facilitate the creation of new products, processes or services that create value. These systems include a simple approval process for obtaining firm resources to pursue innovative ideas.

Exhibit 7.4   Encouraging Innovation and Entrepreneurship

More Innovation and Entrepreneurship	Less Innovation and Entrepreneurship
A strategic direction (mission, vision) that incorporates a strong innovation and entrepreneurship theme	A strategic direction that puts top priority on financial returns or operating efficiency
A culture that encourages creative thinking and risk taking	A culture that rewards conformance and discourages novel ideas
Top management support of entrepreneurship through example and allocation of resources	Top management that encourages maintaining the status quo
Open communications among levels and areas within the firm, supported by an integrated information system	Closed door offices and disorganized and ineffective information system
Valuing the ideas of every employee	Attention given mostly to researchers or managers
Large rewards for internal entrepreneurs who create new value for the company	Harsh penalties for failures such as demotions, salary reductions or termination
Teamwork and collaboration	Authoritarian leadership
A flat management hierarchy with an emphasis on decentralized decision-making	A tall hierarchy with a lot of bureaucratic red tape and many approval levels
Organizational champions who can identify a good idea and gather resources needed to turn it into reality	Approval process that makes it difficult to gather new resources
Focus on learning	Exclusive emphasis on measurable outcomes
Slack resources available to invest in entrepreneurship	Tight finances (high debt, few liquid assets)

Innovative firms learn from their own internal research and development processes, but they also learn from external stakeholders such as customers, suppliers and venture partners.[44] They can learn through communications and transactions with them, and they can pursue new collaborations with them. Collaborative innovation can be defined as "the pursuit of innovations across firm boundaries through the sharing of ideas, knowledge, expertise and opportunities."[45] Collaborations can help smaller firms acquire the resources they need to pursue opportunities. They also help larger firms overcome the challenges they face in exploring for new opportunities:

Vodafone grew into the largest telecom operator primarily on its own. However, with increasing rivalry, the company has changed its attitude. Says CEO Vittorio Colao, "We were a bit naïve thinking everything could be done in-house...the only way to create a fertile environment for innovation is to have open platforms and leverage them." The new philosophy is reflected in a Website called betavine, which allows people to create and test each other's mobile phone applications. The applications can be downloaded on any wireless network. Already users have developed applications that provide real-time train arrival and departure information in Germany and Britain.

Vodafone is looking to its affiliates and subsidiaries for innovation. M-Pesa, developed by a Kenyan company in which Vodafone has a 35% interest, allows people without bank accounts to transfer money through text messages. M-Pesa now has 5 million customers. Vodafone also made an investment in t+ Medical, a British firm that uses cell phones to transmit medical information between doctors and patients.[46]

KEY POINTS SUMMARY

In this chapter, we described the functional strategies and organization structures that are used in implementing strategies. We also discussed organizational culture and explained how a firm can foster innovation and entrepreneurship. The following major points were discussed:

1. Effective strategy implementation requires consistent functional strategies, a supportive organization structure, and a high-performance culture.

2. Strategies are implemented through the day-to-day decisions and actions of employees throughout the organization. Management's challenge is to create a pattern of integrated, coordinated decisions that meets the needs of stakeholders and fulfills the planned strategy of the organization.

3. Functional strategies are represented by the pattern of decisions made by employees in marketing, operations, research and development, human resources, finance, and information systems. Managers must ensure that decisions within each area are consistent with each other, with other functions, and with the stated strategies of the firm.

4. Enterprise resource planning (ERP) systems support a wide variety of functions, such as operations and supply chain management, finance and accounting, human resources, distribution, and customer relationship management from a shared data source.

5. Standard organization structures include functional, divisional, project matrix, or network. The functional structure encourages functional specialization. The divisional structure segments products and markets into smaller, more manageable subunits that may improve service to customers or economies of scale but result in resource duplication. The project matrix structure employs a dual-reporting relationship that is a combination of functional and divisional structures. The network structure is a very decentralized form that is particularly well suited to geographically dispersed offices, stores, or units which, except for some sharing of information and operating policies, operate independently.

6. The strategic business unit (SBU) structure groups related businesses to enhance sharing of information and coordination of activities among them.

7. Foreign subsidiaries play three primary roles in organizations: (1) local implementers that help meet local needs, (2) specialized contributors that play a unique role as a part of an interdependent network, and (3) subsidiaries with a global mandate due that are responsible for an entire global business.

8. An organization's culture and energy play an important role in support of strategy implementation.

9. Innovative firms have a strategic direction, culture and leaders that encourage creativity, learning and risk taking. They also have excellent communications systems, human resources systems that reward entrepreneurial behavior and systems in place to facilitate the creation of new products, processes or services that create value. Financial slack allows a firm the flexibility it may need to pursue promising new ventures.

REFERENCES

1   A. Lashinsky, "Mark Hurd's Moment," *Fortune* (March 16, 2009): 91–100; *Hewlett-Packard 2008 Annual Report*: 3.

2   L.G. Hrebiniak and W. F. Joyce, *Implementing Strategy* (New York: Macmillan, 1984).

3   "Customer Service Champs," *Business Week* (March 2, 2009): 32–33.

4   J. Schienberg, "JetBlue, Continental Tops in Airline Satisfaction," *CNN Money.com*, http://money.cnn.com/2006/06/29/news/companies/airlines/index.htm?cnn=yes (July 28, 2006).

5   R. Hayes and S. Wheelwright, *Restoring Our Competitive Edge: Competing Through Manufacturing* (New York: John Wiley and Sons, 1984).

6   W. Chang, "A Typology of Co-branding Strategy: Position and Classification," *Journal of American Academy of Business* 12 (2008): 220–226.

7   Hayes and Wheelwright, *Restoring Our Competitive Edge*: 30.

8   G. Pallavi, "Going Organic: The Profits and Pitfalls: Organic Foods are Increasingly Popular and Command Premium Prices," *Business Week Online*, http://find.galegroup.com/itx/infomark.do?&contentSet=IAC-Documents&type=retrieve&tabID=T003&prodId=ITOF&docId=A146225033&source=gale&srcprod=ITOF&userGroupName=clemson_itweb&version (May 25, 2006).

9   B. Morris, "The Accidental CEO: She Was Never Groomed to Be the Boss, But Anne Mulcahy is Bringing Xerox Back from the Dead," *Fortune* (June 23, 2003): 58–59.

10   O. Kharif, "Selling Sound: Bose Knows," *Business Week Online*, http://find.galegroup.com/itx/infomark.do?&contentSet=IAC-Documents&type=retrieve&tabID=T003&prodId=ITOF&docId=A145796533&source=gale&srcprod=ITOF&userGroupName=clemson_itweb&version (May 15, 2006).

11   "Summary Financials," http://www.nucor.com/indexinner.aspx?finpage=summaryfinancials, (May 6, 2009).

12   N. Byrnes, "The Art of Motivation," *Business Week* (May 1, 2005): 57.

13   C. Fisher, "Current and Recurrent Challenges in HRM," *Journal of Management* 15 (1989): 157–180.

14   C. Fisher, "Current and Recurrent Challenges in HRM."

15   L.R. Gomez-Mejia and T. Welbourne, "Compensation Strategies in a Global Context," *Human Resource Planning* 14(1) (1991): 29–41.

16   R.H. Hayes, S.C. Wheelwright and K.B. Clark, *Dynamic Manufacturing* (New York: The Free Press, 1988): 61.

17   D.A. Bosse, R.A. Phillips and J.S. Harrison. "Stakeholders, Reciprocity and Firm Performance," *Strategic Management Journal* 30 (2009): 447–456.

18   M. Osheroff, "SOX as Opportunity," *Strategic Finance* (April, 2006): 19–20.

19   C. Dade, "Moving Ahead: How UPS Went From Low-Tech to an IT Power–and Where It's Headed Next," *Wall Street Journal* (July 24, 2006), R4.

20   C. St. John, A. Cannon and R. Pouder, "Change Drivers in the New Millennium: Implications for Manufacturing Strategy Research," *Journal of Operations Management* 19 (2001): 143–160.

21   S. Chou and Y. Chang, "The Implementation Factors that Influence the ERP Benefits," *Decision Support Systems* 46 (2008): 149–157; E.W.T. Ngai, C.C.H. Law and F.K.T. Wat, "Examining the Critical Success Factors in the Adoption of Enterprise Resource Planning," *Computers in Industry* 59 (2008): 548–564.

22   F.W. Gluck, S.D. Kaufman and A.S. Walleck, "Strategic Management for Competitive Advantage," *Harvard Business Review* (July-August, 1980): 154–161.

23   A.D. Chandler, *Strategy and Structure: Chapters in the History of the American Industrial Enterprise* (Cambridge, MA: The MIT Press, 1962).

24   B. Keats and H.M. O'Neill, "Organizational Structure: Looking through a Strategy Lens," in M.A. Hitt, R.E. Freeman and J.S. Harrison, eds., *The Blackwell Handbook of Strategic Management* (Oxford: Blackwell Publishers, Ltd., 2001): 520–542; P.R. Lawrence and J.W. Lorsch, *Organization and Environment* (Homewood, IL: Irwin, 1969): 23–39.

25   A.C. Hax and N.S. Majluf, *The Strategy Concept and Process: A Pragmatic Approach*, (Englewood Cliffs, NJ: Prentice Hall, 1991).

26 Hax and Majluf, *The Strategy Concept and Process.*

27 Keats and O'Neil, "Organizational Structure."

28 J. Galbraith and R. Kazanjian, *Strategy Implementation: Structure, Systems, and Processes* (St. Paul, MN: West Publishing Company, 1986).

29 R.C. Ford and W.A. Randolph, "Cross-Functional Structures: A Review and Integration of Matrix Organization and Project Management," *Journal of Management* 18 (1992): 267–294.

30 J.B. Quinn, *Intelligent Enterprise* (New York: The Free Press, 1992).

31 "Company Structure," http://www.jnj.com/connect/about-jnj/company-structure/?flash=true (May 7, 2009).

32 "Management Discussion and Analysis," *Johnson & Johnson 2005 Annual Report*, http://www.jnj.com/2005AnnualReport/financials/discussion/index.htm (July 15, 2006).

33 M.A. Schilling and H.K. Steensma, "The Use of Modular Organizational Forms: An Industry-Level Analysis," *Academy of Management Journal* 44 (2001): 1149–1168.

34 N. Nohria and S. Ghoshal, *The Differentiated Network* (San Francisco: Jossey-Bass, 1997).

35 J.M. Birkinshaw and A.J. Morrison, "Configurations of Strategy and Structure in Subsidiaries of Multinational Corporations," *Journal of International Business Studies* 26 (1995): 729–754.

36 Some examples in this area include: J.W. Dean, Jr., P. Brandes and R. Dharwadkar, "Organization Cynicism," *Academy of Management Review* 23 (1998): 341–352; R. Cross, W. Baker and A. Parker, "What Creates Energy in Organizations," *MIT Sloan Management Review* 44 (Summer, 2003): 51–56.

37 H. Bruch and S. Ghoshal, "Unleashing Organizational Energy," *MIT Sloan Management Review* 44 (Fall, 2003): 45–51.

38 All of the quotations come from N. Byrnes, "The Art of Motivation," *Business Week* (May 1, 2005): 57.

39 K. Foss and N.J. Foss, "Understanding Opportunity Discovery and Sustainable Advantage," *Strategic Entrepreneurship Journal* 2 (2008): 191–207; R.D. Ireland, M.A. Hitt, and D.G. Sirmon, "A Model of Strategic Entrepreneurship: The Construct and its Dimensions," *Journal of Management* 29 (2003): 963–989.

40 R. Amit, C. Lucier, M.A. Hitt and R.D. Nixon, "Strategies for the Entrepreneurial Millennium," in M.A. Hitt, R. Amit, C. Lucier and R. Nixon, eds., *Creating Value: Winners in the New Business Environment* (Oxford, U.K.: Blackwell Publishers, 2002): 1–12.

41 J.S. Harrison, *Strategic Management of Resources and Relationships* (New York: John Wiley and Sons, 2003).

42 A. Sleptsov and J. Anand, "Exercising Entrepreneurial Opportunities: The Role of Information-Gathering and Information-Processing Capabilities of the Firm," *Strategic Entrepreneurship Journal* 2 (2008): 357–372.

43 J.P. O'Brien, "The Capital Structure Implications of Pursuing a Strategy of Innovation," *Strategic Management Journal* 24 (2003): 415–431.

44 J.S. Harrison, D.A. Bosse and R.A. Phillips, "Managing for Stakeholders, Stakeholder Utility Functions and Competitive Advantage," *Strategic Management Journal* (2010, forth coming).

45 D.J. Ketchen, R.D. Ireland and C.C. Snow, "Strategic Entrepreneurship, Collaborative Innovation, and Wealth Creation," *Strategic Entrepreneurship Journal* 1 (2007): 371.

46 K. Capell, "Vodafone: Embracing Open Source with Open Arms," *Business Week* (April 20, 2009): 52.

8

Strategic Control and Restructuring

U.S. Bank Regulation

Deregulation of the U.S. banking industry has had a significant effect on the way banks operate. The Interstate Banking and Branching Efficiency Act of 1994 eliminated restrictions on bank mergers across state lines. This move facilitated consolidation of the U.S. banking industry. In 1999 Congress passed legislation overturning a Depression-era law that prevented banks from engaging in Wall Street businesses like investment banking. The result of these and other legislative measures was a banking industry comprised of larger companies with a much broader mix of financial products and therefore a much greater influence on the financial sector as a whole.

Another significant trend in banking was beginning to take hold at the turn of the century. Government sponsored Fannie Mae (Federal National Mortgage Association) and Freddie Mac (Federal Home Loan Mortgage Corporation) had established standard procedures for writing mortgages, making them easier to buy and sell. Companies could make money by writing mortgage contracts with homebuyers and then selling them to other companies or to Fannie Mae or Freddie Mac. The more contracts written, the more money was made. During the early years of this century the emphasis on volume was accompanied by a reduction of restrictions on who could qualify for a mortgage. People with lower credit scores or low income levels relative to the size of their mortgages were qualifying to buy homes, resulting in an increase in what were called sub-prime mortgages. Furthermore, many lenders were offering buyers "teaser rates," temporary reductions in interest rates that made houses seem more affordable than they really were. As long as home values continued to rise, the risks were manageable because foreclosure would compensate lenders for most of their losses. Also, Fannie Mae and Freddie Mac continued to buy mortgages of increasingly poor quality.

Many of the sub-prime mortgages were combined into mortgage-backed securities, some of which were structured so that investors would incur significant losses if even a relatively small percentage of the mortgages failed. These investments were traded and sold not only in the United States but around the world. When the U.S. housing market began to drop in value and introductory interest rates expired, a high rate of foreclosures led to significant losses. Because of the interconnectedness of the national and global financial systems and the widespread ownership of mortgage-backed securities, many financial institutions were adversely affected in the United States and elsewhere. Lehman Brothers, with over $600 billion in assets, filed for bankruptcy. Banks became more risk averse, which made it even more difficult for companies to acquire needed capital. By 2009 the world was caught up in a severe economic downturn which was both influenced by and at least partially a result of problems in the banking industry.

Problems in the financial sector led to a reversal of the deregulation trend in the banking industry. As a start, the U.S. Government took steps to both inject the banking industry with needed capital and create rules regarding the way banks do business. The Federal Reserve conducted a "stress-test" of large banks at the height of the crisis, instructing seven of them to raise more capital to offset potential losses. More government involvement and regulation is on the way.[1]

The financial crisis had a great deal to do with control. As the government loosened its control over the banking industry, the banks themselves became responsible for more control of their own operations. Some might argue that the banks were not very good self-regulators. They took on risk levels that, in retrospect, were far too high by creating, trading and holding large numbers of high-risk assets. Of course, government-backed Fannie Mae and Freddie Mac facilitated these actions. Now the government is tightening its control again as a direct response to the financial crisis. The crisis has had far reaching financial implications across all sectors of the global economy. One noticeable outcome is an increase in corporate restructurings in many industries.

Strategic control and restructuring are the central topics of this chapter. In the first half, we will address the development of strategic control systems, which warn managers when performance is off target or when upcoming trends will affect organizational performance. In the second half, we will discuss restructuring methods. Restructuring is used to reorient an organization that has either slipped out of control or must realign itself with environmental trends. We will also discuss how to deal with economic cycles.

STRATEGIC CONTROL SYSTEMS

From the perspective of top executives, a **strategic control system** is "a system to support managers in assessing the relevance of the organization's strategy to its progress in the accomplishment of its goals, and when discrepancies exist, to support areas needing attention."[2] Some existing control systems are based almost exclusively on accounting measures such as return on investment (ROI).[3] Since financial reporting requirements include figures for income, assets and sales, managers can easily calculate ROI or related measures from existing data. In some organizations they are considered as the only important measure of success.

Unfortunately, according to some control experts, accounting-based measures are "too late, too aggregated, and too distorted to be relevant for managers' planning and control decisions."[4] Lateness refers to the long lag times between the organizational transactions themselves and the dates financial reports come out. For example, some companies don't know they are in trouble until so much time has passed that the problem has become very large. The aggregation problem simply means that accounting measures do not contain the detail that is necessary to make meaningful improvements to specific organizational processes. Finally, by relying too heavily on accounting information only, managers can develop a distorted view of organizational performance.[5] Distortion is a particular problem when managers do not understand the effects of the policies that determine the way inventories, plants and equipment are valued and the way overhead costs are allocated to various departments and divisions.

In addition, accounting-based financial measures can prompt managers to behave in ways that are counterproductive over the long run. For example, financial measures such as ROI, if given too much emphasis in the short run, discourage investments in long-term research and development projects because expenses must be paid out immediately while benefits may not accrue until many financial periods later.[6] Also, managers may shut down lines or cancel services that appear to be too costly, placing an emphasis on products and services that are most efficiently produced. These types of decisions are fine as long as customers don't prefer the more costly products and services. However, the end result is often that the overproduced "efficient" goods and services have to be sold at a discount to stimulate customer interest. Consequently, profit margins are eroded and the organization would have been better off keeping the lines or services that were dropped.

Although managers may have difficulty drawing meaningful interpretations from accounting data, shareholders are even more disadvantaged. In 2002, the U.S. Congress passed the Sarbanes-Oxley Act (SOX) which, among other things, requires management to ensure that internal controls are used to make financial statements comparable to other similar companies in the United States. Some executives and accountants are concerned that the reporting requirements of SOX are an overreaction to the wrongdoings of a handful of companies and are suppressing the growth of small businesses, particularly those that would consider transitioning from a private entity to a public company through an Initial Public Offering (IPO).[7] Others argue that SOX is laying the foundation for "continuous improvement to meet the needs of a changing business environment."[8] Since foreign branches of U.S. firms operating in other nations and foreign subsidiaries operating in the United States must comply, the new standards are influencing reporting requirements worldwide. Some foreign firms are taking advantage of SOX compliance to show investors that their financial statements are comparable to similar firms in the United States.

While traditional accounting-based controls do not necessarily need to be eliminated, they should be balanced with other types of controls. It is increasingly common for Chief Financial Officers to be looked to for more than just financial controls. They may be expected to oversee other types of controls and auditing processes, including those related to operations and risk assessment.[9] Some organizations choose to perform periodic operations audits to ensure that managers and employees are following organization procedures and policies. Although these audits are conducted by internal groups, they can be quite effective in surfacing problems. For example, a review of the United Nations' peace-keeping activities conducted by the internal investigative arm uncovered evidence of abuse of procurement policies and a general failure to adhere to the internal controls of the organization.[10]

With advancements in information systems and real-time data collection processes, more companies are employing what can be described as "bottom-up" controls. These types of control systems collect information as close to the customer as possible and rely on operating level employees to make decisions and take actions to correct problems. For these types of systems to work, feedback from customers must be available to members of the work force so that they can make the adjustments that are required for continuous improvement to organizational activities. Bottom-up approaches are, by their nature, flexible and adaptable to the peculiarities of particular systems. The extreme case of bottom-up control is a situation in which customers actually control the activities of the companies they are buying from. For example, Ito-Yokado Co., a company that manages 7-Eleven stores in Japan, controls the product mix, the manufacturing schedule and the delivery of its most important supplies. This process eliminates several wholesale levels. Wal-Mart has similar practices with many of its suppliers. According to the late Peter Drucker, a management scholar, these trends are a result of the availability of better information, "Now that we have real-time information on what goes on in the marketplace, decisions will increasingly be based on what goes on where the ultimate customers, whether housewives or hospitals, take *buying* action."[11]

A comprehensive strategic control model is displayed in Exhibit 8.1. It illustrates three different types of control: feedback, concurrent, and feedforward. **Feedback control** provides managers with information concerning outcomes from organizational activities. **Concurrent control** provides managers with real-time information about processes and activities, so that deviations from plan can be

Exhibit 8.1   The Strategic Control Process

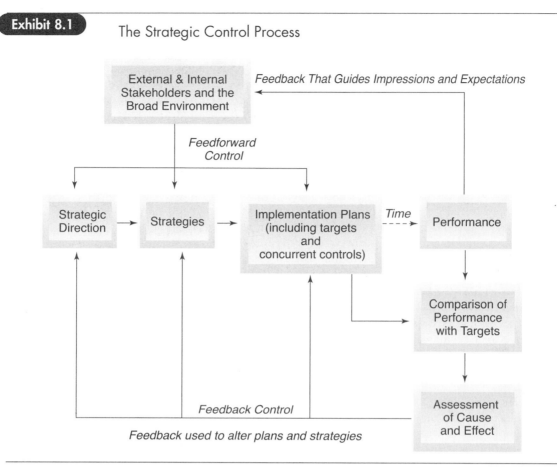

identified before they can affect organizational results. It also includes behavioral controls such as bureaucratic systems and socialization processes. **Feedforward control** helps managers anticipate changes in the external and internal environments, based on analysis of inputs from stakeholders and the broad environment. We will now describe several types of feedback, feedforward, and concurrent control methods and some of their uses.

Feedback Controls

Exhibit 8.1 demonstrates that during the implementation stage of the strategic management process, managers should establish targets (e.g., specific objectives or goals) for areas that are critical to the success of a strategy and the attainment of organizational goals. A time frame for measuring performance is also established. When the appropriate amount of time has elapsed, performance is measured and compared against the targets that were established. If performance is on track with targets, then managers have learned that their expectations concerning performance for that factor are possible, given current organizational and environmental conditions. However, if performance is significantly higher or lower than the established targets, then managers should assess cause and effect in an effort to learn why.

Feedback control systems perform several important functions in organizations.[12] First, creating specific objectives or targets ensures that managers at various levels and areas in the organization understand the plans and strategies that guide organizational decisions. Second, feedback control systems motivate managers to pursue organizational interests as opposed to purely personal interests, because they know they will be held accountable for the results of their actions. Finally, feedback control systems help managers decide when and how to intervene in organizational processes by identifying areas requiring further attention. Exhibit 8.2 provides a description of some common types of feedback controls.

Types of Feedback Controls

Exhibit 8.2

1. **Budgets:** The targets in a budget are the revenue and expense accounts, and managers and employees are held responsible for variations that are greater than established tolerances. Sometimes tolerances are not stated, but are implied or are understood due to past budgeting processes. Budgets may also be used to evaluate the performance of managers; however, this procedure can be problematic because it may discourage investments in training, R&D, or new capital equipment due to their short-term impact on expense accounts. If a budget is used to evaluate managerial performance, organizations should consider adding back these types of investments before evaluation. Another alternative is to create separate accounts for longer-term investment programs that are independent of the rest of the budget.

2. **Ratio analysis:** Financial ratios such as ROI or a current ratio are measured against targets that are established on the basis of past performance or in comparison with competing firms. Although overdependence on this type of control can be dangerous to the long-term performance of firms, in some situations ratio analysis provides good control information. For example, a financial ratio such as the current ratio is important to managing working capital, and debt-to-equity ratio can tell an organization whether it is assuming too much financial risk.

   Sometimes corporate-level managers use ratios such as ROI to evaluate the performance of managers of individual business units. In those cases, top managers should consider adding back long-term investments before calculating ROI to discourage a short-term orientation in decision making. In related diversified firms, ROI-based rewards systems (financial controls) may be inappropriate because they encourage competition among business units instead of the cooperation that is necessary to achieve synergy. Also, because the operations of the various business units should be highly interconnected, it is hard to determine which unit is really most responsible for success. Therefore, in the case of a related diversified firm, ROI is probably an ineffective control measure as it relates to the rewards system.

   However, in an unrelated diversified firm, financial performance ratios may be appropriate for determining the performance of business unit managers. In this situation, organizational managers should only be held accountable for their own financial performance because linkages with other firms in the portfolio are uncommon. Consequently, ROI (after adjustments) may be an appropriate gauge of the performance of business unit managers in unrelated diversified organizations.

3. **Audits:** An audit measures firm conduct and outcomes against established guidelines. Financial audits control accuracy within accounting systems, based on generally accepted accounting principles (GAAP). Social audits control ethical behavior, based on criteria that are established either totally in-house or in conjunction with activist groups, regulatory agencies, or editors of magazines that compile this sort of information (e.g., Business and Society Review). Customer surveys may also be used to generate feedback for control as part of a customer service audit.

4. **Goals and objectives:** Goals and objectives provide performance targets for individuals, departments, and divisions. Specific operating goals are established to bring the concepts found in the mission statement to life—to a level that managers and employees can influence and control. One of the keys to effective goal setting is that the goals must be well integrated from level to level.

Exhibit 8.3   Establishing a Feedback Control System

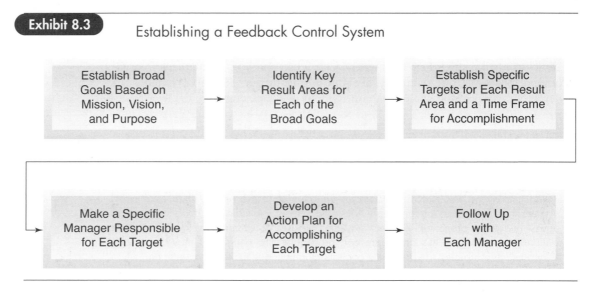

As we mentioned in earlier chapters, the strategies an organization pursues should be directed toward fulfilling the strategic direction of the organization. Effective feedback controls are one way to help ensure that the strategies are indeed moving the organization in an appropriate direction. Exhibit 8.3 contains the steps associated with establishing an effective feedback control system. These steps will now be described in detail.[13]

Establishment of Broad Goals. The major elements of strategic direction that drive an effective feedback control process are the vision, mission and purpose. As described in earlier chapters, a vision articulates where an organization is heading or, more appropriately, where it should be heading. The mission contains a definition of the business and is therefore useful in controlling the scope of an organization's activities. For example, an organization might determine that it is too broadly diversified or not diversified enough to enhance financial performance. The purpose helps articulate precisely what an organization intends to do for particular stakeholders, such as customers, employees, shareholders or the community. Taken together, these elements of strategic direction provide a powerful tool for controlling an organization's processes.

In essence, the key question is, "If we achieve our vision, mission and purpose, who will be affected and how will they be affected?" The answers to this question determine the broad goals of the organization upon which other parts of the feedback control system will be based. For example, a broad goal may be to provide high levels of customer satisfaction. Another goal could be to achieve high returns for shareholders. High employee satisfaction may be a goal for some organizations, as well as a partnering attitude with respect to the community. What is important at this stage is that the broad goals are reflective of the strategic direction of the organization.

Identification of Key Result Areas. The next step in the control process is to identify the areas of the organization that are key to accomplishing the broad goals that were set. For example, an organization may determine that to achieve broad customer goals such as satisfaction, safety, and loyalty emphasis must be placed on R&D, manufacturing, customer service and marketing.

Accomplishment of shareholder goals may involve financial functions, marketing, R&D, and establishment of the appropriate level of diversification.

Establishment of Specific Targets and Time Frames. This phase of the control process identifies precisely what targets must be obtained in each key result area so that the broad goals will be obtained. Unlike the broad goals, these objectives or targets provide specific guidance concerning desired outcomes. The characteristics of effective targets or objectives are listed in Exhibit 8.4.

Assignment of Responsibility. If done correctly, the control process will result in many targets covering a wide range of organizational activities. The only way that anything will actually get done is if responsibility for these targets is assigned to specific managers who have responsibility for the various departments and activities within an organization. Assuming that the establishment of targets was a participative process, the managers to whom responsibility will ultimately be assigned were probably present when the targets were set.

Development of an Action Plan. The next step in establishing a feedback control system is for each manager who was assigned a target to develop a plan of action. The plan consists of the steps that each manager or his/her subordinates

---

Characteristics of Effective Objectives or Targets   **Exhibit 8.4**

1. **They are high enough to be motivating.** If goals are set too low, employees will quickly achieve them and then spend too much time pursuing their own interests on company time.

2. **They are realistic.** If employees believe that goals are too high, they will become discouraged, which will reduce their motivation.

3. **They are specific.** Goals should be established for specific areas or even areas within areas. In other words, broad goals should be divided into smaller goals, which become the responsibility of specific departments and operating units.

4. **They are measurable.** While broad goals are more or less a permanent statement of organizational intent, goals can actually be obtained. Once they are achieved (or not achieved), it is the responsibility of management to reestablish, alter, or discard them. A goal such as, "The organization will be innovative," is not measurable. A better goal would be, "The organization will patent five new products in the next fiscal year."

5. **They are understood by all affected managers and employees.** If employees do not understand a goal, it is as if they never heard it. Effective communication of goals is essential to their attainment.

6. **They are set through participative processes.** If managers and employees who are affected by the goals participate in their creation, they will be more committed to them.

7. **Feedback on performance is a part of the process.** When goals are set and then forgotten, organizational members soon learn that they have no meaning.

8. **Finally, they cover a specific time frame.** Time periods are an essential factor in all good strategic planning.

Sources: G.P. Latham and E.A. Locke, "Goal Setting—A Motivational Technique That Works," *Organizational Dynamics* (Autumn 1979): 68–80; M.D. Richards, *Setting Strategic Goals and Objectives*, 2nd Ed. (West Publishing St. Paul, 1986); M.E. Tubbs, "Goal Setting: A Meta-Analytic Examination of Empirical Evidence," *Journal of Applied Psychology* 3 (1986): 474–475.

must take if the target is to be accomplished by the date specified. This provides a high level of accountability and specifically demonstrates the level of interdependency among units. For example, a large business unit within Lockheed Martin developed a six-month action plan that was approximately 40 oversized pages in length. The targets for each of the managers were contained in the plan, along with the schedule for completion. For other firms, the action plan might be developed for a shorter time interval and consist of just a few succinct pages.

Accountability and Review. The final step in establishing a feedback control system is to close the loop. To ensure that objectives and actions are proceeding as planned, with all interdependencies accounted for, there must be regular oversight and review. In some industries, the review process takes place on a quarterly or annual basis–and involves a combination of written reporting and formal presentation to the management team. In industries that are very fast paced, management may require weekly or monthly updates to ensure progress toward the objectives.

If actions and outcomes are not proceeding as planned, management must determine why and what action should be taken to get back on course. Management may determine, for example, that additional resources are needed, the schedule is too aggressive, or the underlying assumptions that were used to frame the action plan have changed. If management determines that the assumptions have changed, a significant adjustment in the action plan may be required. This is a very common occurrence when a firm is making plans to launch a new product, move into a new market, or open a new facility. Actions of competitors, changes in interest rates, and construction delays are just a few examples of the kinds of uncertainties that can provoke a repositioning of objectives and actions plans.

Concurrent Controls

As demonstrated in Exhibit 8.1, planning for concurrent controls occurs as a part of the implementation process. Concurrent controls are very similar to feedback controls, except that the time horizon is shortened to "real time." For example, the warning systems that are built into navigational equipment on an aircraft tell the pilot immediately if the aircraft has fallen below an acceptable altitude. An aggregate report at the end of the flight telling the pilot how many times the aircraft fell below acceptable standards would not help the pilot manage safety concerns in flight. Aggregate feedback information of that type might be important for designing new navigational systems, but it would not be useful for the pilot during the flight. Within a business environment, real-time feedback is also useful in some instances, but would be a disadvantage in others. Real-time financial feedback, for example, would make managing a business much like operating on the floor of the stock market—frenetic. On the other hand, real-time controls in service delivery environments and in production environments can be very useful.

Some of the most common types of concurrent controls are those associated with production and service processes and with quality standards. Statistical process control involves setting performance standards for specific work activities. The employees performing the activities monitor their own performance and the "outputs" of their efforts. If their work is out of specification, they fix it before handing it off to someone else, as when an automotive worker "stops the line" to prevent a defective automobile from continuing to the next workstation. In those cases, real-time controls work to encourage autonomy and improve quality and efficiency. Other kinds of concurrent controls are those associated with inventory levels and order taking. For example, Amazon.com and Buy.com have real-time inventory systems that allow them to know when stock is low for a particular item so that a new order can be sent to their suppliers as soon as needed. They also use real-time inventory controls to give customers specific information about what items will be shipped, on what day, and when the customer will receive them.

Another category of concurrent controls is associated with control of behavior. Within an organization, managers must depend on employees to perform their duties properly, even when management is not around. Behavioral controls work to encourage employees to comply with organizational norms and procedures. They are "real time" in that they influence employees as their jobs are being performed. Exhibit 8.5 describes two types of behavioral controls.

Feedforward Controls

As we mentioned at the beginning of this chapter, feedforward control systems help managers track and predict changes that occur in their external and internal environments, based on the analysis of inputs from stakeholders and the broad environment (see Exhibit 8.1). They are, in essence, monitoring systems, and in larger firms they typically are managed through the organization's information systems. They might also be called surveillance systems or tracking systems. Some of these systems are comprehensive, covering the entire spectrum of internal and external trends, while others are more focused on particular stakeholders, such as a system that tracks purchasing trends. Good feedforward control systems are important because rapid changes in the social, economic, technological and political environments may require changes to strategies and/or the acquisition of additional organizational resources.[14] Even in stable environments, where environmental changes play a minor role (i.e., production of commodities), feedforward control systems are essential to learning processes that allow organizations to move toward the accomplishment of their goals.

A firm's strategies are established based on premises about the organization and its external environment, including the interests of stakeholders. These premises are assumptions about what will happen in the future. For example, an

---

Behavioral Controls

Exhibit 8.5

Bureaucratic controls and clan controls are two common types of behavioral controls.

Bureaucratic controls: *Rules, procedures, and policies that guide the behavior of organizational members.* Rules provide standards or outline a specific way of doing something, such as check approval. A policy is a more general guide to action, and it provides a framework for decisions that are made routinely. One of the ways McDonald's achieves such a high level of control over its business is by establishing rules and policies that guide the daily decisions and actions of employees. Unfortunately, many companies do not see everyday rules, procedures, and policies as "strategic." However, because bureaucratic controls guide the decisions and actions of employees, they are a major determinant of how well strategies are implemented.

Clan controls: *Socialization processes through which an individual comes to appreciate the values, abilities, and expected behaviors of an organization.* Socialization also makes organizational members more inclined to see things the same way, by espousing common beliefs and assumptions that, in turn, shape their perceptions. Socialization processes for existing employees take the form of intensive training, mentoring relationships and role models, and formal organizational communications including the vision, mission, and values statements.

organization may plan to expand its manufacturing facilities over a period of five years based on the assumption that interest rates will remain approximately the same. If interest rates change dramatically, it could make the planned expansion unprofitable. Also, as discussed in earlier chapters, stakeholder needs and expectations can change—customers may want all transactions conducted over the Internet, suppliers may experience capacity shortages, communities may change their tax and zoning regulations—which will lead managers to evaluate the impact on existing strategies.

These types of situations demonstrate the need for premise control. **Premise control,** a type of feedforward control, involves periodically assessing the assumptions, or premises, that underlie strategic choices. The periodic reevaluation of assumptions is a foundation concept in the iterative, on-going assessment of the environment in strategic management. Premise control helps organizations avoid situations in which their established strategies and goals are no longer appropriate.

The learning processes associated with *both* feedforward and feedback controls form the basis for changes to strategic direction, strategies, and implementation plans. In addition to the traditional measuring and monitoring functions, a study found that top managers use control systems to overcome resistance to change, communicate new strategic agendas, ensure continuing attention to new strategic initiatives, formalize beliefs, set boundaries on acceptable strategic behavior, and motivate discussion and debate about strategic uncertainties.[15] Control systems become one of the "tools of strategy implementation."[16]

So far this chapter has described types of control methods and issues surrounding them. Numerous control methods at multiple levels are necessary to keep an organization and its component parts headed in the right directions. However, they should be integrated in such a way that information can be shared. In other words, information from all parts of the organization should be accessible when and where it is needed to improve organizational processes. The next section discusses the development of comprehensive strategic control systems within organizations.

Comprehensive Strategic Control Systems

Rapidly advancing information technologies have made continuous improvements through control systems possible. Information systems can track large volumes of transactions, operating results, and external data efficiently, providing appropriate reports in a timely fashion to the right people. Enterprise resource planning (ERP) systems, described in the last chapter, are helpful in integrating information from multiple sources.[17] Comprehensive strategic control systems should include feedback, feedforward and concurrent controls. To enhance the quantity and quality of organizational learning, these control systems should have the following characteristics:

1. Information generated by the control systems should be an important and recurring item to be addressed by the highest levels of management.
2. The control process should also be given frequent and regular attention from operating managers at all levels of the organization.
3. Data from the system should be interpreted and discussed in face-to-face meetings among superiors and subordinates.
4. The success of the control process relies on the continual challenge and debate of underlying data, assumptions, and strategies.[18]

For multinational firms, issues to consider when planning strategic control systems involve one additional dimension: national culture. In order to ensure effectiveness, differences in national culture should be considered when designing control systems.[19] Research by Hofstede has shown that national cultures can be distinguished using five dimensions:

1. *Power Distance:* the degree to which members of the society accept and expect uneven power distribution in society and are accepting of authority.
2. *Individualism/Collectivism:* the degree to which the focus of society is on individuals or the group.
3. *Masculine/Feminine:* the degree to which the society draws strong distinctions between gender roles.
4. *Uncertainty Avoidance:* the degree to which members of society are tolerant of uncertainty and ambiguity.
5. *Confucian Dynamics:* the degree to which decisions are focused on the long term versus the short term.[20]

Generally, for strategic control systems to be effective, they should reflect the culture of the nation within which they are applied. For global firms, that may mean designing different control metrics for different nations or regions of the world. Some implications of the national culture dimensions for control systems are shown in Exhibit 8.6.

A comprehensive strategic control system should provide feedback for ongoing, iterative adjustments in direction, resource development and management, and management priorities. When performance suffers, a strategic control system may provide early warnings of performance problems, but it cannot eliminate them completely. Unfortunately some managers find, through their control systems or too late, that their organization's performance does not fit with their

National Culture and Control Systems

Exhibit 8.6

National Culture Dimension	Example Nations	Implications for Control Systems
(1) Power Distance (High)	U.S., UK, Sweden, Norway	Focus on outcomes of decisions
Power Distance (Low)	Asian, Central American, South American nations	Focus on adherence to plan
(2) Individualism	U.S., Australia, Canada, UK	Individual rewards
Collectivism	Colombia, Pakistan, Portugal	Team-based rewards
(3) Masculine	U.S., Japan, Austria, UK	Achievement, heroism, and material success are valued
Feminine	Denmark, Sweden, Norway	Relationships and quality of life are valued
(4) Uncertainty Avoidance	Greece, Portugal	Society expects control over management risk taking
Uncertainty Tolerance	U.S., Denmark, Singapore	Less rule based
(5) Long-term Orientation	Hong Kong, South Korea	Focus on sales growth and customer satisfaction
Short-term Orientation		Focus on profits

Source: J.C. Lere and K. Portz, "Management Control Systems in a Global Economy," *The CPA Journal* 75 (9) (September 2005): 62–64.

expectations, or the expectations of their interested stakeholders. To correct an organization that has deviated sharply off course, managers must initiate some sort of restructuring. Restructuring is the topic of the next section.

STRATEGIC RESTRUCTURING

It is well known that no strategy or organization design works indefinitely. If a firm is successful with its strategies, that success alone will create a need for change, because the increases in sales volume and organization size will demand different management methods and organizational structures. What is just as typical, however, is for customers, competitors, and technologies to interact to create a changing business environment, which will require that the organization make changes also. Unless a firm is the permanent sole participant in a no-growth industry (which is extremely unlikely), change is constant and should be assumed. The iterative, on-going strategic management process described in this book, with its continuous scanning of the internal and external environments and its reevaluation of strategies and implementation methods, is all about the management of change over time. For example, global pharmaceutical giant Bristol Myers Squibb embarked on a significant multi-year restructuring plan a few years ago to reduce costs system-wide. Over five years, they reduced the number of sales people in the United States and Europe by 30%, outsourced their information technology division, and reorganized R&D.[21]

Researchers have observed that as organizations evolve over time they tend to move through a period of convergence, followed by a period of reorientation or radical adjustment, and then convergence again. This cycle repeats over time.[22] During the convergence stage, the organization makes minor adaptive changes to strategies, but follows a consistent approach. The structure and systems are stable, and performance, for the most part, is acceptable.

For many organizations, successes reinforce a certain way of doing business. During the convergence stage, managers develop certain mental models, or mindsets, about how the industry and the organization work. **Mental models** represent the knowledge managers have about the industry and the organization, and how specific actions relate to desired outcomes.[23] They reflect what managers understand to be true about the organization and its industry. Mental models are derived from experiences, with past successes and failures contributing to the overall picture. As long as the premises that underlie these mental models do not change, the mental models represent useful experience that should be brought to bear on decisions. When premises do change, however, the established mental models may prevent the executives, managers, and employees from recognizing the need for change at all.

A few well-known examples illustrate this point. In the automobile industry, the movie and music production industries, film/camera industry, and in many retailing segments, established management mental models have contributed to a sluggish response to industry change.[24] In these industries, the established competitors achieved extraordinary, sustained success over many decades. They developed effective strategies, useful structures, and strong cultures. However, when the assumptions underlying their industries changed, the existing competitors were slow to recognize what was happening. In the U.S. automotive industry many years ago, the major companies failed to recognize the demographic, economic, and social trends driving demand for fuel-efficient economy cars. Music and movie production companies were caught off-guard by both the role of digital download services and the stay-at-home entertainment trend. In retailing, bricks and mortar distributors and retailers were shocked by the success of dot-com entrants, particularly in the higher-value niche market segments.

Not only were these companies slow to recognize the need for change, they were also slow to make changes once the need was recognized. Their mental models were no longer congruent with the requirements for success in their industries. Reinforced by established organizational structures, resources, and processes, their mental models led to high levels of inertia, which caused reluctance to change. Even when managers recognized the need for change, they often believed they were constrained in their ability to respond.

A period of convergence can continue indefinitely, as long as the industry conditions and organization characteristics are not significantly out of alignment.[25] However, when gradual drift results in a substantial misalignment or an environmental discontinuity does occur, the organization will be forced to reorient itself. Sometimes a crisis can help the firm make the changes it needs to make. Sony's CEO Sir Howard Stringer saw just such an opportunity in the economic crisis of 2008–2009: "When this crisis came along, for me it was a godsend, because I could reorganize the company without having to battle the forces of the status quo."[26]

Restructuring, transformation, renewal, and reorientation are all words that describe the same general phenomenon: a significant change in how business is conducted.[27] Restructuring typically involves a renewed emphasis on the things an organization does well, combined with a variety of tactics to revitalize the organization and strengthen its competitive position. Popular restructuring tactics include refocusing corporate assets on distinctive competencies, retrenchment, leveraged buyout, and changes to the organization's internal structure. In some extreme cases, a firm may be forced to consider reorganization under Chapter XI of the bankruptcy code. Organizations may use any one or a combination of these strategies in restructuring efforts.

Refocusing Corporate Assets

Refocusing activities generally are viewed favorably by external stakeholders such as the financial community.[28] Refocusing entails trimming businesses that are not consistent with the strategic direction of the organization. This type of refocusing is often called downscoping. **Downscoping** involves reducing diversification through selling off nonessential businesses that are not related to the organization's core competencies and capabilities.[29]

Researchers have discovered that most restructuring companies are moving in the direction of reducing their diversification as opposed to increasing it.[30] Furthermore, when new CEOs are hired into poorly performing companies, they are much more likely to divest a poor performing unit than CEOs who participated in the original decisions to invest in or acquire the unit.[31] A **divestiture** is a reverse acquisition. The businesses that should be divested during a restructuring include those that have little to do with the distinctive competencies of the organization.

One type of divestiture is a **sell-off**, in which a business unit is sold to another firm or, in the case of a leveraged buyout, to the business unit's managers.[32] For example, Perkin-Elmer sold its aerospace division to Eaton Corporation as part of a strategy to refocus its efforts on its Health Sciences and Photonics businesses, which are positioned in markets that serve genetic screening and medical imaging.[33] Also, Rockwell Automation divested its Reliance Electric motor business and Dodge

Mechanical Services, two units representing one-fifth of its revenues, as part of a plan to refocus from motors and gears to high-tech factory automation systems.[34]

Spin-offs are another form of divestiture. One form of spin-off gives current shareholders a proportional number of shares in the spun-off business. For instance, if a shareholder owns 100 shares of XYZ company and the company spins off business unit ABC, the shareholder would then own 100 shares of ABC company and 100 shares of XYZ company. The key advantage of a spin-off relative to other divestiture options is that shareholders still have the option of retaining ownership in the spun-off business. For example, Electrolux AB spun off Husqvarna AB, which makes lawn mowers and chain saws.[35] Research has shown that firms tend to select a spin-off or sell-off strategy for divestiture based on which strategy they have used in the past. Also, the experience firms obtain with a particular strategy can increase their subsequent performance.[36]

Initial public offerings also can be used to spin off a business. For example, eBay determined that its Skype Internet-phone business was not a good fit with its core operations. They could not find an offer attractive enough to sell off the business, so they initiated an IPO. John Donahoe, CEO of eBay said the IPO "will give Skype the focus and resources required to continue its growth and effectively compete."[37]

Retrenchment

Retrenchment is a turnaround strategy. It can involve such tactics as work force reductions, closing unprofitable plants, outsourcing unprofitable activities, implementation of tighter cost or quality controls, or new policies that emphasize quality or efficiency. For instance, the Chelyabinsk Forge-and-Press Plant in Russia is taking advantage of a recession to boost productivity. Andrey Gartung, CEO, cut staff from 4,400 to 3,500, ordered each department to cut costs by 15%, and asked workers to reduce waste wherever they find it, with prizes for those who do. Says Gartung, "The companies that will survive are the ones that are efficient."[38]

Work force reductions, or downsizing, are a very common feature in retrenchment strategies. Historically, many work force reductions have been targeted toward hourly workers, but today middle management layoffs are common. Evidence is mounting that "downsizing does not reduce expenses as much as desired, and that sometimes expenses may actually increase."[39] Certainly, severance packages are one reason for the increase. Also, many organizations cut muscle, as well as fat, through layoffs. A study of "white-collar" layoffs in the U.S. automobile industry found that most companies experienced problems such as a reduction in quality, a loss in productivity, decreased effectiveness, lost trust, increased conflict, and low morale.[40] Other studies have shown that the "surviving" employees experience feelings of guilt and fear which may hurt productivity or organizational loyalty.[41] It is not surprising, then, that the stock market often reacts unfavorably to announcements of major layoffs.[42] Research has shown that long-term financial performance is higher when downsizing is accompanied by a comprehensive redesign of the organizational structure, strategies, and processes, rather than just personnel reductions.[43]

Chapter XI Reorganization

An organization that is in serious financial trouble can voluntarily file for Chapter XI protection under the Federal Bankruptcy Code: "Chapter XI provides a proceeding for an organization to work out a plan or arrangement for solving its financial problems under the supervision of a federal court. It is intended primarily for debtors who feel they can solve their financial problems on their own if given sufficient time, and if relieved of some pressure."[44] Numerous Chapter XI reorganizations have occurred recently in the automotive, airline and banking industries. The newspaper business also has seen several reorganizations:

> The bloodied newspaper business keeps getting redder all over. On Feb. 21, Journal Register, owner of 20 daily newspapers including the *New Haven Register*, declared bankruptcy. The company was staggering under $692 million in debt, much of it taken on through the 2004 acquisition of four papers in economically depressed Michigan. Two days after Journal Register's filing, Philadelphia Media Holdings, which bought the *Philadelphia Inquirer* and *Philadelphia Daily News* from McClatchy in 2006, also filed for Chapter 11. And on Feb. 24, Hearst said it may shut down the *San Francisco Chronicle* if costs can't be cut or a buyer found.[45]

One of the major disadvantages of Chapter XI is that, after filing, all subsequent managerial decisions of substance must be approved by a court. Thus, managerial discretion and flexibility are reduced. In a study of firms that had voluntarily filed for Chapter XI protection, only a little over half of the firms were "nominally successful in reorganizing," and "two-thirds of those retained less than 50 percent of their assets on completion of the reorganization process."[46]

Leveraged Buyouts

Leveraged buyouts (LBOs) involve the private purchase of a business unit by managers, employees, unions or private investors. For example, Mexican broadcasting firm Grupo Televisa SA partnered with a group of U.S. private-equity investors to purchase a 25% stake in Spanish-language broadcaster Univision Communications Inc.[47] These types of deals are called "leveraged" because much of the money that is used to purchase the business unit is borrowed from financial intermediaries (often at higher-than-normal interest rates). Because of high leverage, LBOs are often accompanied by selling off assets to repay debt. Consequently, organizations typically become smaller and more focused after an LBO.

During the late 1970s and early 1980s, LBOs gained a reputation as a means of turning around failing divisions. For instance, Hart Ski, once a subsidiary of Beatrice, was revived through an LBO led by the son of one of its founders. Also, managers and the union joined forces to turn around American Safety Razor, a failing division of Philip Morris. These LBOs benefited many of these organizations' stakeholders, including employees and local communities.[48]

Nevertheless, some researchers have discovered that LBOs stifle innovation and research and development, similar to mergers and acquisitions.[49] Others have found that LBO firms have comparatively slower growth in sales and employees and that they tend to divest a larger proportion of both noncore and core businesses, compared to firms that remained public.[50] Also, some executives who initiate LBOs seem to receive an excessive return. For example, John Kluge made a $3 billion profit in two years through dismantling Metromedia following an LBO.[51] Consequently, some business people are starting to wonder if LBOs are really in the best interests of all stakeholders. Plant closings, relocations and work force reductions are all common results from LBOs. Not surprisingly, reports of failed LBOs are not uncommon. Successful LBOs require buying a company at the right price with the right financing, combined with outstanding management and fair treatment of stakeholders.[52]

Structural Reorganization

Organizational structure, which was discussed in detail in Chapter 7, can be a potent force in restructuring efforts. As organizations diversify, top managers have a more difficult time processing the vast amounts of diverse information that are needed to appropriately control each business. Their span of control is too large. Consequently, one common form of structural reorganization occurs when an organization that is functionally structured moves to a divisional structure. The end result is more managers with smaller spans of control and a greater capacity to understand each of their respective business areas. For example, following the acquisition of Chiron Corporation, Novartis initiated several changes in organizational structure to accommodate the many new activities. The company created a new vaccines and diagnostics business unit, which included the Novartis Vaccines group as well as activities of the Chiron acquisition that were focused on diagnostics. The portion of Chiron that was involved in biopharmaceuticals was integrated into the Novartis Pharmaceutical business unit and the early stage research group was merged with the Novartis Institute for Biomedical Research.[53]

Organizations frequently combine restructuring approaches. For instance, a company may use an LBO to downscope its businesses, thus emerging as a stronger, more focused firm. The General Motors restructuring combines Chapter XI protection with retrenchment and changes to organizational structure, including dividing the lowest performing and higher-performing manufacturing units into separate companies.[54] Also evident is very heavy government involvement during the entire process, including billions of dollars in "bailout" money.

> GM's bankruptcy caps a frenetic few months in which the Obama administration scrambled to salvage GM as well as Chrysler LLC, the country's first- and third-largest car makers, at a cost to taxpayers of over $62 billion. GM officials portrayed the bankruptcy—No. 2 in asset size among industrial concerns to WorldCom's filing in 2002—as an unprecedented opportunity to reverse decades of decline. GM said it would close 17 factories and parts centers and lop off 20,000 more jobs by the end of 2011 in Michigan, Indiana, Ohio and Tennessee.[55]

DEALING WITH ECONOMIC CYCLES

Economic cycles are a well-known phenomenon. Although government actions may influence the severity of economic downturns and the speed and size of the ensuing recoveries, it is unlikely that they will ever be eliminated completely. Forces of supply and demand, coupled with both anticipated trends and unanticipated shocks, such as wars, mean that there will be times when the economy is growing well and other times when it is growing slowly or shrinking.

During periods of rapid economic growth, consumer demand is increasing, which acts as an incentive to producers to increase their supply of goods and services. They also provide higher levels of employment and possibly higher wages to attract more workers. They buy more materials and supplies. More income for companies and their workers reinforces demand, and the cycle continues. During such periods, although some firms experience strategic failures, growing demand means that it is easier to achieve success. However, as economic growth slows, firms with weaker resource positions and less effective strategies, as well as firms in industries most affected by economic cycles, tend to experience market and financial stress. Most firms make adjustments to at least some aspects of their strategies during economic cycles.[56]

There is some question as to whether business cycles are predictable enough so that firms can plan for them. A research team at the University of California, Irvine, studied the strategies of nearly 200 companies going into and out of the 2001 recession. One of their conclusions was that "successfully managing the business cycle *does not necessarily depend on the ability to accurately forecast its movements at all*. Rather, all that is required in some instances is that one firm has a set of capabilities that allows it to respond more swiftly than its rivals to key business cycle turning points and movements."[57] These capabilities are referred to as a firm's **business cycle orientation**, and they include the following:

1. *Business Cycle Literacy:* Top management team members are outwardly focused on macroeconomic events and business cycle movements. They are also aware of how movements influence their own industry.
2. *Forecasting Resources*: The firm has sufficient resources to track economic indicators that are important to its industry.
3. *A Facilitative Organizational Structure*: The organizational structure facilitates the timely acquisition, processing and dissemination of important information and allows timely decision making.
4. *Business-cycle Sensitive Management Principles*: Guidelines for dealing with business cycles pertaining to marketing and pricing, production and inventory control, human resource management, risk management, capital expenditure programs, and timing of acquisitions and divestitures.
5. *Supportive Organizational Culture*: Employees at all levels of the organization are willing to accept the changes that are necessary as a result of dealing with the business cycle.[58]

In the automobile industry, Hyundai took advantage of the recession to gain market advantage:

> It is not just America's ailing carmakers that have been clobbered by the recession and the corresponding collapse in demand for new vehicles: every other car maker is suffering too. Even luxury car marques such as Mercedes-Benz, Lexus and BMW, which are usually less affected by economic downturns, have reported plunging sales. All of which makes the achievements of South Korea's Hyundai particularly remarkable. It has managed to increase its car sales in America ... and it has done so, in part, by moving into the luxury car market. The idea of a luxury Hyundai may sound like an oxymoron to many people, given the brand's low-cost image ... but Hyundai has benefited from consumers' desire to "trade down" in hard times.[59]

Of course, it also helps to have a strategic position that is attractive in a tight economic period. For instance, discount retailer Wal-Mart took advantage of the economic downturn of 2008–2009 and used its considerable operating and marketing expertise to increase its market share. Similarly, deep-discounter Dollar Tree experienced record sales.[60] Even Target, known for their "cheap chic" merchandise, did a good job of managing expenses and inventory levels, allowing the company to weather the recession fairly well.[61]

There is also some research evidence that firms are able to achieve higher returns from acquisitions during a downturn. This probably results from the relatively low prices of specific companies whose share prices are adversely affected by the downturn. Also, acquiring firms may discover that implementing restructuring strategies is relatively easier because people are less resistant to change. Retrenchments frequently follow acquisitions.[62]

Economic cycles are only one of the many managerial challenges that lie ahead. It is hard to predict with precision the kind of business environment the next generation of managers will face. However, judging from the recent past, it will almost certainly be associated with increasing global complexity and inter-connectedness, fueled by advancements in information management, communications and other technologies. In addition, successful firms are even more likely to depend on specialized, mobile and diverse labor pools, some of which are found in countries outside their home countries. As education levels, income levels, and access to capital grow around the world, new powerful competitors will continue to enter the global marketplace.

Increased globalization will come with increased scrutiny and interest in ensuring that corporations exhibit appropriate conduct, which may eventually result in more widely held global standards of social responsibility. As the banking industry example found at the beginning of this chapter demonstrated, governments are also more likely to increase their control of businesses through regulations and other means.

Managers will face challenges in several areas—retaining valuable employees, creating and preserving competitive advantage, holding back new entrants, serving increasingly demanding customers, choosing and timing technology investments at a time when change is so rapid. Also, major shocks associated with terrorism, new diseases and wars will create new threats as well as opportunities for those firms that are best able to deal with them. The challenges that managers will face are extraordinary—but never dull. It is a very exciting time to be in business. We hope the tools, theories and techniques found in this book will help you become an effective leader in this newly emerging century.

KEY POINTS SUMMARY

This chapter treated the important topics of strategic control and restructuring. The following are some of the key points that were discussed:

1. Strategic controls are systems to support managers in tracking progress toward organizational goals and ensuring that organizational processes and the behavior of organizational members are consistent with those goals.

2. Organizations should not rely exclusively on accounting-based, top-down controls because, according to some control experts, accounting-based measures are too late, too aggregated, and too distorted to be relevant for all of a manager's planning and control decisions. In addition, too much reliance on accounting-based financial measures can prompt short-sightedness among managers.

3. Feedback control provides managers with information concerning outcomes from organizational activities, which is then used as a basis for comparison with the targets that have been established.

4. Concurrent controls provide managers with real-time information for managing performance (e.g., process controls), or serve as a real-time source of influence over the behavior of employees (e.g., bureaucratic and clan controls).

5. Feedforward controls help managers anticipate changes in the external and internal environments, based on the analysis of inputs from internal and external stakeholders and the broad environment.

6. The learning processes associated with all types of control form the basis for changes to

strategic direction, strategies, and implementation plans.

7. As a result of performance problems and/or pressure from stakeholders, many firms are now restructuring. The restructuring techniques that were described in this chapter included refocusing assets, retrenchment, Chapter XI reorganization, leveraged buyouts and changes to organization structure. These methods can also be used in combination.

8. Most firms make adjustments to at least some aspects of their strategies during economic cycles. Successful management of business cycles is more likely for firms that have a strong business cycle orientation, which means that they have a high level of business cycle literacy, sufficient forecasting resources, a facilitative organizational structure, well-developed business-cycle-sensitive management principles, and a supportive organizational culture.

REFERENCES

1 D. Solomon, D. Enrich and D. Paletta, "Banks Need at Least $67 Billion in Capital," *Wall Street Journal* (May 7, 2009): A1, A2; D. Henry and M. Goldstein, "The Perils of Global Banking," *Business Week* (May 18, 2009): 38–43; C.W. Calomiris and P.J. Wallison, "Blame Fannie Mae and Congress for the Credit Mess," *Wall Street Journal* (September 23, 2008): A29; A. Zardkoohi and D.R. Fraser, "Geographical Deregulation and Competition in U.S. Banking Markets," *The Financial Review* 33: 85–98; Y. Brook, R. Hendershott and D. Lee, "The Gains from Takeover Deregulation: Evidence from the End of Interstate Banking Restrictions," *Journal of Finance* 53: 2185–2199; D. Solomon, D. Paletta, H.N. Moore and R. Sidel, "Bank Bailout Plan Revamped," *Wall Street Journal* (February 2, 2009): A1, A2.

2 P. Lorange, M.F. Scott Morton and S. Ghoshal, *Strategic Control* (St. Paul: West Publishing Company, 1986): 10.

3 J.F. Weston and E.F. Brigham, *Essentials of Managerial Finance*, 7th ed. (Hinsdale, IL: The Dryden Press, 1985): 154.

4 H.T. Johnson and R.S. Kaplan, *Relevance Lost* (Boston: Harvard Business School Press, 1987): 1.

5 D.E.W. Marginson, "Management Control Systems and Their Effects on Strategy Formation at Middle-Management Levels: Evidence from a U.K. Organization," *Strategic Management Journal* 23 (2002): 1019–1031.

6 R.E. Hoskisson and M.A. Hitt, "Strategic Control and Relative R&D Investment in Large Multiproduct Firm," *Strategic Management Journal* 6 (1988): 605–622.

7 L. Stephens and R.G. Schwartz, "The Chilling Effect of Sarbanes-Oxley: Myth or Reality?" *The CPA Journal* 76 (6) (2006): 14–19.

8 M. Osheroff, "SOX as Opportunity," *Strategic Finance* (April, 2006): 19–20.

9 R. Angel and H. Rampersad, "Improving People Performance: The CFO's New Frontier" *Financial Executive* 21 (8) (2005): 45–48; D.R. Campbell, M. Campbell and G.W. Adams, "Adding Significant Value with Internal Controls," *The CPA Journal* 76 (6) (2006): 20–25.

10 M. Turner, "UN Review Finds Procurement Abuse," *The Financial Times* (January 21, 2006): 1.

11 P.F. Drucker, "The Economy's Power Shift," *The Wall Street Journal* (September 24, 1992): A1.

12 M. Goold and J.J. Quinn, "The Paradox of Strategic Controls," *Strategic Management Journal* 11 (1990): 43–57.

13 This discussion and our model are most heavily influenced by the work of R.E. Freeman, *Strategic Management: A Stakeholder Approach* (Boston: Pittman, 1984) and R.S. Kaplan and D.P. Norton, "Putting the Balanced Scoreboard to Work," *Harvard Business Review* (September-October, 1993): 134–147.

14 Lorange, Scott Morton and Ghoshal, *Strategic Control*: 2–8.

15 R. Simons, "How New Top Managers Use Control Systems as Levers of Strategic Renewal," *Strategic Management Journal* 15 (1994): 169–189.

16 R. Simons, "Strategic Orientation and Management Attention to Control Systems," *Strategic Management Journal* 12 (1991): 49–62.

17 S. Chou and Y. Chang, "The Implementation Factors that Influence the ERP Benefits," *Decision Support Systems* 46 (2008): 149–157; E.W.T. Ngai, C.C. H. Law and F.K.T. Wat, "Examining the Critical Success Factors in the Adoption of Enterprise

Resource Planning," *Computers in Industry* 59 (2008): 548–564.

18   Simons, "Strategic Orientation": 50.

19   J.C. Lere and K. Portz, "Management Control Systems in a Global Economy," *The CPA Journal* 75 (9) (2005): 62–64.

20   G. Hofstede, *Culture's Consequences* (Beverly Hills, CA: Sage, 1980); G. Hofstede, "National Cultures in Four Dimensions," *International Studies of Management and Organization* 13 (1983): 46–74; G. Hofstede, *Cultures and Organizations: Software of the Mind* (New York: McGraw Hill, 1991).

21   D. McCormick, "Bristol Myers Squibb to Cut Costs by $500 Million," *Pharmaceutical Technology* 30 (2) (2006): 24.

22   C.J. Gersick, "Revolutionary Change Theories: A MultiLevel Exploration of the Punctuated Equilibrium Paradigm," *Academy of Management Review* 16 (1991): 10–37; M.I. Tushman and E. Romanelli, "Organizational Evolution: A Metamorphosis Model of Convergence and Reorientation," in E.E. Cummings and B.M Staw, eds., *Research in Organizational Behavior* (Greenwich, Conn: JAI Press, 1985): 171–222.

23   N.A. Wishart, J.J. Elan and D. Robey, "Redrawing the Portrait of a Learning Organization: Inside Knight-Ridder, Inc.," *Academy of Management Executive* (February, 1996): 7–20; J.P. Walsh, "Managerial and Organizational Cognition," *Organization Science* 6 (1995): 280–321.

24   A. Saxenian, *Culture and Competition in Silicon Valley and Route 128* (Cambridge, MA: Harvard University Press, 1994).

25   Gersick, "Revolutionary Change Theories"; Tushman and Romanelli, "Organizational Evolution."

26   "Sir Howard Stringer Believes He is Finally In a Position to Fix Sony," *The Economist* (March 7, 2009): 73.

27   Gersick, "Revolutionary Change Theories"; Tushman and Romanelli, "Organizational Evolution."

28   C. Markides, "Consequences of Corporate Refocusing: Ex Ante Evidence," *Academy of Management Journal* 35 (1992): 398–412.

29   R.E. Hoskisson and M.A. Hitt, *Downscoping: How to Tame the Diversified Firm* (New York: Oxford University Press, 1994): 3.

30   R.E. Hoskisson and R.A. Johnson, "Corporate Restructuring and Strategic Change: The Effect on

Diversification and R&D Intensity," *Academy of Management Executive* (May, 1991): 7–21; Hoskisson and Hitt, *Downscoping.*

31   M.L.A. Hayward and K. Shimizu, "De-commitment to Losing Strategic Action: Evidence from the Divestiture of Poorly Performing Acquisitions," *Strategic Management Journal* 27 (6) (2006): 541–557.

32   D.D. Bergh, R.A. Johnson and R. Dewitt, "Restructuring Through Spin-off or Sell-off: Transforming Information Asymmetries into Financial Gain," *Strategic Management Journal* 29 (2008): 133–148.

33   "Perkin Elmer Announced December 6 That It Had Completed the Sale of its Aerospace Business to Eaton Corporation," *Pharmaceutical Discovery* (Nov–Dec, 2005): 14.

34   "Rockwell Automation, Inc.: Mechanical and Motor Units to Be Sold Amid Business Shift," *Wall Street Journal* (June 21, 2006): B1.

35   "Electrolux AB: Net Falls 2.6% after Spinoff of Outdoor-Products Division," *Wall Street Journal* (July 19, 2006): B1.

36   D.D. Bergh and E.N. Lim, "Learning How to Restructure: Absorptive Capacity and Improvisational Views of Restructuring Actions and Performance," *Strategic Management Journal* 29 (2008): 593–616.

37   G.A. Fowler, "EBay to Unload Skype In IPO, Citing Poor Fit," *Wall Street Journal* (April 15, 2009): B1.

38   J. Bush, "Russia's Factories Shift Gears," *Business Week* (May 18, 2009): 51.

39   W. McKinley, C.M. Sanchez and A.G. Schick, "Organizational Downsizing: Constraining, Cloning, Learning," *Academy of Management Executive* (August, 1995): 32.

40   K.S. Cameron, S.J. Freeman and A.K. Mishra, "Best Practices in White-Collar Downsizing: Managing Contradictions," *Academy of Management Executive* (August, 1991): 57–73.

41   J. Brockner, S. Grover, T. Reed, R. DeWitt and M. O'Malley, "Survivors' Reactions to Layoffs: We Get By with a Little Help from Our Friends," *Administrative Science Quarterly* 32 (1987): 526–541.

42   D.L. Worrell, W.N. Davidson III and V.M. Sharma, "Layoff Announcements and Stockholder Wealth," *Academy of Management Journal* 34 (1991): 662–678.

43   E.G. Love and N. Nohria, "Reducing Slack: The Performance Consequences of Downsizing by Large Industrial Firms, 1977–1993," *Strategic Management Journal* 26 (2005): 1087–1108.

44   D.M. Flynn and M. Farid, "The Intentional Use of Chapter XI: Lingering Versus Immediate Filing," *Strategic Management Journal* 12 (1991): 63–64.

45   "Extra! Chapter 11!" *Business Week* (March 9, 2009): 8.

46   W.N. Moulton, "Bankruptcy as a Deliberate Strategy: Theoretical Considerations and Empirical Evidence," *Strategic Management Journal* 14 (1993): 130.

47   D. Luhnow and J. Lyons, "Televisa to Join U.S. Group That Will Vie for Univision," *Wall Street Journal* (April 27, 2006): A3.

48   K.M. Davidson, "Another Look at LBOs," *Journal of Business Strategies* (January/February, 1988): 44–47.

49   A good review of these studies is found in S.A. Zahra and M. Fescina, "Will Leveraged Buyouts Kill U.S. Corporate Research and Development?" *Academy of Management Executive* (November, 1991): 7–21.

50   M.F. Wiersema and J.P. Liebeskind, "The Effects of Leveraged Buyouts on Corporate Growth and Diversification in Large Firms," *Strategic Management Journal* 16 (1995): 447–460.

51   K.M. Davidson, "Another Look at LBOs," *Journal of Business Strategies* (January/February, 1988): 44–47.

52   M. Schwarz and E.A. Weinstein, "So You Want to Do a Leveraged Buyout," *Journal of Business Strategies* (January/February, 1989): 10–15.

53   P. Van Arnum, "Novartis Creates New Vaccines Division Following Close of Chiron Deal," *Pharmaceutical Technology*, (June, 2006): 20.

54   J. McCracken and M. Spector, "Remnants of 'Old GM' to Linger," *Wall Street Journal* (June 1, 2009): A15.

55   N.K. King, Jr. and S. Terlep, "GM Collapses into Government's Arms," *Wall Street Journal* (June 2, 2009): A1.

56   B. Mascarenhas and D.A. Aaker, "Strategy Over the Business Cycle," *Strategic Management Journal* 10 (1989): 199–210.

57   P. Navarro, "The Well-Timed Strategy: Managing the Business Cycle," *California Management Review* 48 (Fall 2005): 72–73.

58   Navarro, "The Well-Timed Strategy."

59   "Hyundai's Surprising Success," *The Economist* (March 7, 2009): 71.

60   "Many a Mickle," *The Economist* (March 7, 2009): 39.

61   "Target Looks Bulletproof," *Business Week* (April 27, 2009): 68.

62   N. Pangarkar and J.R. Lie, "The Impact of Market Cycle on the Performance of Singapore Acquirers," *Strategic Management Journal* 25 (2004): 1209–1216.

Appendix—Preparing a Strategic Analysis

Strategic management is an iterative, ongoing process designed to position a firm for competitive advantage in its ever-changing environment. To manage an organization strategically, a manager must understand and appreciate the desires of key organizational stakeholders, the industry environment, and the firm's position relative to its stakeholders and industry. This knowledge allows a manager to set goals and direct the organization's resources in a way that corrects weaknesses, overcomes threats, takes advantage of strengths and opportunities, and, ultimately, satisfies stakeholders. This book contains a foundation for understanding these strategic management processes.

With case analysis, you can practice some of the techniques of strategic management. Case analysis, to some extent, mirrors the processes managers use to make real strategic decisions. The main advantages managers have over students who analyze cases are that they have more information and more experience. For example, managers have ongoing relationships with internal and external stakeholders, from whom information can be gathered. They may also have a business intelligence system and staff to help them make decisions. In addition, managers usually have substantial experience in the industry and company. Nevertheless, managers must still make decisions without full information. Like students, they never have all of the facts or the time and resources to gather them. In case analysis, you must sort accurate, relevant information from that which is inaccurate or irrelevant.

The authors of cases have attempted to capture as much information as possible. They typically conducted extensive interviews with managers and employees and gathered information from public sources such as annual reports and business magazines. Many cases include a detailed description of the industry and competitors as well as an extensive profile of one organization. You can supplement this information through your own library research, *if* your instructor thinks this is appropriate.

Case analysis typically begins with a brief introduction of the company. The introduction, which sets the stage for the rest of the case, should include a brief description of the defining characteristics of the firm, including some of its outstanding qualities, past successes, failures, and products or services. The industries in which the firm is involved are also identified.

The next section of a case analysis can be either an environmental analysis or an internal analysis. Opportunities are defined as conditions in the broad and task *environments* that allow a firm to take advantage of *organizational* strengths, overcome *organizational* weaknesses, or neutralize *environmental* threats. Consequently, both environmental and organizational analyses are required before all of the organization's opportunities can be identified. We have chosen to treat environmental analysis first because it establishes the context in which firm strategies and resources can be understood. However, reversing the order of analysis would not be incorrect and is even preferred by some strategic management scholars.

Environmental analysis is an examination of the external environment, including external stakeholders, the competition, and the broad environment. Systematic external analysis will help you draw conclusions about the potential for growth and profit in the industry and determine keys to survival and success in the industry.

An organizational analysis, which follows the external analysis, is designed to evaluate the organization's strategic direction, business- and corporate-level strategies, resources, capabilities, and relationships with internal and external stakeholders, and then determine the strengths, weaknesses, vulnerabilities, and sources of competitive advantage exhibited by the firm. These determinations must be made against a background of knowledge about the external environment so that the full range of opportunities and threats can also be identified.

STRUCTURING AN ENVIRONMENTAL ANALYSIS

An analysis of the external environment includes an industry analysis and an examination of key external stakeholders and the broad environment. Findings are then summarized, with an emphasis on identifying industry growth and profit potential and the keys to survival and success in the industry. Some organizations are involved in more than one industry. Consequently, a separate industry analysis is done for each of the industries in which a firm is involved.

Industry Analysis

Environmental analysis should begin with an industry analysis. The first step in industry analysis is to provide a basic description of the industry and the competitive forces that dominate it. Porter's Five Forces are evaluated, along with other relevant issues:

1. What is the product or service? What function does it serve? What are the channels of distribution?

2. What is the industry size in units and dollars? How fast is it growing? Are products differentiated? Are there high exit barriers? Are there high fixed costs? These are some of the forces that determine the strength of competition among existing competitors.
3. Who are the major competitors? What are their market shares? In other words, is the industry consolidated or fragmented?
4. Who are the major customers of the industry? Are they powerful? What gives them power?
5. Who are the major suppliers to the industry? Are they powerful? What gives them power?
6. Do significant entry barriers exist? What are they? Are they effective in protecting existing competitors, thus enhancing profits?
7. Are there any close substitutes for industry products and services? Do they provide pressure on prices charged in this industry?
8. What are the basic strategies of competitors? How successful are they?
9. To what extent is the industry global? Are there any apparent advantages being involved in more than one nation?
10. Is the industry regulated? What influence do regulations have on industry competitiveness?

External Stakeholders and the Broad Environment

A complete environmental analysis also includes an assessment of external stakeholders and the broad environment. The identity and power of competitors, suppliers, and customers was already established during the industry analysis. At this stage of the analysis, other important stakeholders should also be identified and their influence on the industry determined (see Chapter 2). If any of the external stakeholders pose a threat or opportunity, this also should be identified. One of the outcomes of this part of the analysis should be the establishment of priorities for each external stakeholder group. High-priority stakeholders will receive greater attention during the development of the strategic plan.

The broad environment should also be evaluated. Four of the most important factors are current social forces, global economic forces, global political forces, and technological innovations. Remember that each of these forces is evaluated only as they relate to the industry in question. Forces in the broad environment may also pose threats or provide opportunities.

After describing the industry as it exists now, it is important to capture the underlying dynamics that will create industry change and require new strategic approaches. One useful way to accomplish this is to group factors that influence the industry into two categories: those that create and influence industry demand and those that create and influence industry cost structures and profit potential. The findings from this part of the analysis will help you decide whether the industry is "attractive" (growing and profitable) and worthy of further investment (i.e., time, money, resources). It will also help you identify areas in which the firm may be able to excel in an effort to create a competitive advantage.

Factors that Influence Demand and Cost Structures

There are many industry factors and stakeholder actions that create and influence demand for products and services. Some of the factors are part of the broad environment of the firm, such as the state of the economy. Other factors are part of the task environment, most of which are related to the actions of two key stakeholder groups: customers and competitors. If the underlying factors that create demand are changing, then it is likely that demand patterns will change. For example, demand for washing machines is a function of household formations and replacements. To predict future demand, you would study the numbers of people in the household-forming age bracket, durability of washers, and economic conditions.

Some of the industry factors and stakeholder actions that create and influence demand and growth prospects in an industry include:

1. The function(s) served by the product.
2. The stage of the product life cycle (i.e., degree of market penetration already experienced).
3. Economic trends, including income levels and economic cycles (i.e., recession, boom).
4. Demographic trends (part of social trend analysis) such as population and age.
5. Other societal/cultural trends, including fads and commonly held values and beliefs.
6. Political trends, which may include protectionist legislation such as trade barriers.
7. Technological trends, including new applications, new markets, and cost savings that make prices more competitive.
8. Programs developed by firms in the industry, such as new product introductions, new marketing programs, new distribution channels, and new functions served.
9. Strong brand recognition, domestically or worldwide.
10. Pricing actions that stimulate demand.

After analyzing the factors that create and influence demand, you should be able to draw some conclusions about industry growth prospects for the industry and firm. Since you can never be certain about the timetable and ultimate outcome of a trend that, by definition, is changing over time, one technique that may be useful is to develop alternative demand scenarios. For example, if the health of the economy is a major driver of a product's demand, you could consider the upside and downside of an economic recovery using the following type of format: If the economy recovers within six months, then industry demand for the product could be the highest in five years. If the recovery does not materialize, then demand might linger at last year's levels.

After determining growth prospects for the industry, you will want to determine the cost structure and profit potential of the industry. As with demand, there are various factors and stakeholder actions that create and influence cost/profit structures in an industry. Among these factors are the following:

1. *Stage of the product life cycle.* In the early stages of the life cycle, firms have large investments in product development, distribution channel development, new plant and equipment, and workforce training. In the latter stages, investments are more incremental.
2. *Capital intensity.* Large investments in fixed costs such as plants and equipment make firms very sensitive to fluctuations in demand—high levels of capacity utilization are needed to cover or "spread" fixed costs. Industries that have a lower relative fixed cost investment but higher variable costs are able to control their costs more readily in turbulent demand periods.

3. *Economies of scale*. Larger-sized facilities can achieve lower costs per unit than smaller facilities in some instances because of lower per-foot construction costs, more efficient use of equipment, and more efficient use of indirect labor and management. If a facility is so large that additional equipment and management are needed, economies of scale may be lost.
4. *Learning/experience effects*. With repetition and an environment that encourages and rewards learning, employees can become more productive over time.
5. *The power of customers, suppliers, competitive rivalry, substitutes, and entry barriers*. Powerful customers, suppliers, competitive rivalry, substitutes, or low entry barriers can erode profit potential. The forces, which are part of Porter's Five Forces Model, were discussed in detail in Chapter 2.
6. *The influence of other stakeholders*. These may include powerful foreign governments, joint venture partners, powerful unions, strong creditors, etc.
7. *Technological changes that provide opportunities to reduce costs*. Technological innovations can allow a firm to invest in new equipment, new products, and new processes or to alter the balance of investments between fixed and variable costs.

After systematically profiling the factors and stakeholder actions that influence cost structures and profits, you should be able to draw conclusions about industry profit potential. After the basic environmental analysis is complete, the next step is to perform a more detailed examination of the major strategic issues facing the industry.

Strategic Issues Facing the Industry

A thorough environmental analysis provides the information needed to identify factors and forces that are important to the industry in which your organization is involved and, therefore, your organization. These factors and forces may be categorized as follows:

1. *Driving forces in the industry*, which are trends that are so significant that they are creating fundamental industry change, such as the opening up of Eastern Europe or networked computer communications. Of course, each industry will have its own unique set of driving forces.
2. *Threats*, defined as noteworthy trends or changes that threaten growth prospects, profit potential, and traditional ways of doing business.
3. *Opportunities*, which are important trends, changes, or ideas that provide new opportunities for growth or profits.
4. *Requirements for survival*, identified as resources and capabilities that all firms must possess to survive in the industry. An example in the pharmaceutical industry is "product purity." These factors do not command a premium price. They are necessary, but not sufficient to be successful.
5. *Key success factors*, which are factors firms typically should possess if they desire to be successful in the industry. An example in the pharmaceutical industry is the ability to create products with new therapeutic qualities. This ability may lead to high performance.

Having completed an analysis of the external environment, you are ready to conduct a more specific analysis of the internal organization.

STRUCTURING AN ORGANIZATIONAL ANALYSIS

Understanding industry trends, growth prospects, cost structures, profit potential, and key strategic issues can help you critique an organization's strategies and evaluate its strengths and weaknesses. For example, what might qualify as strength in one industry may be an ordinary characteristic or a weakness in another industry. A good organizational analysis should begin with a general evaluation of the internal organization.

Evaluation of the Internal Environment

The following questions are useful in assessing the internal organization:

1. What is the company's strategic direction, including its vision, mission (including business definition), enterprise strategy (purpose), and long-term goals. If some of these factors are contained in a formal mission statement, share it.
2. How has the strategic direction changed over time? In what way? Has the evolution been consistent with the organization's capabilities and planned strategies?
3. Who are the principal internal stakeholders? In particular, who are the key managers and what are their backgrounds? What are their strengths and weaknesses? Are they authoritarian or participative in their management style? Is this appropriate for the situation? What seems to drive their actions?
4. Who owns the organization? Is it a publicly traded company with a board of directors? If there is a board and you know who is on it, is the composition of the board appropriate? Is there an individual or group with a controlling interest? Is there evidence of agency problems? How active are the owners and what do they value?
5. What are the operating characteristics of the company, including its size in sales, assets, and employees, its age, and its geographical locations (including international operations)?
6. Are employees highly trained? If a union is present, how are relations with the union?
7. How would you describe the organization's culture? Is it a high-performing culture? Is it supportive of the firm's strategies?

Most instructors also require a financial analysis to identify financial strengths and weaknesses, evaluate performance, and identify financial resources available for strategy implementation. A financial analysis should include a comparison of ratios and financial figures with major competitors or the industry in which the organization competes (cross-sectional) as well as an analysis of trends in these ratios over several years (longitudinal). Some commonly used financial ratios are specified in Chapter 3.

When analyzed superficially, ratios can be more misleading than informative. For example, in comparing return-on-assets for two firms in the same industry, the one with the higher ratio could have superior earnings or devalued assets from too little investment. Two firms can differ in return-on-equity because of different debt-equity financing policies rather than from true performance reasons. When accurately interpreted and considered in the larger organization context, the analysis may also uncover strengths, weaknesses, or symptoms of larger organizational problems.

Identification of Resources and Capabilities

The foregoing analysis of the internal environment provides an excellent starting point for identifying key resources and capabilities. For example, outstanding resources and capabilities may result from (1) superior management, (2) well-trained employees, (3) an excellent board of directors, (4) a high-performance culture, (5) superior financial resources, or (6) the appropriate level and type of international involvement. However, these potential sources of competitive advantage barely scratch the organizational surface.

You should also evaluate the organization's primary value chain activities to identify resources and capabilities. These activities include its (7) inbound logistics, (8) operations, (9) outbound logistics, (10) marketing and sales, and (11) service, as well as the support activities of (12) procurement, (13) technology development, (14) human resource management, and (15) administration. Chapter 3 provided a description of how to use the value chain.

In addition, an organization may have (16) an excellent reputation, (17) a strong brand name, (18) patents and secrets, (19) excellent locations, or (20) strong or valuable ties (i.e., alliances, joint ventures, contracts, cooperation) with one or more external stakeholders. All of these potential resources and capabilities (and many others) are discussed in this book. They form a starting point that you can use to help identify the potential sources of competitive advantage. Each company will have its own unique list.

Evaluation of Strategies

The next step in internal analysis is to describe and critique the organization's past strategies. In critiquing strategies, you will need to describe them in detail, discuss whether they have been successful, and then *evaluate whether they fit with the industry environment and the resources and capabilities of the organization.*

1. What is the company's *pattern* of past strategies (corporate, business, functional, international)?
2. How successful has the company been in the past with its chosen strategies? How successful is the company now?
3. For each strategy, what explains success or failure? (Use your environmental and organizational analyses to support your answer.)

Many instructors require their students to evaluate the success of an organization on the basis of both qualitative and quantitative (financial) measures. The financial measures were developed during your financial analysis, so you only need to make reference to them here. Some common qualitative measures include product or service quality, productivity, responsiveness to industry change, innovation, reputation, and other measures that indicate key stakeholder satisfaction (i.e., employees, customers, managers, regulatory bodies, society).

Identification of Sources of Competitive Advantage

You are now ready to consolidate your internal and external analyses into lists of strengths and weaknesses, as well as expand and revise your lists of opportunities and threats. In Chapter 1, strengths were defined as firm resources and capabilities that can lead to a competitive advantage. Weaknesses, on the other hand, were described as resources and capabilities that the firm does not possess, resulting in a competitive disadvantage. Consequently, each of the resources and capabilities identified during the organizational analysis should be measured against the factors identified in the environmental analysis. The next paragraph describes how this can be done.

Resources and capabilities become strengths if they have the potential to lead to a competitive advantage. This happens when (1) they are valuable, which means that they allow the firm to exploit opportunities and/or neutralize threats arising from the external environment, and (2) they are unique, meaning that only a few firms possess the resource or capability. Using these criteria, a list of strengths should be assembled. Strengths become sources of competitive advantage when an organization is aware of their value and has organizational systems in place to take advantage of this potential. If the strength is also hard to imitate, then it can lead to a *sustainable* competitive advantage; consequently, these types of strengths should be highlighted. Weaknesses also should be listed. These are resources and capabilities the firm does not possess that, according to your environmental analysis, lead to a competitive disadvantage.

Opportunities are conditions in the external environment that allow a firm to take advantage of organizational strengths, overcome organizational weaknesses, or neutralize environmental threats. Consequently, now that the organizational analysis is complete, you should re-evaluate your list of opportunities to determine whether they really apply to your organization. You also should evaluate threats to make sure they are applicable to your firm. Threats are conditions in the broad and task environments that may stand in the way of organizational competitiveness or the achievement of stakeholder satisfaction.

At this point, you also may want to add to your list of opportunities some of the potential linkages and alliances that the firm could develop with external stakeholders. For example, if your company is strong in production but weak in foreign marketing, you may see an opportunity to enter a new foreign market through a joint venture with a strong marketing company. Another example may involve neutralizing a threat of new government regulation by forming an alliance with competitors to influence the regulating body.

DEVELOPING A STRATEGIC PLAN

Your environmental and organizational analyses helped you to (1) draw conclusions about the growth prospects and profit potential in the industry and any trends that are critical to the firm, (2) evaluate the past strategies and strategic direction of the firm, and (3) develop a list of strengths, weaknesses, opportunities, and threats. The next step is to make recommendations concerning the strategies the firm may want to pursue in the future. If the firm is not a stellar performer, this should be an easy task. However, even firms that have been highly successful in the past should consider taking advantage of opportunities and should respond to threats. History has taught us that firms that are unwilling to progress eventually decline.

Strategic Direction and Major Strategies

You should probably begin your strategic recommendations by focusing on the strategic direction and major strategies of the firm. Based on your earlier analyses, you may want to consider adjustments to the mission of the firm, including its vision, business definition, or enterprise strategy. Of course, the business definition also helps identify the growth orientation of the business. Are the growth plans taking advantage of industry opportunities? If the industry is becoming mature, should horizontal integration be pursued rather than market penetration alone?

If you determined earlier that the business strategy is not as successful as it should be, what adjustments should be made? Could the company have more success by focusing on one segment of the market? Or if the company were pursuing a focus strategy, would broadening the target market be appropriate? If the company were pursuing cost leadership, would a differentiation strategy work better? If differentiation doesn't seem to be working very well, would a cost leadership strategy be better? Or, would a best-cost strategy be the most appropriate?

Finally, you should examine the corporate strategy (concentration, vertical integration, related or unrelated diversification). Is your corporate strategy still appropriate, given your environmental analysis? Is your dominant industry stagnant? Is it over-regulated? Is competition hurting profitability? Should you consider investing in other industries? If so, what are their defining characteristics? What core competencies and capabilities could be applied elsewhere? What opportunities could be explored that relate to the corporate strategy?

It is possible that you may want to leave the strategic direction and major strategies alone, especially if the organization has enjoyed recent success. Regardless of whether you altered the direction and strategies, at this point you have now established what you think they should be. The direction and corporate- and business-level strategies provide guidance for fine-tuning an organization's strategies. Each of the recommendations you make from this point on should be consistent with the strategic direction and major strategies of the organization. At this point, it is time to explore strategic opportunities further.

Evaluation of Opportunities and Recommendations

Using the strategic direction and corporate- and business-level strategies as guides, strategic opportunities should be evaluated further. These alternatives were generated during earlier analyses. They include the following:

1. *Opportunities that allow a firm to take advantage of organizational strengths.* These opportunities may involve alternatives such as better promotion of current products and services, new products or services, new applications for existing products and services within existing markets, exploring new domestic or foreign markets, diversifying into areas in which strengths can be applied, or creation of joint ventures with companies with complementary strengths. These are only a few examples.
2. *Opportunities for the firm to overcome organizational weaknesses.* Do any of the organizational weaknesses relate to an area that you described in your industry analysis as essential for survival? Do any of the weaknesses relate to key success factors? Firms can overcome their weaknesses through strategies such as learning from joint venture partners, creating new alliances with organizations that are strong where the organization is weak, or fixing problems internally through R&D, better controls, efficiency programs, IT, TAM, etc. Again, these are only a few examples.
3. *Opportunities for the firm to neutralize environmental threats.* These often involve creation of strategic alliances to offset the influence of a powerful stakeholder such as a government regulator, a strong union, a powerful competitor, or an influential special interest group. The firm may form an

alliance *with* the powerful stakeholder or with other stakeholders in an effort
to balance the power. Firms may also form alliances to help cope with threats
emerging from the broad environment.

Evaluation of opportunities means much more than simply accepting them on
the basis of earlier environmental and organizational analyses. They also should
be evaluated based on factors such as the following:

1. *Cost/benefits analysis.* Do the financial benefits of pursuing the opportunity
   appear to outweigh the financial costs?
2. *Ethical analysis.* Is pursuit of this strategy consistent with the enterprise
   strategy (purpose) of the organization? Could there be negative effects on the
   firm's reputation?
3. *Protection of other strengths.* Does pursuit of this opportunity in any way
   detract from or weaken other strengths? For example, could it damage a
   brand name? Could it weaken a strong financial position?
4. *Implementation ability.* Will implementation of this strategy be easy or
   difficult? In other words, does the strategy "fit" the capabilities, structure,
   systems, processes, and culture of the organization?
5. *Stakeholder analysis.* How will this strategy affect key stakeholders? Which
   ones are likely to support it? Are they high priority? Which ones are likely to
   oppose it? Are they high priority? What are the strategic ramifications of their
   support or opposition?
6. *Future position.* Will the strategy continue to be viable as the industry and the
   broad environment undergo their expected changes? Will it provide a
   foundation for survival or competitive success?

The result of this analysis should be a recommendation or recommendations
that the organization should pursue. Many evaluation tools can facilitate the
evaluation process, such as a pay-off matrix that provides an evaluation of several
alternatives based on a standard set of criteria (see Appendix Exhibit 1). However, the tools should never act as substitutes for in-depth analysis of the alternatives themselves. In other words, even if a numeric score-keeping system is used,
the numbers should be explained based on detailed strategic analysis.

You may not be required by your instructor to conduct a formal analysis of
alternatives based on a standard set of criteria; however, you should still make
recommendations concerning changes the organization should make to remain
or become competitive and satisfy its stakeholders. Through this entire process,
remember that many companies identify areas of strength that are no longer

A Pay-Off Matrix Approach to Evaluating Opportunities   **Appendix Exhibit 1**

	Criteria			
	Criterion 1	Criterion 2	Criterion 3	Total
Opportunity 1	−2	1	2	1
Opportunity 2	2	1	−1	2
Opportunity 3	1	2	1	4

Note: In this matrix, −2 means that the opportunity is very weak based on the criterion, −1 means weak, 0 means
neutral, 1 means strong, and 2 means very strong.

capable of giving the company a competitive edge. What was a key to success yesterday may be a requirement for survival today.

Implementation and Control

Recommendations should always be accompanied by an implementation plan and basic controls. The following are major questions that should be addressed during this section of a case analysis. Items 7 and 8 relate specifically to control.

1. How do the recommendations specifically address concerns that were identified during the analysis?
2. What will be the roles and responsibilities of key internal *and* external stakeholders in carrying out the recommendations and how are they expected to respond? What actions should be taken to smooth out the transition period or avoid stakeholder discontent?
3. Does the organization have the resources (funds, people, skills) to carry out the recommendations? If not, how should the organization proceed in developing or acquiring those resources?
4. Does the organization have the appropriate systems, structures, and processes to carry out the recommendations? If not, how should the organization proceed in creating the appropriate systems, structures, and processes?
5. What is the appropriate time horizon for implementing recommendations? What should the organization and its managers do immediately, in one month, in six months, in a year, etc.?
6. What are the roadblocks the organization could encounter while implementing the recommendations (i.e., financing, skilled labor shortages)? How can the organization overcome these roadblocks?
7. What are the desired outcomes or changes the organization should expect once the recommendations have been implemented? How will the organization know if the recommendations have been successful? In other words, what are the objectives associated with your recommendations?
8. What were some of the major assumptions you made with regard to the external environment? Which of these factors, if different from expected, would require an adjustment to your recommendations?

Following the implementation section, you may want to update your audience (your instructor or other students) concerning actions the firm has taken since the case was written. If a case update is required, it should center on actions that pertain to the focus of your case analysis. If you do an update, remember that what the organization did, even if it appears to have been successful, may not have been the optimal solution.

A NOTE TO STUDENTS

If you are reading this appendix early in the course, you will have the rest of the semester or quarter to practice the case analysis process and study the chapter readings. If you are reading this appendix later in the course, we encourage you to go back to earlier chapters and refresh your memory concerning the concepts that were covered. Just as this course integrates material you learned during your years of business study, the case analysis process integrates material from all sections of the strategic management course.

The material in this appendix represents the way we teach case analysis. Since there is not a standard method for analyzing cases, your instructor may teach a method of case analysis that differs from our approach. Also, cases can be treated in many different formats, including class discussions (complete with discussion questions to be answered before coming to class), written papers, formal presentations, and class debates. After reading this appendix, check with your instructor for specific instructions and requirements.

Index

Note: Page numbers in *Italic* indicate figures or exhibits.